Grammatical Variation of Pronouns in
Nineteenth-Century English Novels

Hituzi Linguistics in English

No. 4	*A Historical Study of Referent Honorifics in Japanese*	Takashi Nagata
No. 5	*Communicating Skills of Intention*	Tsutomu Sakamoto
No. 6	*A Pragmatic Approach to the Generation and Gender Gap in Japanese Politeness Strategies*	Toshihiko Suzuki
No. 7	*Japanese Women's Listening Behavior in Face-to-face Conversation*	Sachie Miyazaki
No. 8	*An Enterprise in the Cognitive Science of Language*	Tetsuya Sano et al.
No. 9	*Syntactic Structure and Silence*	Hisao Tokizaki
No. 10	*The Development of the Nominal Plural Forms in Early Middle English*	Ryuichi Hotta
No. 11	*Chunking and Instruction*	Takayuki Nakamori
No. 12	*Detecting and Sharing Perspectives Using Causals in Japanese*	Ryoko Uno
No. 13	*Discourse Representation of Temporal Relations in the So-Called Head-Internal Relatives*	Kuniyoshi Ishikawa
No. 14	*Features and Roles of Filled Pauses in Speech Communication*	Michiko Watanabe
No. 15	*Japanese Loanword Phonology*	Masahiko Mutsukawa
No. 16	*Derivational Linearization at the Syntax-Prosody Interface*	Kayono Shiobara
No. 17	*Polysemy and Compositionality*	Tatsuya Isono
No. 18	*fMRI Study of Japanese Phrasal Segmentation*	Hideki Oshima
No. 19	*Typological Studies on Languages in Thailand and Japan*	Tadao Miyamoto et al.
No. 20	*Repetition, Regularity, Redundancy*	Yasuyo Moriya
No. 21	*A Cognitive Pragmatic Analysis of Nominal Tautologies*	Naoko Yamamoto
No. 22	*A Contrastive Study of Responsibility for Understanding Utterances between Japanese and Korean*	Sumi Yoon
No. 23	*On Peripheries*	Anna Cardinaletti et al.
No. 24	*Metaphor of Emotions in English*	Ayako Omori
No. 25	*A Comparative Study of Compound Words*	Makiko Mukai
No. 26	*Grammatical Variation of Pronouns in Nineteenth-Century English Novels*	Masami Nakayama
No. 27	*I mean as a Marker of Intersubjective Adjustment*	Takashi Kobayashi

Hituzi Linguistics in English

26

MASAMI NAKAYAMA

―

Grammatical Variation of Pronouns in Nineteenth-Century English Novels

HITUZI
SYOBO

Copyright © Masami Nakayama 2018
First published 2018

Author: Masami Nakayama

All rights reserved. Except for the quotation of short passages for the purposes of criticism and review, no part of this publication may be reproduced, stored in a retrieval system, or transmitted in any form or by any means, electronic, mechanical, photocopying, recording or otherwise, without the written prior permission of the publisher.

In case of photocopying and electronic copying and retrieval from network personally, permission will be given on receipts of payment and making inquiries. For details please contact us through e-mail. Our e-mail address is given below.

Hituzi Syobo Publishing

Yamato bldg. 2F, 2-1-2 Sengoku Bunkyo-ku
    Tokyo, Japan 112-0011
Telephone: +81-3-5319-4916
Facsimile: +81-3-5319-4917
e-mail: toiawase@hituzi.co.jp
http://www.hituzi.co.jp/
postal transfer: 00120-8-142852

ISBN978-4-89476-901-4
Printed in Japan

Preface and acknowledgements

One reads novels in various ways. What interested as well as puzzled me while reading English novels written a couple of centuries ago was that the grammatical usage of English differed from what I had learned at school. That was the beginning of the present research. I soon found that there were differences in use of grammar between characters in novels and also between different authors, and that several linguistic factors were complexly intertwined in the use of grammatical variants. Based on these findings, I would like to illustrate, in a small way at least, multiple facets of the usage of variants commonly seen in the novels of that day.

The aim of this book is to investigate the grammatical variation in pronouns in English novels written in the 19th century from multiple linguistic perspectives and to reveal what kinds of linguistic factors are involved in the use of pronominal variants. I decided to focus on the behavior of pronouns since pronouns have many variants with a relatively high frequency of appearance, which I thought was suitable for quantitative and qualitative analyses. The study shows which linguistic factors best account for the use of pronominal variants in the 19th-century English novels examined and how pronominal usage in 19th-century English is possibly different from that in Present-day English or that in the previous centuries.

This monograph is based on my PhD thesis, presented to the Department of Language and Information Sciences of the Graduate School of Arts and Sciences at the University of Tokyo in 2015. Some sections in the book, though not quite in the same form, have appeared in the following four articles: section 2.1.2 was published as "The Complex Behavior of the Second Person Pronoun *Ye* in 19th-Century English Novels," *Studies in English Literature: English Number* 55, 95-115; section 2.2.2 corresponds to "The Weakened Form *'em* of *them* in 19th-Century English Novels," *ERA, New Series* 32, Nos. 1 & 2, 59-75; "*It is I* vs. *It is me* in 19th-Century English Novels," *Studies in Modern English* 30, 1-23, contains much of section 3.1; and section 5.1 parallels "*Who* vs. *Whom* in 19th-Century English Novels," *Studies in Modern English: The Thirtieth Anniversary Publication of the Modern English Association*, Ed, Ken Nakagawa, Tokyo: Eihōsha, 435-450. The publication of this monograph was supported by JSPS KAKENHI Grant Number JP17HP5058, Grant-in-Aid for Publication of Scientific Research Results.

I would like to thank all those people who have helped me with the completion of the dissertation and the publication of the work. First and foremost, I wish to extend my heartfelt gratitude to my supervisor, Professor Jun Terasawa, for his support throughout the course of my doctoral studies. Without his supervision and unfailing encouragement this work would not have been possible. To my committee members, Professor Shiro Yamamoto, Professor Hiroto Ueda, Professor Yoshifumi Saito and Professor Harumi Tanabe, I am sincerely grateful for giving insightful comments on an earlier draft and broadening my research horizons. My profound thanks also go to Professor Roger Robins, who read the entire manuscript very carefully to check my English and gave me numerous invaluable suggestions.

In addition, I would like to express my deep appreciation to Dr Matsuji Tajima, Emeritus Professor of Kyushu University, under whose tutelage I completed an MA thesis at Kyushu University. He paved the way for me to study in the field of philology while teaching the importance of reading a primary source text closely.

Finally, I wish to give my warmest gratitude to my parents for their moral support and to my husband and daughters for their constant assistance.

Contents

Preface and acknowledgements		V
List of tables and figures		XII

CHAPTER 1
Introduction

1.1	Aim and scope	1
1.2	Previous studies	3
1.3	Methodological framework	6
1.3.1	Corpus	6
1.3.2	Grammar books	9
1.3.3	Multifaceted approach	10
1.3.3.1	Sociolinguistic analysis	10
1.3.3.2	Stylistic analysis	12
1.3.3.3	Regional parameters	14
1.3.3.4	Outline of the study	14

CHAPTER 2
Dialectal Variation of Personal Pronouns

2.1	Second person	18
2.1.1	*Thou*	18
2.1.1.1	Overview	18
2.1.1.2	Data	19
2.1.1.3	"Power" as a key to the use of *THOU*	21
2.1.1.4	"Emotion" which triggers *THOU*	31
2.1.1.5	Summary	35
2.1.2	*Ye*	36
2.1.2.1	Overview	36
2.1.2.2	Data	37
2.1.2.3	Complex behavior of *ye*	38

2.1.2.4	Distribution of two types of *ye* and how to tell the difference	50
2.1.2.5	Summary	51
2.2	Third person	51
2.2.1	Third person singular	52
2.2.1.1	Nonstandard forms for *he*	52
2.2.1.2	Nonstandard forms for *she*	55
2.2.1.3	Nonstandard forms for *it*	59
2.2.1.4	Summary	68
2.2.2	Third person plural *'em* for *them*	69
2.2.2.1	Overview	69
2.2.2.2	Data	70
2.2.2.3	Sociolinguistic analysis	71
2.2.2.4	Syntactic and phonological analyses	73
2.2.2.5	Summary	80
2.3	Reflexive pronouns	80
2.3.1	Overview	80
2.3.2	Data and observation	81
2.3.2.1	The *–sel'* type	82
2.3.2.2	The *–seln/–sen* type	84
2.3.2.3	The *hisself* type and others	85
2.3.3	Summary	87

CHAPTER 3
Case Problems of Personal Pronouns

3.1	*It is I* vs. *It is me*	91
3.1.1	Overview	91
3.1.2	Data	92
3.1.3	Analysis	93
3.1.4	*I!* vs. *Me!*	99
3.1.4.1	Data	99
3.1.4.2	Analysis	100
3.1.5	Summary	105
3.2	*Than I* vs. *than me*	105
3.2.1	Overview	105
3.2.2	*Younger than I* vs. *younger than me*	106
3.2.3	*Than myself*	113
3.2.4	Summary	116
3.3	*As I* vs. *as me*	116

3.3.1	Overview	116
3.3.2	*As tall as I* vs. *as tall as me*	116
3.3.3	*Such as he* vs. *such as him*	120
3.3.4	*As myself*	122
3.3.5	Summary	124
3.4	*But, except, save*	125
3.4.1	Overview	125
3.4.2	Data and analysis	125
3.4.3	Summary	128
3.5	*You and I* vs. *you and me*	129
3.5.1	Overview	129
3.5.2	Nominative position	129
3.5.3	*Between you and me*	133
3.5.4	Summary	137
3.6	Overall Summary	138

CHAPTER 4
The Nonstandard Usage of Demonstrative Pronouns

4.1	*Them books* for *those books*	141
4.1.1	Overview	141
4.1.2	Data and analysis	142
4.2	*Them that* for *those that*	146
4.2.1	Overview	146
4.2.2	Data and analysis	147
4.3	Summary	154

CHAPTER 5
The Rivalry between Relative Pronoun Variants

5.1	*Whom* vs. *who*	158
5.1.1	Overview	158
5.1.2	Interrogative and relative pronouns	159
5.1.2.1	Interrogative *whom/who*	161
5.1.2.2	Relative *whom/who*	164
5.1.3	Summary	168
5.2	*Of which* vs. *whose*	169
5.2.1	Overview	169
5.2.2	Genitive *whose* and its alternative variants	170

5.2.3	*Of which* vs. *whose* for non-personal antecedents	172
5.2.3.1	Chronological and sociolinguistic analyses	173
5.2.3.2	Spoken and written	175
5.2.3.3	Types of antecedents	176
5.2.3.4	Syntactic factors	183
5.2.4	Summary	186

CHAPTER 6
Concord with Indefinite Pronouns

6.1	Pronoun-verb concord	190
6.1.1	Overview	190
6.1.2	The *everybody* type	191
6.1.3	The *every man* type	198
6.1.4	Spoken and written	199
6.2	Pronominal co-reference	200
6.2.1	Overview	200
6.2.2	The *everybody* type	201
6.2.3	The *every man* type	204
6.2.4	Spoken and written	205
6.2.5	Sociolinguistic analysis	206
6.2.5.1	The *everybody* type	206
6.2.5.2	The *every man* type	212
6.3	Discrepancy in number	213
6.4	Summary	215

CHAPTER 7
Conclusion

7.1	Linguistic factors involved in the choice of pronominal variants	219
7.2	Influence of prescriptive grammar	224
7.2.1	Archaic/dialectal use	224
7.2.2	Casual use	225
7.2.3	Solecism criticized by grammarians	225
7.3	How the grammatical change in pronouns proceeded in the 19th century	228
7.4	Further investigation	229

Appendix	230
Bibliography	237
Index	249

List of tables and figures

Tables

Table 2.1: Forms of the personal pronouns in Late Modern English	17
Table 2.2: Distribution of *THOU* and the numbers of speakers who use it according to text	20
Table 2.3: Relationship between the speaker and the addressee in use of *THOU*	22
Table 2.4: Senior-to-junior relationship in use of *THOU*	23
Table 2.5: Man-to-man relationship in use of *THOU*	27
Table 2.6: Power balance and emotions in use of *THOU*	32
Table 2.7: Distribution of the second person pronoun *you* and its variants	37
Table 2.8: Distribution of nonstandard second person pronouns	37
Table 2.9: Case variation of *yo/ye* in *North and South*	38
Table 2.10: Case variation of *yah/ye* in *Wuthering Heights*	40
Table 2.11: Case variation of *ye* in the 15 texts concerned	49
Table 2.12: Position of the pronoun *ye/'ee/yer* in the nominative	50
Table 2.13: Distribution of old/recent variants *ye*	50
Table 2.14: Nonstandard variants for the third person singular male pronoun	52
Table 2.15: Variation of the *'t* form in the nominative case according to text	60
Table 2.16: Distribution of the *'t* form combined/not combined with *n't* in spoken/written language	61
Table 2.17: Number of characters who use the *'t* form (with *n't/not*) classified according to social class	62
Table 2.18: Variation of *'t* form in the objective case according to text	67
Table 2.19: Distribution of *'em* and *them* in the objective position according to text	71
Table 2.20: : Number of characters who use *'em* classified according to social class and sex	71
Table 2.21a: Verbs preceding *'em*	74
Table 2.21b: Prepositions preceding *'em*	75
Table 2.22a: Distribution of verbs preceding *'em/them* in the dialogue of the 14 texts concerned	75
Table 2.22b: Distribution of 10 perpositions preceding *'em/them* in the dialogue of the 14 texts concerned	76
Table 2.23a.: Distribution of 20 verbs preceding *'em/them* according to final sound	77
Table 2.23b.: Distribution of 10 prepositions preceding *'em/them* according to final sound	77
Table 2.24: Variation of nonstandard reflexive pronouns according to text	81
Table 3.1: Variation of *it is* in the construction *It is I/me*	94

Table 3.2: Distribution of *It is I/me* according to register	94
Table 3.3a: Number of characters who use Type *It is I* classified according to social class and sex	94
Table 3.3b: Number of characters who use Type *It is me* classified according to social class and sex	95
Table 3.4: Syntactic elements following *It is I/me* in written/spoken language	96
Table 3.5: Examples of *It is I/me* in dialogue classified according to social class and syntactic element	97
Table 3.6: Distribution of *I!/Me!* according to register	101
Table 3.7: Distributions of *It is I/me* and *I!/Me!* in written/spoken language	101
Table 3.8a: Number of characters who use Type *I!* classified according to social class and sex	102
Table 3.8b: Number of characters who use Type *Me!* classified according to social class and sex	102
Table 3.9: Characters who use both *I!* and *Me!*	103
Table 3.10: Number of characters who use Type *dear me* according to social class and sex	104
Table 3.11: Variation of the construction *than* in comparison between subjects according to register	109
Table 3.12: Variation of predicates of the preceding subject in Types *than I am* and *than I*	112
Table 3.13: Distribution of *than I am /than I/than me* and *than myself* according to sex	114
Table 3.14: Distribution of *as I am/as I/as me* according to register	117
Table 3.15: Number of characters who use the nominative forms in the *as – as* construction classified according to social class and sex in written/spoken language	119
Table 3.16: Case variation in the construction with *as*	120
Table 3.17: Case variation in the construction with *as* in the subject/complement and object positions	122
Table 3.18: Distributions of the reflexive and non-reflexive pronouns in the construction with *as*	122
Table 3.19: Distribution of the reflexive pronoun in the construction with *as* according to register	123
Table 3.20: Distribution of *as I am/as I/as me* and *as myself* according to sex	124
Table 3.21a: Pronoun type after *but, except, save* in the objective function	125
Table 3.21b: Pronoun type after *but, except, save* in the nominative function	126
Table 3.22: Distribution of *but, except, save* in the nominative function according to the subject/object territories	127
Table 3.23: Number of characters who use *you and me* in the nominative function classified according to social class and sex	130

Table 3.24: Variation of *you and me* in standard/nonstandard forms   132
Table 3.25: Number of characters who use *between you and me* classified according to social class and sex   133
Table 3.26: Variation of the coordinated pronouns in *between A and B*   134
Table 3.27: Distribution of *between A and B* with/without reflexive pronouns according to sex   137
Table 4.1: Number of characters who use *them books* classified according to social class and sex   143
Table 4.2: *Them/they* modified by restrictive relative clauses classified according to register   148
Table 4.3: *Those/them/they* modified by restrictive relative clauses in the subject position   150
Table 4.4: *Those/them* modified by restrictive relative clauses in the object position   152
Table 5.1: Distribution of the objective *whom/who* in the relative/interrogative pronoun   159
Table 5.2: Distribution of the relative and interrogative pronouns *whom/who* in written/spoken language   160
Table 5.3: Number of characters who use the interrogatives *whom/who* in the objective function classified according to social class   161
Table 5.4: Number of users of the relative *whom* classified according to social class and register   165
Table 5.5: Distribution of genitive relative *whose* and its variant forms for persons/non-persons   171
Table 5.6: Chronological difference in the use of *of which* and *whose* for non-persons   174
Table 5.7: Distribution of *of which* and *whose* for non-persons according to sex   174
Table 5.8: Distribution of *of which* and *whose* with male authors according to chronological difference   174
Table 5.9: Numbers of characters who use *of which/whose* for non-persons classified according to social class and sex   175
Table 5.10: Distribution of non-personal relatives *of which/whose* according to register   175
Table 5.11: Non-personal antecedents of *of which* and *whose*   177
Table 5.12: Syntactic functions of the headword   184
Table 5.13: Distribution of *of which* and *whose* according to the headword's function and antecedents' type   185
Table 6.1: Number concord between indefinite pronouns and verbs   191
Table 6.2: Pronoun-verb concord: *either/neither* with/without an *of*-phrase   194
Table 6.3: Pronoun-verb concord: *none* in the construction with/without an *of*-phrase   196

Table 6.4: Pronoun-verb concord: *none* in the existential sentences   197
Table 6.5: Pronoun-verb concord in written/spoken language: the *everybody* type   199
Table 6.6: Number concord of pronominal co-reference: the *everybody* type   201
Table 6.7: Number concord of pronominal co-reference: compounds with *every/any/some/no*   202
Table 6.8: Co-referential pronouns: indefinites + *of us/you*   203
Table 6.9: Number concord of pronominal co-reference: the *every man* type   205
Table 6.10: Number concord of pronominal co-reference in written/spoken language   206
Table 6.11: Number concord of pronominal co-reference according to sex   207
Table 6.12: Relationship between the referent's sex and the co-referential pronoun   209
Table 6.13a: Number concord of pronominal co-reference according to the authors' sex: MALE and FEMALE   210
Table 6.13b: Number concord of pronominal co-reference according to the authors' sex: BOTH   210
Table 6.14: Relationship between the referent's sex and the co-referential pronoun: the *every man* type   212
Table 6.15a: Number concord of pronominal co-reference for MALE and FEMALE according to the authors' sex   213
Table 6.15b: Number concord of pronominal co-reference for BOTH according to the authors' sex   213
Table 6.16: Shift from singular to plural forms in written/spoken language   214
Table 7.1: Linguistic factors involved in the use of pronoun variants   221
Table 7.2: Distribution of nominative/objective forms in different types of case problems   226
Table 7.3: Distribution of *them/those books* and *them/they/those* + rel.   226
Table 7.4: Distribution of *whom/who* in the objective position   226
Table 7.5: Distribution of *of which/whose* for (non-)personal antecedents   226
Table 7.6: Distribution of number concord with indefinite pronouns   226

Figures

Figure 2.1: The axis of social distance (adapted from Bruti 2000: 35)   31
Figure 2.2: The axis of emotional attitude (adapted from Bruti 2000: 35)   31
Figure 3.1: Distribution of *It is I/me* according to text   93
Figure 3.2: Distribution of *I!/me!* according to text   100
Figure 3.3: Distribution of *than I am/than I/than me* in comparison between subjects according to text   107
Figure 3.4: Distribution of *than oneself* (as the subject of a clause) according to text   114

Figure 3.5: Distribution of *as I am/as I/as me* in the construction *as – as* according to text ... 117
Figure 3.6: Distribution of coordinated pronouns *you and I/me* according to text ... 130
Figure 3.7: Distribution of the reflexive pronouns used in *between A and B* ... 136
Figure 4.1: Distribution of *those books* and *them books* according to text ... 142
Figure 4.2: Distribution of *those/them/they* modified by restrictive relative clauses according to text ... 147
Figure 5.1: Frequencies of the relative pronoun *whom* per 10,000 words ... 164
Figure 5.2: Distribution of *of which/whose* for non-persons ... 173
Figure 5.3: Non-personal antecedents of *of which* and *whose* ... 178
Figure A2.1: Dialectal demarcation presented by Wright (1905) (adapted from Hirooka 1965: xlvii) ... 234
Figure A2.2: Geographical demarcation of Great Britain (2014) ... 235

CHAPTER 1

Introduction

1.1 Aim and scope

The study of Late Modern English grammar had been long neglected by historical linguists on the assumption that the syntax in this period was little different from that of Present-day English. Since the shortage of research on Late Modern English (1700–1900) was pointed out by scholars such as Mats Rydén (1979: 34) and Manfred Görlach (1999), however, interest in this period of English has increased to yield a number of publications and fill the gap of data. Among those publications recently issued were two collections of essays focusing on English in the Late Modern English period with a direct reference to the relevant centuries in their titles: *Eighteenth-Century English: Ideology and Change* (Hickey, 2010) and *Nineteenth-Century English: Stability and Change* (Kytö, Rydén and Smitterberg, 2006).[1] The proceedings of the Late Modern English conferences — *Insights into Late Modern English* (Dossena and Jones, 2003), *'Of Varying Language and Opposing Creed': New Insights into Late Modern English* (Pérez-Guerra, González-Álvarez, Beuno-Alonso and Rama-Martínez, 2007) and *Current Issues in Late Modern English* (Tieken-Boon van Ostade and van der Wurff, 2009) — carry the innovative works by international scholars. Thus Late Modern English is now considered an important area in the midst of exploration.

Preceding this prosperity, in the late 1950's through the 1960's, the historical study of English had been criticized as merely describing the development of language and lacking theoretical analysis of data (Rissanen 1986: 97). In overcoming this problem, the variationist approach has been applied to the historical study of English.[2] Suzanne Romaine (1982) made a foundation for the socio-historical approach, which encompasses historical linguistics and sociolinguistics, to investigate a particular speech community.[3] Similar approaches were observed in Merja Kytö (1993) and Terttu Nevalainen and Helena Raumolin-Brunberg (2003). In recent years, pragmatics has also contributed to the studies of linguistic change by scrutinizing historical data from a contextual standpoint (e.g., Taavitsainen and Jucker eds. 2003),[4] which tends to be neglected in quantitative research.

Through the studies of historical sociolinguistics, scholars' attention has been increasingly paid not only to standard language but also to "nonstandard" language on the assumption that, in order to investigate linguistic variation, it is necessary to study both standard and nonstandard languages (e.g., Trudgill 1975; Andersson and Trudgill 1990; Milroy 2000). This trend is obviously seen in the publication of *Writing in Nonstandard English* (Taavitsainen, Melchers and Pahta, 1999).[5]

The present work, which features the grammatical variation of the pronoun in 19th-century English novels with the application of a multi-dimensional approach, is a modest attempt to respond to needs that have been observed and recommendations that have been suggested in the field of historical linguistics over the past two decades. Although the pronoun is one of the significant parts of speech in a sentence and has many variables even in Late Modern English, unlike the verb system its grammatical variation has attracted less attention, probably because linguistic change in the pronominal system has been considered even more subtle.

The purpose of the present thesis is threefold: firstly, to illustrate the grammatical changes in pronouns attested in 19th-century English novels; secondly, to reveal which linguistic factors are involved in the pronominal changes by analyzing the usage of the target variable from several linguistic standpoints, such as syntactic, morphological, phonological, stylistic, sociolinguistic and pragmatic ones; thirdly, to consider how a prominent upsurge of normative grammar influenced the change of the English language in the century. With regard to the grammatical change of pronouns, the following are often noted by researchers: the archaic second person singular pronoun *thou*; the case problems (e.g., *it is I/me, younger than I/me, who/whom* in the object position; *between you and me/I*); the use of demonstrative *them* for *those* (e.g., *them books*); and disagreement in number such as singular *they* (e.g., *Everyone* has a book in *their* bags.). These pronominal variables are to be dealt with in this study.

It is often said that women spoke or wrote less grammatically than men did, e.g., McKnight (1928: 519–521); Tieken-Boon van Ostade (2006: 259). Taking Jane Austen's language as an example, McKnight states that her works afford abundant illustration of the form of language "controlled by social usage rather than by book rule" (1928: 521). It is interesting that, in one of her works, as though agreeing with his statements, protagonist Catherine says, "As far as I have had opportunity of judging, it appears to me that the usual style of letter-writing among women is faultless, except in three particulars.... . A general deficiency of subject, a total inattention to stops, and a very frequent ignorance of grammar" (*Northanger Abbey*, p. 13). In the present study, I would like to examine how the male and female authors of our 19th-century novels differ in grammatical use of pronoun.

1.2 Previous studies

There are only a few books which exclusively focus on Late Modern English from a historical point of view. Görlach overviews 18th- and 19th-century English in two works: *Eighteenth-Century English* (2001) and *English in Nineteenth-Century England: An Introduction* (1999). Other general linguistic introductions to Late Modern English, though different in size, are covered in George H. McKnight (1928: 405–538), Hayashi Ono and Hiroyuki Ito (1993), Richard Bailey (1996), Joan C. Beal (2004), Lynda Mugglestone (2006) and Ingrid Tieken-Boon van Ostade (2006, 2009).[6] In these studies, spelling, grammar, vocabulary and pronunciation in this period are identified and explained though linguistic variables, if mentioned, are not sufficiently identified and analyzed.

Grammatical usage of 19th-century English is also discussed in historical and comprehensive studies of grammar, such as Otto Jespersen's *Modern English Grammar on Historical Principle* (1909–49), Hendrik Poutsma's *Grammar of Late Modern English* (1914–29), F. Th. Visser's *Historical Syntax of the English Language* (1963–73), and David Denison's *Cambridge History of the English Language*, Vol. 4: 1776–1997 (1998). However, these studies do not pay any particular attention to 19th-century English itself; examples from the 19th-century are usually treated as those of (Late) Modern English without being separated from those of the previous centuries. Denison focuses on change during the Late Modern English period (1776-present day) but not on change within the period. Furthermore, in his study, while he spares many pages for the verbal group and the structure of clauses and sentences, he only briefly deals with the usage of pronouns.

Linguistic research on a particular novelist's English has been conducted since the middle of the 20th century. Studies on the language of 19th-century authors include K. C. Phillipps (1970) on Jane Austen, Phillipps (1978) on Thackeray, John W. Clark (1975) on Anthony Trollope, G. L. Brook (1970), Takao Yoshida (1980), Robert Golding (1985), Knud Sørensen (1985) and Osamu Imahayashi (2006) on Dickens, and Hideo Hirooka (1983) on Thomas Hardy. In those works, the language of individual authors is analyzed with reference to style, regional and/or social dialect, grammar and vocabulary. *In search of Jane Austen* (2014) is a recent work in which Tieken-Boon van

Ostade analyzes various aspects of Austen's letter writing from a sociolinguistic standpoint, focusing on her spelling, vocabulary and grammar.

Regarding dialectal variants and their grammatical usage in England, Scotland, Ireland and Wales, Joseph Wright's *English Dialect Dictionary* (1898–1905) and *English Dialect Grammar* (1905) are essential to consult for morphological and syntactic variation. Philologists have taken little interest in dialects, except for G. L. Brook's *English Dialects* (1963) and N. F. Blake's *Non-standard Language in English Literature* (1981). Brook studied the dialectal usage in different periods of English, including class and occupational dialects, dialect and literature, and so on. Blake presents a historical survey of the way in which nonstandard language is used in literary texts from Chaucer to modern times. *Studies in British Dialects* by Itsuki Hosoe (1956), though not completed, includes the dialectal usage of Hardy and the Brontës. In *Dialects in English Literature*, Hirooka (1965) studied regional dialects in English Literature from Old English to Modern English. Hosoe (1935), who based his study on George Eliot's works, revealed the usage of the Midland dialect from phonetic, syntactic and lexical perspectives. Lieselotte Anderwald (2002) investigates a range of morphosyntactic features of negation, offering a new understanding of regional and social variation in Present-day English. Her study is based on the British National Corpus (BNC).[7] Katie Wales (2006) focuses on Northern speech and culture in the context of identity, iconography, mental maps, boundaries and marginalization, emphasizing their richness and variety. In this work, Northern English grammar is briefly discussed in terms of "erosion."

There are some researchers who have paid attention to how use of language differed according to social classes in Late Modern English. In *Common and Courtly Language* (1986), a pioneering work of this kind, Carey McIntosh gave his insights into courtly-genteel and lower-class styles of language found in 18th-century novels, journals and letters. In *Language and Class in Victorian England* (1984), Phillipps observes the vocabulary, pronunciation and grammar in the upper and lower classes in Victorian England on the basis of data taken from fiction as well as non-fiction works. He describes the characteristic styles of language of both classes in Victorian society but does not give the detailed statistics.

In the limited number of works featuring specific grammatical variation in Late Modern English, relatively greater scholarly interest has been placed on the variation of the English verb system. Mats Rydén and Sverker Brorström (1987) survey the historical development of the *be/have* paradigm in English on the basis of letters and plays written in the 18th and 19th centuries. With a sociohistorical-linguistic approach, Tieken-Boon van Ostade (1987) shows that the transition of the use of the auxiliary *do* was not completed in 18th-century

English. Nobuko Suematsu (2004), using Jane Austen's six novels and her letters as a corpus, sheds light on the verb system in Austen's English by presenting numerical data. Anita Auer (2009) discusses the development of the subjunctive in 18th-century English and German with reference to the grammar books, actual usage, and the different socio-political contexts in which these developments occurred. Her research is based on A Representative Corpus of Historical English Registers (ARCHER).[8] Erik Smitterberg (2005) and Svenja Kranich (2010) both research the development of the progressive; Smitterberg focuses on the progressive in a process of integration into English grammar in the 19th century by using the Corpus of Nineteenth-Century English (CONCE)[9] while Kranich examines the development of the function of the progressive in Modern English by using ARCHER-2.[10] As noted in Auer, Smitterberg and Kranich, the development of diachronic corpora such as ARCHER and CONCE has been playing an important role for research on Late Modern English.

Regarding personal pronouns, Wales (1996) observes the usages of "the most recent generation" in *Personal Pronouns in Present-day English*. She uses her own extensive files of examples of pronouns from the 1980s until January 1995 as well as the corpora of English usage housed at University College London. Her approach is empirical, and sometimes pragmatic and functional, as her concern lies in social, political and rhetorical issues of culture, relationships and power. However, she does not present any statistical data to support her discussion.

Among others, the complex use of the second pronouns *thou* and *you* has been attracting the interest of historical linguists for several decades. Many of studies deal with the usage of these second person pronouns in Early Modern English with reference to R. Brown and A. Gilman (1960) as a landmark article. Corpus-based statistical analysis has recently become an important trend: Ulrich Busse issued *Linguistic Variation in the Shakespeare Corpus: Morpho-Syntactic Variability of Second Person Pronouns* (2002) and Terry Walker presented Thou *and* You *in Early Modern English Dialogues: Trial, Depositions, and Drama Comedy* (2007). Busse discusses the variation of second person pronouns in the Shakespeare Corpus from a syntactic perspective while Walker, using *A Corpus of English Dialogue 1560–1760*, attempts to ascertain which extra-linguistic factors are relevant to the choice between *thou* and *you*. As for the relative pronoun, Mats Rydén (1966) observes relative constructions in early 16th-century English. Tieken-Boon van Ostade (1994) analyzes the pronominal usage in 18th-century English; by using private letters as a corpus, she deals with the constructions in which the subject pronominal appears in the object position and the object pronominal appears in the subject position. She also discusses the usage of non-reflexive *–self* forms in the relevant constructions.

As we have observed above, there is little research which intensively treats the usage of pronouns in 19th-century English, using a certain amount of linguistic corpus to yield statistical data. To my best knowledge, there is no intensive research of grammatical change in regard to the pronoun usage in 19th-century English except for Xavier Dekeyser's *Number and Case Relations in 19th Century British English: A Comparative Study of Grammar and Usage* (1975). Using works published in the 19th century (about 3,000,000 words), Dekeyser thoroughly investigates number-and-case relations in this period in terms of chronological (before 1850 or after 1850) and stratified ("written conversational English" or "narrative, descriptive and informative prose") standpoints and gives syntactic analysis to each phenomenon. In the first half of his book, he deals with number relations (e.g., collectives, indefinites and multiple head phrases, subject heads modified by post posed plural adjuncts.) while in the second half he discusses case relations (e.g., the subject of the gerund, *who* vs. *whom*, nominative forms and objective forms of personal pronouns, and case relations in multiple head phrases). Dekeyser concludes that, as far as number-and-case relations in 19th-century English are concerned, grammatical doctrine has failed to thwart the development of usage, saying that "these allegedly correct forms are employed, not because they are prescribed, but because they are the ones which are inherent to the intrinsic laws of usage" (p. 269). Since his interest lies in "number-and-case relation" in general, the pronoun is accordingly treated under this theme. I will deal with the same issues, using different corpora in Chapter 3, Section 5.1 and Chapter 6, to confirm whether my statistical data agree with his results.

Dekeyser partially applies a sociolinguistic approach; as to the usage of agreement with the pronoun, he presents the statistical data to suggest that women use the singular *they* more often than men. I would like to probe more deeply into such problems by closely examining the contexts of individual examples. As for the case issues concerning the personal pronoun as well as the relative pronoun, the analyses of the characters' social background and the situations in which they are speaking, which are not dealt with in Dekeyser's research, may reveal another dimension of the pronominal usage at that time.

1.3 Methodological framework

1.3.1 Corpus

In order to exemplify the norms of spoken conversational English, it may not be appropriate to use dialogue from novels and plays, since several kinds of historical corpora covering 19th-century English in various genres are now available. Fictional speech is indeed not real spoken language. All the dialogues in novels are composed by the authors in order to create their characters' features, such as social backgrounds, education and personalities. In this sense, language written in novels may be called a thorough invention by the authors. Therefore, many may well think that there are indisputable disadvantages to using novels as linguistic materials. Nevertheless, if one attempts to conduct linguistic research, especially on 19th-century English, when the genre of fiction had reached the height of popularity, the novel could be a useful material for its own merits as follows:

a. The 19th century is regarded as the century of the novel's full arrival, since it is both quantitatively and qualitatively rich in the publication of novels. People of every rank in society appear in works written in this century, providing a variety of speech. Some authors are said to have recorded the spoken language of the time, such as Jane Austen, "who is usually credited as the first to record colloquial language in her novels" (Tieken-Boon van Ostate 2006: 249). Also, some Victorian authors knew the dialect firsthand, either regional or social, including Elizabeth Gaskell, the Brontës, George Eliot, Thomas Hardy and Dickens. Dialectal variants appearing in novels are mostly listed in Wright's *English Dialect Dictionary* (1898–1905). These facts suggest that the characters' dialectal speech is not the authors' arbitrary creation.
b. Generally, the novel has a variety of style, such as narrative and dialogue, formal and informal. There are also various situations called speech events in dialogue,[11] which are profitable for pragmatic and psychological analyses.
c. While authors generally choose language to illustrate the characteristics of people in their novels, they occasionally reveal their own habitual usage or predilection without noticing it. This enables us to conduct two different kinds of sociolinguistic analyses by examining two versions of the author's language: intentional linguistic representations and unintentional linguistic instinct.

Given the above mentioned merits, the novel is far from worthless as a corpus to help investigate linguistic change in the 19th century.

In preparing our corpus, several points were taken into account so that it would cover various aspects of the usage of pronouns in this period. Firstly, major novels were selected throughout the century including those of eight female authors to find possible differences in language between the male and female authors. Secondly, in order to cover dialectal usage of pronouns as much as possible, our texts contain works of the seven authors stated above who were acquainted with regional dialectal speech. Although I tried to compile a balanced corpus in various ways, the present one could not be regarded as such. When we choose one novel from all the works written by a novelist, it is difficult or perhaps impossible to decide which one is the most suitable for research of this kind. The twenty texts I have selected here vary in size and style. The ages at which the authors wrote their texts range from 21 to 55 years old. Most female authors' works belong to the earlier period of the 19th century. It is not known how these elements could affect the results of research. We should therefore use our corpus just as one sample of the English novels written in the 19th century.

The present corpus consists of the following twenty texts, or about 2,400,000 words, which would be adequate in size both for quantitative and qualitative analysis of pronominal variants. The twenty works used for our research are arranged according to the authors' date of birth as below:

[Authors and works]	[Approximate numbers of words]
Jane Austen (1775–1817): *Pride and Prejudice* (1813)	121,900
Mary Shelly (1797–1851): *Frankenstein* (1818)	75,100
Elizabeth Gaskell (1810–1865): *North and South* (1854–55)	183,100
W. M. Thackeray (1811–1863): *Vanity Fair* (1847–48)	304,300
Charles Dickens (1812–1870): *Great Expectations* (1860–61)	185,500
Anthony Trollope (1815–1882): *Barchester Towers* (1857)	198,600
Charlotte Brontë (1816–1855): *Jane Eyre* (1847)	186,400
Emily Brontë (1818–1848): *Wuthering Heights* (1847)	116,600
George Eliot (1819–1880): *Silas Marner* (1861)	71,500
Charles Kingsley (1819–1875): *The Water Babies* (1863)	68,400
Anne Brontë (1820–1849): *The Tenant of Wildfell Hall* (1848)	170,800
Lewis Carroll (1832–1898): *Alice's Adventures in Wonderland* and *Through the Looking-Glass* (1865 and 1872)	56,100
Thomas Hardy (1840–1928): *Jude the Obscure* (1895)	145,400
Robert Louis Stevenson (1850–1894): *Treasure Island* (1883)	68,900
Oscar Wilde (1854–1900): *The Picture of Dorian Gray* (1891)	79,100
Marie Corelli (1855–1924): *The Sorrows of Satan* (1895)	164,200
George Gissing (1857–1903): *The Private Papers of Henry Ryecroft* (1903)	61,900
Arthur Conan Doyle (1859–1930): *A Study in Scarlet* (1887)	43,400
Rudyard Kipling (1865–1936): *Captains Courageous* (1897)	53,400
H. G. Wells (1866–1946): *The Invisible Man* (1897)	48,800
Total	2,403,400

For other necessary information about the authors (e.g., birthplace, education) and the works (e.g., publication year, main setting of the story, narrator), see appendix 1. I also utilized the electronic texts of our authors provided by Project Gutenberg (http://www.gutenberg.org/) to make our statistic data accurate.

1.3.2 Grammar books

Although the first grammars were written in the late 16th century, comprehensive grammar books were compiled by the two 18th-century pioneer grammarians, Joseph Priestley, a schoolmaster and scientist who issued *Rudiments of English Grammar* in 1761, and Robert Lowth, later Bishop of London, who prepared *The Short Introduction to English Grammar* in 1762. Their works were followed by a long line of English grammars leading up to Lindley Murray's *English Grammar*, published in 1795, a culmination in the grammatical and rhetorical labors of the 18th century. From the end of the 18th century through the 19th century, when England was in the midst of the Industrial Revolution, people studied grammar more intensively than at any other time. In the geographically and socially mobile society, they had to prove the social status to which they claimed they belonged in terms of their language. People's craving for "good" language was so great that there was an increase in the production of grammar books during the second half of the 18th century, with some of the influential works reissued in the 19th century (cf. Tieken-Boon van Ostade 2008: 1–14).

There was no uniform guiding principle among the 18th and 19th-century grammarians. While many grammarians, including Lowth, aimed to apply the principles of universal grammar to the English language, Murray's theory was more liberal, placing importance on usage (McKnight 1928: 394). It may be all the more appropriate to refer to Priestley (1769), Lowth (1769) and Murray (1806) as chief grammar books written in the 18th centuries.[12] In addition, for 19th-century grammar, I consulted William Hazlitt, Goold Brown and William Cobbett. Hazlitt, an essayist, wrote *A New and Improved Grammar of the English Tongue: For the Use of Schools* in 1809.[13] Cobbett, a politic and forceful journalist, produced *A Grammar of the English Language, in A Series of Letters* in 1819. In 1851, Brown compiled an encyclopedic work, *The Grammar of English Grammars*, which covers various views of many preceding grammarians on the controversial usage of a given subject.

In the history of English, it occasionally happens that nonstandard variants become standard in course of time and vice versa. In this research, the terms "standard" and "nonstandard" are used for the usage which is regarded as such in contemporary grammars.

1.3.3 Multifaceted approach

Language change involves a complexity of factors, "interwoven sociolinguistic and psycholinguistic factors which cannot easily be disentangled from one another" (Aitchison 2001: 249). Grammatical change of the pronoun is no exception. In this study, several approaches will be applied to the analysis of pronominal variation, including the chronological, syntactic, stylistic, morphological, phonological, sociolinguistic, and pragmatic perspectives.

First of all, I will view overall distribution of the target variants from a chronological standpoint to obtain the historical development of the pronoun from the Late Modern English period through the Present-day English period. The distribution of target variants might have changed in the course of the 19th century, which will be also examined. I would then like to consider which kinds of factors are involved in their occurrence. The factors determining linguistic variation are basically of two types: one is language-internal factors such as syntactic, morphological and phonological factors and the other is language-external factors such as chronological, social, regional, stylistic and psychological factors. These factors, either external or internal, often work together in the course of linguistic transition, which in turn requires us to examine a certain variable with reference to a couple of parameters. As regards external factors, a close examination of contexts is the best strategy. In order to make the best and the most objective use of our data possible, we need to set certain standards for the classification of variants, which are discussed below.

1.3.3.1 Sociolinguistic analysis
Sex (or gender) and age are essential elements in socio-historical studies. Alongside these two elements, social class is another significant parameter for investigation of language since it is revealed in speech as well as in manners, education, clothing and a sense of values.

Since in novels there are many characters whose exact age is unknown, I will simply put people into three groups, male, female and child, by combining two elements (sex and age) into one. "Child" stands for those of school age or under. Married characters are considered "male" or "female" no matter how young they are. In our texts, there are some characters who appear as a child and grow up in the course of the story. Such characters will be differently classified according to their growing stages. The authors' sex is also subject to sociolinguistic analysis whenever necessary.

Strictly speaking, England had only two classes: aristocrats (who inherited titles and land) and commoners (everyone else). However, concerning social class in 19th-century English society, or Victorian society,[14] historians agree that it was three-tiered (the upper, middle and lower classes),[15] although there is no consensus on the exact composition of those classes. This English class system continued into the 20th century.

Before deciding on the definition of social class for our study, we would like to have a look at which kinds of analyses have been conducted on the basis of social class. Alan S. C. Ross (1956) is known to be the first to deal with languages in terms of social class. He coined the terms "U" and "non-U," representing "upper class" and "non-upper class" respectively. In his article he is concerned with the linguistic demarcation of the upper class (1956: 13). The debate does not refer to the speech of the working class or linguistic difference between the middle and lower classes. McIntosh (1986) uses the terms "upper-class English" and "lower-class English" in discussing the stylistics of social class in 18th-century English literature.

Even with 19th-century English society, researchers tend to employ a two-layer demarcation. In *Language and Class in Victorian England*, Phillipps (1984) discusses different usage between "the upper classes" and "the lower orders," focusing on variables used by those in these two different categories respectively. "The upper classes" consist of the nobility and gentry and "the lower orders" stand for all the other people below the rank of the gentry, both in country and in town. The classifications mentioned above illustrate that the central concern of historical linguists has been placed on language particular to the upper class. On the other hand, in sociolinguistic studies working-class people have collected a lot of attention. Trudgill (1974), for instance, applies a more detailed classification to his study on the use of the third-person singular form without -s in Norwich. He assigns his subjects to five social classes ranging from upper middle class to lower working class[16] on the basis of their occupation, education, income, and other factors. This method is common among sociolinguists but would not be practical in dealing with many characters in novels whose detailed social and economic background is difficult to define.

Imahayashi (2007a) divides the 19th-century society into two groups but his approach is different from Phillipps (1984). He divides people into "the working class" and "non-working class," focusing on the characteristic usage among working-class people. A two-layer classification like his may be helpful to discuss the use of "nonstandard" language and to avoid the troublesome work of drawing a line between the upper and the middle on the one hand and another line between the middle and the lower on the other. Still, I would like to sort the 19th-century society into three groups, since this classification more faithfully represents the society at that time and could reveal possible difference between the three classes.

In order to decide how to divide the characters in our novels into three social classes, let us consider the social class system of 19th-century England once again in more detail. Generally speaking, Victorian people consisted of "the aristocracy and landed gentry, or those who did not have to work for a living," "the middle classes" and "the working classes" (cf. Mitchell 1996). The boundary between two classes was ambiguous, as mentioned above. Within the middle class, those with the highest social standing were the professionals, referred to as "upper middle class." In England, the sons and daughters of peers were commoners, and the eldest son would become an aristocrat only after his father died. The younger sons had to earn their living in professions such as clergymen and commissioned officers. Social contact and intermarriage between the two groups were possible. This was the same with the border between the middle and the lower classes. Business success or failure would sometimes change one's social status dramatically within a lifetime.[17] The middle class grew in size and significance during the 19th century owing to the Industrial Revolution. The aspiring middle class made up about 15 percent of the population in 1837 and 25 percent in 1901 (Mitchell 1996: 20). The categorization of social class at the beginning of the 19th century would be different from that at the end of the century. In the 20th century, on top of the aristocracy and the landed gentry, the upper class contained high-ranking officials, clergymen, barristers and other professionals (Hatanaka et al. 1983: 27).

Taking all these elements into account, I will put the characters of our 19th-century texts in the three groups as follows: the upper class includes the aristocracy of large landowners, the gentry, the clergy, barristers, physicians and high-rank officers; the middle class includes tenant farmers, schoolmasters and school teachers, scientists, manufacturers, merchants, traders, surgeons, police officers, governesses, clerks, sea captains and butlers; placed in the lower class are innkeepers, factory workers, artificers, farmers, domestic servants, fishermen, seamen, other laborers, buccaneers and convicts. Some upper-middle-class people, such as the clergy, military and naval officers, physicians,[18] and barristers, are grouped into the upper class since these are regarded as aristocratic professions.[19] A male character's status is decided by his occupation and by the family into which he was born. A female character who has an occupation is decided in the same way, while a married woman's status depends on her husband. The status of children is determined by their family.

1.3.3.2 Stylistic analysis

Brook (1973: 81) notes that "[t]here are some varieties of language which can be associated neither with groups nor individuals but with the occasions when they are used," calling these varieties registers. He states that the study of these varieties or registers may be regarded as the examination of language in the context within which it is used. Although the definition of "register" varies from scholar to scholar, many agree that there are three major elements which stand out. According to M.A.K. Halliday (1978: 33), concepts needed for describing what is linguistically significant in the context of situation are the "field," the "tenor" and the "mode." As summarized by John Pearce in Doughty et al. (1972: 185–186), "field" refers to the institutional setting in which language occurs, and embraces the subject-matter at hand and the whole activity of the speaker or participant in a setting; "tenor" refers to the relationship between participants, variation in formality, the length of the relationship and the degree of emotional charge in it; "mode" refers to the channel of communication adopted, i.e., the choice between spoken and written medium. The terminology used by scholars sometimes differs but the idea of the three elements for register is almost the same.[20]

All these elements, no matter what they are named or how they are technically defined, are essential for explaining why the speaker (or the writer) uses a particular variant in a particular occasion. For stylistic or contextual analysis, we will consider linguistic genre of language (religious, poetic, etc.), difference in use between spoken and written language, the relationship between a speaker and his or her addressee, and the speaker's psychological condition (emotion in particular). In most cases, I use the term "register" in dealing with language in spoken or written contexts.

We will perhaps need some definition for spoken and written languages in the novel. Our 19th-century texts contain languages of various styles, such as dialogue, letter, note, diary, poetry and narrative.[21] It is safe to regard dialogue as a written representation of spoken language, as it is agreed that dialogue is fictional speech. Letters, diaries, notes and poetry written by the characters are considered written language. In the present study, I will therefore regard dialogue as spoken language and treat the other genres (e.g., narrative, letter, note, diary and poetry) as subcategories within the written category.

The linguistic context for "narrative" is difficult to determine. There are traditionally two types of narrative: first-person narrative by one of the novel's characters and third-person narrative by an omniscient narrator. Since omniscient narrators are usually out of the story, they do not typically use the first person singular pronoun *I* in their narration. There are, however, some exceptional cases: As seen in *Vanity Fair* and *Barchester Towers*, even omniscient narrators may sometimes use the first person pronoun in reference to themselves as if they were part of the story. Still, I will regard the narrative of these novels as third-person narrative in its totality.

Narrative is conducted in a variety of styles, especially in first-person narrative. Some narratives are written in the way of a letter, journal or diary, while others are delivered in monologue or discourse to another character. It is not rare that one text has more than one narrator, each narrating in a different style. There are also cases in which a text contains more than one type of narrative, as seen in *Wuthering Heights* and *Frankenstein*.[22] As complex as narrative can be, in terms of register, all kinds of narrative will be regarded as written language to avoid excessively complicated categorization. Even when narrative is conducted in interview or monologue, its language is closer to written language because, in general, stories told in narrative are not spontaneous, as in dialogue, but previously prepared. It sometimes happens that uneducated narrators sometimes use nonstandard language in writing as if they were speaking. A case in point is *The Adventure of Huckleberry Finn* by Mark Twain (1884). The narrator is a street urchin called Huck and the premise is that he wrote the story after his "adventures."[23] The narrative conducted by an uneducated narrator such as Huck should be dealt with as written language as well, notwithstanding the fact that his English is broken and would be subject to careful sociolinguistic analyses.

In our study, as far as the main narrative is concerned, regardless of the style in which it is conducted, the language will be called narrative. For instance, in *Treasure Island* and *A Study in Scarlet*, the narrative is carried out in journals, and in *The Tenant of Wildfell Hall*, the narrator delivers the whole story in letters to his relative, who does not actually appear in the story. These narratives are all treated as narrative instead of journal or letter, save for a couple of exceptions. The narrative of *The Private Papers of Henry Ryecroft* (henceforth referred to as *Henry Ryecroft*) is supposed to have been written by a retired writer named Henry Ryecroft, as its title illustrates. I classify his language as diary. In *Frankenstein*, although the discourse of the scientist Frankenstein and that of the monster, both of which are related in the letters by Walton to his sister, are regarded as narrative, the language of Walton is classified as letter since it appears in an exact form of letter to his sister.

1.3.3.3 Regional parameters

In classification of the modern English dialects, Wright (1905:3) divides England (and Wales) into five divisions: the Northern, Midland, Eastern, Western and Southern dialects. Since there is only a limited regional variation in our 19th-century corpus, Wright's categorization will be quite sufficient. I will discuss dialectal usage for some variables even more simply according to North vs. South, as used in Bernd Kortmann (2008: 490). Kortmann identifies a north-south divide for a range of morpho-syntactic properties, with the core of the North constituted by Scottish English, Orkney/Shetland and the dialects of North England, and the South constituted by the Southwest, the Southeast and East Anglia. For the dialectal map of Modern English presented by Wright and the demarcation of Great Britain today, see Appendix 2.

1.3.3.4 Outline of the study

This work consists of seven chapters including the present chapter. From

Chapter 2 through Chapter 6, I will show which linguistic factors are involved in the choice of certain pronominal variants: Chapter 2 explains dialectal variation of personal pronouns; Chapter 3 considers the case problems of personal pronouns; Chapter 4 focuses on the nonstandard usage of demonstrative pronouns; Chapter 5 treats the rivalry between relative pronoun variants as seen in the choice between *whom* and *who* in the objective function and the choice between *of which* and *whose* for non-persons; Chapter 6 discusses number agreement in the case of indefinite pronouns. In each of these five chapters, quantitative analysis is first conducted on the relevant variables followed by qualitative analysis from several standpoints. Summaries are given at the end of each major section. In the concluding Chapter 7, as an overall summary of the present study, I examine what kinds of linguistic factors influence the target variants analyzed in the previous five chapters and consider how the prescriptive grammar affected the pronominal changes in 19th-century English.

Notes
1 The former, which consists of ten detailed case studies, concerns the relationships between English, its users, and 19th-century society. It also discusses major structural aspects of nineteenth-century English, such as nouns, verbs and adjectives, and vocabulary (Germanic vs. Romance). The latter, containing sixteen papers, deals with such issues as linguistic ideology, the grammatical tradition and the contribution of women to the writing of grammars.
2 Included in pioneering works of language variation are William Labov's *Social Stratification of English in New York City* (1966) and Peter Trudgill's *Social Differentiation of English in Norwich* (1974).
3 In *Socio-historical Linguistics*, she presented a detailed analysis of the development of relative clause formation strategies in Middle Scots.
4 In *Diachronic Perspectives on Address Term Systems* (2003), address term system and their diachronic developments in European languages are discussed. Several contributions deal with the complex usage of *thou* and *you/ye* in English from pragmatic perspectives.
5 This work consists of articles which deal with both literary and nonliterary texts and explore a variety of approaches in mainstream linguistics, sociolinguistics and dialectology, and research of nonstandard English.
6 Tieken-Boon van Ostade (2006) features 18th-century English, Bailey (1996) and Mugglestone (2006) cover 19th-century English, while McKnight (1928), Ono and Ito (1993), Beal (2004) and Tieken-Boon van Ostade (2009) deal with English in both centuries.
7 The BNC is a 100-million-word corpus of current British language, written (90%) and spoken (10%), from a wide range of sources. Anderwald's data are based on the spoken section of this corpus.
8 ARCHER, first constructed by Douglas Biber and Edward Finegan in the 1990s, is a multi-genre corpus of British and American English covering the periods 1600-1999.
9 CONCE is divided into three periods (1800-1830, 1850-1870, and 1870-1900), and seven genres (Debates, Drama, Fiction, History, Letters, Science, and Trials).
10 ARCHER-2 is the expanded version of ARCHER. ARCHER 3.1 was completed in 2006 and

the current version known as ARCHER 3.2 was completed in 2013. For versions of ARCHER, see http://www.projects.alc.manchester.ac.uk/archer/archer-versions/[accessed May 29, 2017].

11 According to George Yule (1996: 135), speech event is "[a] set of circumstances in which people interact in some conventional way to arrive at some outcome."

12 In 1769, Priestley issued his expanded edition with a supplement entitled "Notes and Observations, for the Use of Those Who have made some Proficiency in the Language," and Lowth issued a new corrected edition that year as well. In 1806, Murray's fifteenth edition was issued.

13 The publication year printed on the text was 1810.

14 Social class in 19th-century England could be represented by that in Victorian society (1837-1901) because of the length of time.

15 According to Julia Prewitt Brown (1985: 7), in 1803, the upper class comprised about 27,000 families (or 2 % of the population); the middle ranks made up about 635,000 families; the lower ranks about 1,347,000 families.

16 Trudgill's five social classes are: the upper middle class (UMC), the lower middle class (LMC), the upper working class (UMC), the middle working class (MWC) and the lower working class (LWC).

17 Geoffrey Crossick (1991: 153) states that "[t]he early nineteenth century then witnessed a critical transition in political economy as the settled nature of Smith's three orders yielded, ... Landlords, capitalist, and labourers transposed easily into higher, middle, and lower classes, ..."

18 Julia Prewitt Brown (1985: 61) states that "younger sons of the gentry and aristocracy usually considered entering either the Army or the Church."

19 Regarding court presentation, *The Habits of Good Society* writes that "the wives and daughters of the clergy, of military and naval officers, of physicians and barristers, can be presented. These are the aristocratic professions but the wives and daughters of general practitioners and solicitors are not entitled to a presentation. The wives and daughters of merchants, or of men in business (excepting bankers), are not entitled to presentation ..." (cited by Hughes (1998: 179))

20 For instance, "style" is used instead of "tenor" (Joos 1961:11; Halliday, McIntosh and Strevens 1964). David Crystal and Derek Davy (1969: 61) use the terms "tenor," "field" and "mode" as stylistic elements.

21 Robert Scholes and Robert Kellogg (1966: 4) define narrative as "all those literary works which are distinguished by two characteristics: the presence of a story and a story-teller."

22 This is called Chinese-box narrative.

23 In his monologue, Huck says that "so there ain't nothing more to write about, and I am rotten glad of it, because if I'd a knowed what a trouble it was to make a book I wouldn't a tackled it and ain't agoing to no more." (p. 262)

CHAPTER 2
Dialectal Variation of Personal Pronouns

The system of personal pronouns in Present-day English was established in the 16th century after three changes had taken place: "the disuse of *thou, thy, thee*; the substitution of *you* for *ye* in a nominative case; and the introduction of *its* as the possessive of *it*" (Baugh and Cable 2002: 242). These changes, however, had not been fully completed in Late Modern English. The personal pronouns in this period are illustrated as below.

Table 2.1: Forms of the personal pronouns in Late Modern English

	1st. Person		2nd Person.		3rd Person.			
	Sing.	Plur.	Sing.	Plur.	Sing.			Plur.
					Masc.	Fem.	Neut.	
Nom.	I	we	thou	ye	he	she	it	they
Obj.	me	us	thee	you	him	her	it	them
Poss.	my	our	thy	your	his	her	its	their

(Adapted from Poutsma 1916: ch. XXXII,1)

The difference between Late Modern English and Present-day English is that the archaic second person pronouns *thou, thee,* and *thy* in the singular and *ye* in the plural are retained in the former. By 19th-century English, the use of *thou* and *ye* had already become extremely limited. Roger Lass (2006: 98) states that "by the end of the eighteenth (century) *thou* is not an option in ordinary speech, though it remains in special register like poetry and prayer." Hazlitt (1810: 49), a 19th-century grammarian, also stated that "[i]n common and familiar discourse we always employ the second person plural (*you*) instead of the singular (*thou*)." As these descriptions suggest, both *thou* and *ye* found in our 19th-century texts had become so marginal that they may be no longer called standard forms at that time. In this chapter, I would like to focus on the personal pronouns which are out of the paradigm today, that is, archaic and/or dialectal forms. Nonstandard use of the reflexive pronouns is also discussed here.

2.1 Second person

2.1.1 *Thou*

2.1.1.1 Overview

The second person pronouns *thou* and *ye/you* have an interesting history. The archaic singular form *thou* (OE *þu*) had been used from the Old English period through the Modern English period but has been replaced by *you* in Present-day English. The form *you* was originally an objective case (OE *eow*) but has been used as a nominative case as well as an objective case. The difference in the use of *thou* and *ye* went beyond mere number. In the 13th century, the singular form *thou* was used among familiars and in addressing children or persons of inferior rank, while the originally plural form *ye* began to be used as singular and as a mark of respect in addressing a superior (Baugh and Cable 2002: 242). The singular use of the plural *ye/you* was increasingly promoted by the idea that the plural pronoun was a more polite way to address a single person than the singular *thou*. By the middle of the 14th century, *you* was well on the way to becoming neutral, and *thou* "marked," and then the form *thou* was gradually replaced by *you* and had fallen out of use in ordinary speech by the 18th century (Lass 2006: 97).

While the pronoun *thou* is no longer used in present-day standard English, it was preserved in certain fields and can still be found today. In local dialects, the form was used to express familiarity, as in Shakespeare, and Quakers retained the familiar singular form in their speech for religious reasons (Brook 1963: 109; Jespersen 1933:§14.5). Trudgill (1999: 92–93) states that there are two major "Tradition Dialect" areas of England which have preserved the *thou/you* distinction mentioned above, though sparsely: one northern area (the Lower North, the Lancashire and Staffordshire areas) and one western area (the Northern Southwest and the Western Southwest). In dialect, the form *thou* is limitedly used in idiomatic phrases: In some Northern dialects, *thee/thou* forms are attested in an imperative starting with *thee* like *Thee shut up!* (Brook 1963: 109) or in set phrases such as the stereotypical Yorkshire leave-taking *Sithee* 'I'll see you' (Beal 2010: 41). In addition to dialectal speech, it is known that the archaic form was used in Christian prayers well into the 20th century, and therefore was kept in religious and poetic language.

On the usage of *thou* and *you*, numerous studies have been conducted, especially with reference to Shakespeare's drama. Many researchers, including Brown and Gilman (1960), Charles Barber (1981), Anne Carvey Johnson (1966),[1] Joan Mulholland (1967), Busse (2002) and Penelope Freedman (2007), attempted to analyze the rivalry between *thou* and *you* in Early Modern English from syntactic, sociolinguistic and stylistic standpoints. Brown and

Gilman's famous "power and solidarity" rule in the selection of *thou/you* has been applied to many European languages and has become a fundamental theory. Researchers focusing on the usage of *thou/you* in spoken language are Jonathan Hope (1994) and Terry Walker (2007). Walker, closely investigating *thou* and *you* in three speech-related genres — trials, deposition and drama comedy — in *A Corpus of English Dialogues 1560–1760*, shows how extralinguistic factors such as sex, age and rank influence pronominal usage. She argues that in unemotional familiar address, the higher ranks tended to exchange *you*, but that no sufficient evidence indicates that the lower ranks would tend to exchange *thou*; in terms of sex parameter, power based on sex in husband/wife relations affected pronominal usage in comedy, and parental authority could encourage *thou* in depositions and comedy. In recent years, besides the conventional linguistic approaches as given above, pragmatic perspectives have been introduced in order to explain the cases that the previous studies treated as deviation (e.g., Bruti 2000; Busse 2003; Mazzon 2003). In these studies textual analysis is integrated with some basic socio-pragmatic considerations. Bruti proposes two axes for the selection of *you/thou* in Shakespeare's English: an axis for social distance and one for emotional attitude, to which I will return for the discussion of *thou* in our texts. Since the transition of *thou* to *you* was thought to have been completed by 1700, the usage in Late Modern English has hardly attracted interest and little has been studied from any perspective. However, it would nevertheless be worthwhile to investigate how the remainder of *thou* was used in the 19th-century, when it was extremely limited in frequency. Since in previous studies "power and solidarity" and "emotion" are often treated as significant elements in the choice of *thou*, particularly in Elizabethan works, it would be reasonable to examine how these elements are involved in its use in our corpus from sociolinguistic and pragmatic perspectives. For discussing the use of the old form *thou* in 19th-century English, however, the possibility of dialectal use as well as stylistic effect (e.g., religious, poetic, etc.) cannot be ignored. Such factors will be considered when necessary.

2.1.1.2 Data

For the sake of convenience, I will hereafter use *THOU* for *thou, thine, thy* and *thyself* and *YOU* for *you/ye, your* and *yourself*. The occurrence of *THOU* is extremely low in our 19th-century texts. A brief examination of our corpus shows the instances of *THOU* and *YOU* are 406 (1.1%) and 36713 (98.9%) respectively. This indicates that *YOU* is undoubtedly the norm as second person pronoun both as singular and as plural. Our texts yield quite a few examples of *THOU* in mere quotation from literature in the earlier periods. With these examples excluded, the occurrence of *THOU* is reduced to 272.[2] Given the absolutely dominant use of *YOU*, overall statistical analysis of the rivalry between the two forms would not be fruitful, but it is valuable to examine whether the choice of the form *THOU* is habitual for the individual, especially in the case of dialect speakers. With that point in mind, I would like to consider the characteristic behavior of the "marked" *THOU* commonly observed in our texts. The twenty texts under research are arranged in order of the authors' year of birth from top to bottom.[3]

Table 2.2: Distribution of *THOU* and the numbers of speakers who use it according to text

	Absolute frequency	Frequency per 10,000 words	Number of speakers
Pride			
Frankenstein	46	6.13	2
N and S	50	2.73	8
Vanity	10	0.33	3
Great			
Barchester	49	2.47	2
Jane	5	0.27	2
Wuthering	31	2.66	6
Silas			
Water	32	4.68	3
Wildfell	4	0.23	2
Alice			
Jude	6	0.41	3
Treasure			
Dorian			
Satan	36	2.19	3
Ryecroft	3	0.48	1
Scarlet			
Captains			
Invisible			
Total	272	1.13	35

Note: Examples of *THOU* found in quotation are omitted from this table.

According to the frequency of *THOU* per 10,000 words, the pronoun *THOU* is attested more often in the earlier period of the century. In view of literary genre or style of the texts, it is found that the texts with *THOU* in higher frequency include Gothic novels such as *Frankenstein* and *The Sorrows of Satan*, *The Water Babies*, a fantasy novel, and *Henry Ryecroft*, which is written in the style of a diary. In contrast, *Pride and Prejudice*, which makes a realistic description of the daily life of upper middle class families, has no relevant examples, though it is the oldest of all our texts under examination. Thus, it can be assumed that, as is the case in the 20th century, *THOU* was no longer used in daily life in the 19th century.

The table indicates a possible involvement of dialectal factors in the use of *THOU*. The eleven texts in which *THOU* is attested include three works by the Brontë sisters, who are from Northern England, and *North and South*, which is set in the northern part of England. In terms of the number of speakers of

THOU, more than half belong to these North-related texts. These findings suggest that the form *THOU* symbolizes the Northern speech. However, it is significant that the form is not habitually used by any of the eighteen users of *THOU* in these texts, whether they speak local dialect or standard English. In the Brontës' works, there appear some characters who speak Yorkshire dialect, with Joseph, a local servant in *Wuthering Heights*, being a typical case. However, even for those dialect speakers, *THOU* is not the regular second person singular form, though they sometimes keep the archaic second person nominative plural *ye* (see 2.1.2 Ye).

2.1.1.3 "Power" as a key to the use of *THOU*

In order to investigate how the form *THOU* is used in individual instances, let us first examine the relationship between the speaker and the addressee. In order to distinguish the "power difference" between two people, age and sex would be two important elements. For the sake of simplicity, when there is more than one factor involved in the relation, the most influential one is applied: when there is an age gap between the speaker and the addressee, as in the case of parent and child, they are considered "senior" and "junior" even if the younger one is a grownup; when characters are similar in age, they are differentiated by sex even if they are both children and it follows that the relationship between two boys is regarded as that between "two men." Nonhuman entities, such as spiritual beings and nature, and narrators are also considered.[4] The number of combinations stands for that of the combinations of the speaker and the addressee; for instance, when character X addresses character Y as *THOU* and Y also addresses X as *THOU*, the number of combinations amounts to two (one is X→Y and the other one is X←Y) in one pair (X&Y). Table 2.3 shows the absolute frequency of *THOU* and the number of combinations for each relation.

As demonstrated in the table, when employed between human characters, *THOU* seems more likely to be used from senior to junior and male to female and less likely in the opposite relations (i.e., from junior to senior and female to male). Although there is no example of the master and servant relationship, the table surely indicates the tendency that *THOU* is used from a person in a socially higher or sexually stronger position to one inferior in that respect in our 19th-century texts.

Table 2.3: Relationship between the speaker and the addressee in use of THOU

	Speaker	Addressee	Combination	Token
a	Senior	Junior	14	66
b	Junior	Senior	3	6
c	Male	Female	6	13
d	Female	Male	1	1
e	Male	Male	12	80
f	Female	Female	1	3
g	Nonhuman entity	Character (human)	4	67
h	Character (human)	Nonhuman entity	8	17
i	Narrator	Character (human)	6	17
j	Narrator	Reader	1	2
Total			56	272

As to the relationship between a character and a nonhuman entity, the number of combinations is greater in cases in which *THOU* is used from a character to a nonhuman entity than in the reversed direction. The absolute frequency, however, is much higher in the nonhuman-entity-to-character relationship, with 67 tokens compared to 17 for the opposite direction. This suggests that there is not a clear disparity in the use of *THOU* between these two sides — an interesting phenomenon in that, although nonhuman entities are greater in power than mortals, human characters can similarly address their more powerful counterparts as *THOU*. This matter will be considered later in more detail. Omniscient narrators call their characters or readers *THOU*. Power belongs to the narrator. There is no example of the use of *THOU* given in the opposite direction.

The results show that Brown and Gilman's power theory is generally applicable to our 19th-century novels; power is significantly relevant to the use of *THOU*. It is true, however, that there are instances in which *THOU* is employed from one in lesser power (e.g., Junior, female, human character) to one in greater power (e.g., senior, male, nonhuman entity, respectively). Let us next see how power theory works or does not work by taking a close look at the individual examples of each relationship.

a [Senior → Junior]

To start with, the use of *THOU* from senior to junior will be examined. There are fourteen different combinations for this relationship, which are displayed in Table 2.4.

Table 2.4: Senior-to-junior relationship in use of THOU

Speaker	Addressee	Combination	Token
Father	Daughter	4	25
Father	Son	2	8
Mother	Son	1	3
Uncle	Nephew	1	2
Aunt	Nephew	1	4
Servant	Master's son	3	6
Old woman	Boy	1	13
Employer	Boy	1	5
Total		14	66

Although the pronoun is mostly used from a senior to a junior in a family ([1] and [2]), it is also used from a servant to his or her master's son (3), from an employer to his junior employee (4), and from an old woman to a boy whom she had met for the first time (5). This demonstrates that an age difference is quite important in use of THOU.

(1) 'The blessing of God be upon *thee*, my child!'[5]
     <Mr. Hale → Margaret: Daughter>   (*N and S*, p. 40)
(2) 'It would ha' been a blessing if Goddy-mighty had took *thee* too wi' *thy* mother and father, poor useless boy! ...' <Mrs. Fawley → Jude: Nephew>
                                              (*Jude*, p. 7)
(3) "Hareton, it's Nelly — Nelly, *thy* nurse."
     <Nelly → Hareton: Master's son>   (*Wuthering*, p. 97)
(4) '*Thou* come along,' said Grimes; 'what dost want with washing *thyself*? *Thou* did not drink half a gallon of beer last night, like me.'
     <Mr. Grimes → Tom: Employee>   (*Water*, p. 12)
(5) 'Water's bad for *thee*; I'll give *thee* milk.'
     <Old woman → Tom: Stray child>   (*Water*, p. 36)

b [Junior → Senior]

We will next see the opposite relations, i.e., the junior-to-senior relationship. Compared to the examples of *THOU* used from adult to child, its use is extremely restricted in the reversed direction; there are only six examples and the number of combinations is three. Let us see these exceptional cases. In example (6), Bessy, a daughter of Nicholas in *North and South*, addresses her father as *THOU*. She is trying to prevent her father from telling the police on Boucher, his coworker, who has thrown a stone at their master's sister. The sentence "I dunno' where I got strength" describes her unusually frantic condition, in which she gained bravery to use *THOU*.

(6) I dunno' where I got strength, but I threw mysel' off th' settle and clung to him. "Father, father!" said I. "*Thou*'ll never go peach on that poor clemmed man. I'll never leave go on *thee*, till *thou* sayst *thou* wunnot."
<Bessy → Nicholas: Father> (*N and S*, p. 201)

Though Bessy utters *THOU* in an emphatic way, she does not have any hostility towards her father. To the contrary, her use of the pronoun is based on their trust and love. This leads Bessy to use *THOU* to address her father against the power restriction and her request is successfully accepted; without becoming indignant, Nicholas soothes his daughter, saying "Dunnot be a fool, ... I never thought o' telling th' police on him; ..." (*N and S*, p. 201).

The other examples of *THOU* from junior to senior are found in Hareton addressing Nelly, his old nurse, and Isabella, his relative in *Wuthering Heights*. His use of *THOU* makes a striking contrast with Bessy's above. In example (7), while Nelly sees her old master's son with pleasure, he is quite rude to her because he has no idea who she is. In this case, Hareton's "thee!" in addressing Nelly shows animosity. He is annoyed when chided by a strange woman for his bad words. All his attention is poured on the orange Nelly has in her hand and her meddling with his affair is the last thing he wants. A similar usage is found in (8). When meeting Isabella, a stranger who has suddenly come to live in his house, he unreservedly expresses hostility to her, as is illustrated with the word "authoritatively." Unlike the relationship between Bessy and Nicholas, Hareton apparently does not feel any familiarity or trust towards these elder people. The reason he addresses Nelly as *THOU* is not because he thinks that Nelly is socially inferior to him but because he has not been educated in manners.

(7) "Who has taught you those fine words, my barn," I inquired, "The curate?"
"Damn the curate, and *thee*! Gie me that," he replied.
<Hareton → Nelly: Old nurse> (*Wuthering*, p. 97)
(8) "Now, wilt *tuh* be ganging?" he asked authoritatively.
<Hareton → Isabella: Aunt> (*Wuthering*, p. 121)

In the cases where children use *THOU* towards their seniors, however, the dialectal factor may also be considered. The two juniors who exceptionally use *THOU* towards seniors, Bessy and Hareton, are both from Northern England and both speak a dialect more or less. One point to be noted here is that neither Bessy nor Hareton uses *THOU* habitually: Hareton usually says *you* for the second person pronoun and Bessy, *yo* (see §2.1.2). Thus, in light of their use of the second person pronoun, it is safe to say that *THOU* is the marked form for them, as it is for others who speak standard English, and that they try to convey some special feelings by employing it, whether consciously or not.

c [Male → Female]
"Power" is observed as an important factor in the male-to-female relationship just as in the senior-to-junior relationship, although its absolute frequency is not as high. The numbers of combinations of the male-to-female relationship and the female-to-male relationship are six and one respectively. This disparity can be explained by social status; man had more power than woman in 19th-century English society.[6] The six relevant combinations of the male-to-female relationship are "a husband to his wife" (2 exx.), "a landowner to a governess" (1 ex.), "Monster to a girl" (1 ex.), "a millworker to a young woman" (1 ex.) and "a boy to a girl" (1 ex.). The use of *THOU* from a husband to his wife is found in example (9) from *The Tennant of Wildfell Hall* (hereafter referred to as *Wildfell Hall*). In this scene, Mr. Hattersley, who has shown affection to another woman, is trying to persuade his wife, Milicent, to believe that the only woman he truly loves is her. This type of usage is commonly seen in male-to-female relations. Interestingly, a quite similar usage is found in a scene in *The Merchant of Venice* by Shakespeare, where Bassanio, apologizing to Portia for losing the betrothal ring, makes a pledge not to do such a thing again for all the world. Note the following two examples:

(9) 'You said you adored her.'
     'True, but adoration isn't love. I adore Annabella, but I don't love her; and I love *thee*, Milicent, but I don't adore *thee*.'
     <Mr. Hattersley → His wife; Milicent>   (*Wildfell*, p. 276)
     Cf. Pardon this fault, and by my soul I swear I never more will break an oath with *thee*. <Bassanio → Portia> (*The Merchant of Venice*, 5, 1, 247–49)

Just as Bassanio shifts from *YOU* to *THOU* in addressing Portia when he is making a promise, Mr. Hattersley chooses *THOU* to appeal to his wife's leniency. In either case, *THOU* is used as a marker by the male to express sincere affection to the woman.

Manifestation of attachment is similarly attested in the relationship between lovers. In example (10) in *Jane Eyre*, Rochester's longing for Jane is expressed by his *thee*'s. After a few lines, when he is back to a less emotional state, he uses *you* to address her. Example (11) is the utterance from the monster to a girl in *Frankenstein*. Although *THOU* is usually used between a man and a woman who are in a close relation, the monster, who comes to a barn after committing murder, expresses warm emotion towards an unfamiliar woman sleeping there in addressing her as *THOU*. The terms "lover," "affection" and "my beloved" in his utterance illustrate that he is craving for something to pacify his distressed feeling, regarding her as somebody like his beloved angel. This example illustrates that *THOU* can express affection beyond solidarity as often established between husband and wife or lovers.

(10) I longed for *thee*, Janet! Oh, I longed for *thee* both with soul and flesh! <Mr. Rochester → Jane> (*Jane*, p. 447)

(11) "Awake, fairest, *thy* lover is near — he who would give his life but to obtain one look of affection from *thine* eyes: my beloved, awake!" <Monster → Young woman in a barn> (*Frankenstein*, p. 143)

d [Female → Male]
Women rarely use *THOU* to address a man. As mentioned above, there is only one example of this type, which belongs to Arabella in *Jude the Obscure*. She is probably one of the wives who exceptionally have power over their husbands in the male-dominated Victorian society. Although she enticed Jude to marry her, she is not happy to be with him. In example (12), she straightforwardly expresses her feeling that their marriage is now troublesome for her. In this scene, Jude is lying flat in his sickbed with no other person to nurse him. This example reveals that Arabella has advantage over him, both physically and psychologically. Arabella speaks some Southeastern dialect, but she usually employs *you* for the second person. In the following example, she is addressing Jude as *thee* in giving vent to her dissatisfaction.

(12) 'I've got a bargain for my trouble in marrying *thee* over again!" Arabella was saying to him. 'I shall have to keep *'ee* entirely, — that's what 'twill come to! ...' <Arabella → Jude> (*Jude*, p. 373)

e [Male ↔ Male]
The number of the examples in which *THOU* is used in the male-to-male relationship is the largest in absolute frequency and the second largest in the number of combinations. It is known that in the Elizabethan period *THOU* was used by men of higher social status to address those of lower status. Such examples are not found in our 19th-century texts. Rather, when *THOU* is used between two men in this period, they are often equal in social class and this is why the use of *THOU* is more often bilateral in this category. Out of the twelve combinations, *THOU* is mutually used in eight combinations in four pairs.

Table 2.5: Man-to-man relationship in use of *THOU*

Speaker	Addressee	Combination	Token
Scientist	Monster	1	3
Monster	Scientist	1	32
Scientist	Genevan magistrate	1	2
Worker	Worker	3	16
Worker	Employer	1	2
Student	Student	2	6
Boy	Boy	1	5
Gatekeeper	Chimney sweep	1	8
Chimney sweep	Gatekeeper	1	6
Total		12	80

In Middle English and Early Modern English, lower-rank people usually call each other *THOU*. Such usage is found in two pairs, as shown in examples (13) and (14).

(13) Grimes rang at the gate, and out came a keeper on the spot, and opened. 'I was told to expect *thee*,' he said. 'Now *thou*'lt be so good as to keep to the main avenue, and not let me find a hare or a rabbit on *thee* when *thou* comest back. I shall look sharp for one, I tell *thee*.'
'Not if it's in the bottom of the soot-bag,' quoth Grimes, and at that he laughed; and the keeper laughed and said: 'If that's *thy* sort, I may as well walk up with *thee* to the hall.' <Keeper vs. Chimney-sweep>
(*Water*, p. 14)

(14) 'We must take the tickets for her concert,' Fritz said. 'Hast *thou* any money, Max?'
'Bah,' said the other, 'the concert is a concert *in nubibus*. Hans said that she advertised one at Leipzig: and the *Burschen* took many tickets. But she went off without singing. She said in the coach yesterday that her pianist had fallen ill at Dresden. She cannot sing, it is my belief: her voice is as cracked as *thine*, O *thou* beer-soaking Renowner!' (Italicized "in nubibus" and "Burschen" in the original) <German university students>
(*Vanity*, p. 842)

In example (13) from a once-upon-time story narrated in *The Water Babies*, a chimney-sweep and a gatekeeper address each other as *THOU*. The description "to Tom's surprise that he [the keeper] and Grimes chatted together all the way quite pleasantly" illustrates that these two men know each other and regularly address each other as *THOU*. Example (14) from *Vanity Fair* is an interesting one. The speakers are both German students. In German, the intimate form *du* and the respectful form *Sie* are used for the second person. It is therefore natural for them to address each other as *THOU* even when speaking in

English.

f [Female → Female]
There is only one combination in which the pronoun *THOU* is used between female characters. In his analysis of *YOU/THOU* in terms of social ranks in 17th-century English, Johnson (1966: 268) states that women of all ranks employ *YOU* more frequently than men, which is also supported by our findings. In example (15) from *North and South*, the speaker is Bessy, a millworker's daughter, and the addressee is Margaret, a clergyman's daughter from the South of England. Though belonging to different social classes, they are congenial to each other. In this scene, Bessy, who has been ill for long, says how welcome it would be to be released from suffering by death soon. Her *THOU* does not seem to be used to express either anger or affection towards Margaret, but it sounds seriously and solemnly persuasive. Although she speaks a Northern dialect, Bessy does not always use the second person singular pronoun. In the earlier example (6), she uses *THOU* in addressing her father to make a strong request, and here in addressing Margaret as *THOU* she is trying to make herself clearly understood. It is interesting to note that she first uses *yo*, which is the norm for her, and as her emotion becomes heightened, she switches to *THOU* in her utterance.

(15) 'If yo'd led the life I have, and getten as weary of it as I have, and thought at times, "maybe it'll last for fifty or sixty years — it does wi' some," — and got dizzy and dazed, and sick, as each of them sixty years seemed to spin about me, and mock me with its length of hours and minutes, and endless bits o' time — oh, wench! I tell *thee thou*'d been glad enough when th' doctor said he feared *thou*'d never see another winter.' <Bessy → Margaret>   (N and S, p. 89)

g [Nonhuman entity → Character]
The relationship between a nonhuman entity and a human is similar to that between an adult and a child, as seen in such expressions as "men call God 'Father'" and "people are children of God." Among nonhuman entities who address a character as *THOU* are God, Satan and a character's inner voices. In example (16), God is blessing Helen in *Wildfell Hall*, in (17) from *The Sorrows of Satan*, Satan is tempting Geoffrey, the protagonist and writer, to give up God and take Satan. In (18) from *Barchester Towers*, an inner voice is encouraging Bishop Proudie, who is always controlled by his wife, not to obey her but to follow his own decision. In all three examples, the speaker clearly addresses the hearer as *THOU* with authority, and particularly in (16) and (17), in which God and Satan are the speakers, respectively, the archaic form *THOU* is used

in a religious context.

(16) 'I will never leave *thee*, nor forsake *thee*,'⁷ seemed whispered from above their myriad orbs. <God → Helen>   (*Wildfell*, p. 292)
(17) 'Man, deceive not *thyself*!' he said — 'Think not the terrors of this night are the delusion of a dream or the snare of a vision! *Thou* art awake — not sleeping — *thou* art flesh as well as spirit! ...' <Satan → Geoffrey>
(*Satan*, p. 378)
(18) Now, bishop, look well to *thyself*, and call up all the manhood that is in *thee*. <Monitor → Dr. Proudie>   (*Barchester*, I, p. 160)

h [Character → Nonhuman entity]
God is universally addressed as THOU both in the earlier centuries and in the 19th century. Similar usage is attested with other nonhuman entities. There are eight combinations of this type in our texts, where five nonhuman entities (God, wind, country, night and superstition) are addressed as THOU by the characters. The form is used either in religious or poetic contexts in all the cases.

(19) 'So help me God! man alive — if I think not I'm doing best for *thee*, and for all on us... .' <Nicholas → God>   (*N and S*, p. 155)
(20) 'Blow, blow, *thou* winter wind!' *Thou* canst not blow away the modest wealth which makes my security. <Ryecroft → Wind>   (*Ryecroft*, p. 154)
(21) My country, my beloved country! who but a native can tell the delight I took in again beholding *thy* streams, *thy* mountains, and, more than all, *thy* lovely lake! <Frankenstein → Country>   (*Frankenstein*, p. 75)
(22) and by *thee*, O Night, and the spirits that preside over *thee*, to pursue the dæmon, who caused this misery, until he or I shall perish in mortal conflict. <Frankenstein → Night>   (*Frankenstein*, p. 202)
(23) "Down superstition!" I commented, as that spectre rose up black by the black yew at the gate. "This is not *thy* deception, nor *thy* witchcraft: it is the work of nature. She was roused, and did — no miracle — but her best." <Jane → Superstition>   (*Jane*, p. 420)

In terms of power, nonhuman entities are generally thought to be far more powerful than people. However, despite the indisputable imbalance in power against characters, they nevertheless address nonhuman entities as THOU. Why do characters use THOU rather freely to the opponent whom they most fear? As often indicated, this is probably because many of those in the 19th century were familiar with *The King James Version* of the Bible (1611) or the *KJV*, which preserved the second person pronouns *ye* and *thou*, along with other versions of the Bible at that time.[8] Barbara M. H. Strang (1970: 140) says that "its [*thou*'s] preservation in the *KJV* carried the implication that religious address, especially to the Deity, required special forms." The usage of *THOU* in addressing God is, therefore, often treated separately from its use for people in the previous studies. It would not be in doubt that the use of *THOU* to the Deity in a religious style in the 19th century reflects its old-fashioned usage seen in the earlier Bible. In addition to this text-based reflex, it might be also possible that human characters feel freer to use *THOU* to nonhuman entities than to human superiors. In dialogue between people, speakers tend to avoid using *THOU* to address the hearer because formality and politeness usually play no small role in the speaker's style. When addressing people in socially higher or stronger positions, emotional tones or terms tend to be checked by formality as much as possible. In speech to nonhuman entities, however, since characters do not have to be bound by formality, they can use *THOU* freely.

I [Narrator → Character] & J [Narrator → Reader]
Omniscient narrators sometimes talk to their characters. Such examples are found in *Vanity Fair* and *Barchester Towers*. In examples (24) and (25), the narrator addresses the character as *THOU* in a religious context, as the terms "heathen" and "Christian," respectively, illustrate.

(24)   Peace to *thee*, kind and selfish, vain and generous old heathen! — We shall see *thee* no more. <Narrator → Miss Crawley>   (*Vanity*, p. 437)
(25)   Ah, *thou* weak man; most charitable, most Christian, but weakest of men! Why couldst *thou* not have asked herself? <Narrator → Mr. Harding>
(*Barchester*, II, p. 4)

The narrator of *Barchester Towers* uses *THOU* for the reader as well. In example (26), he is calling on the reader to imagine how Mr. Quiverful feels in this situation with sympathy.

(26)   He [Mr. Quiverful] thought of these things; and do *thou* also, reader, think of them, and then wonder, if *thou* canst, that Mr. Slope had appeared to him to possess all those good gifts which could grace a bishop's chaplain. <Narrator → Reader>   (*Barchester*, I, p. 240)

It is interesting to note that while the narrators seem to prefer *THOU* in addressing the character or the reader in pitiful moods, they employ *YOU* in more casual contexts or in descriptive narratives, as in the following examples.

(27)   Good-bye, Colonel — God bless *you*, honest William! — Farewell, dear

Amelia — Grow green again, tender little parasite, round the rugged old oak to which *you* cling!
<Narrator → Colonel Dobbin/Amelia>   (*Vanity*, p. 871)

(28) *You* and I, my dear reader, may drop into this condition one day: for have not many of our friends attained it? <Narrator → Reader>
(*Vanity*, p. 484)

2.1.1.4 "Emotion" which triggers *THOU*

The previous section has indicated that even in some exceptional cases in which the rule of power seems to be violated, the speakers use the form for a good reason. That is, in order to fully explain the usage of *THOU*, it is necessary to consider some elements other than power. Jan Svartvik and Geoffrey Leech's study of Elizabethan English (2006: 55) may suggest that the usage of *THOU* in our 19th-century texts is related to "tone" and "attitude":

> The choice between *thou* and *you* in Elizabethan English has been much debated, but it was clearly a matter of tone and attitude, not hugely different from today's choice between *tu* and *vous* in French, *du* and *Sie* in German, or *ni* and *nín* in Chinese.

What sort of "tone" can cause the use of *THOU*? Bruti (2000: 35), analyzing forms of personal reference in some of Shakespeare's works from a pragmatic perspective, proposes to redefine *THOU*'s markedness and observe the direction of switch between *YOU* and *THOU* along two axes: the axis of social distance and the axis of emotional attitude, as shown below.

	Social distance	
	Address to	
Inferiors	Equals	Superiors
Thou	*(y/t)*	*You*

Figure 2.1: The axis of social distance (adapted from Bruti 2000: 35)

	Emotional attitude	
anger/contempt	indifference/neutrality	familiarity/intimacy
Thou	*You*	*Thou*

Figure 2.2: The axis of emotional attitude (adapted from Bruti 2000: 35)

Although the social use of *THOU/YOU* disappeared in 19th-century English, the social-rank-based axis in Figure 2.1 is applicable to some of our sample. The regular usage of *THOU*, or the unmarked form *THOU*, is found in six combinations. Two combinations are seen in the senior-junior relationship; Mr. Grimes and an old woman invariably address a little chimney sweep as

THOU in an old story narrated in *The Water Babies*. The remaining four are found in mutual use in the male-to-male relationship: two lower-class males in *The Water Babies* and German students in *Vanity Fair*. The uses of THOU found in the case of those six speakers are fully explained by the axis of social distance in Figure 2.1. As for the other examples, the emotion-based axis in Figure 2.2 is quite helpful. The directions of "anger/contempt" and "familiarity/intimacy" on the axis can be called negative and positive directions in emotional attitude respectively. I would like to apply these emotional directions to

Table 2.6: Power balance and emotions in use of THOU

		Positive			Negative		
		Comb.	Token		Comb.	Token
Strong–to-Weak						
S → J	affection, love	3	18	anger, indignation	3	12
	pity	2	5	hatred	3	12
				mockery	1	1
M → F	affection, love	2	5	hatred	1	1
	persuasion	1	2	contempt	1	2
				hostility	1	3
No → Ch	admonition	1	34			
	temptation	1	13			
Na → Ch	admonition	3	13			
	pity	3	4			
Na → R	admonition	1	2			
Subtotal		17	96		10	31
Equal relations						
M → M	persuasion	2	10	hostility	2	34
				curse	1	3
				anger	1	5
				hatred	2	8
F → F	persuasion	1	3			
Subtotal		3	13		6	50
Weak-to–Strong						
J → S	appeal	1	4	anger	1	1
				defiance	1	1
F → M				hatred	1	1
Ch → No	appeal	1	2	hatred	1	2
	love	1	3			
	request	1	2			
Subtotal		4	11		4	5
Total		24	120		20	86

S: Senior, J: Junior, M: Male, F: Female, No: Nonhuman entity, Ch: Character, Na: Narrator, R: Reader the categorization of our data. Here I exclude the examples of unmarked *THOU*, including its biblical use between God and humans, which reduces the relevant examples to 206 divided into 44 combinations. The speaker's emotion in each case is determined by consulting the linguistic contexts in which the form is used. For instance, specific words such as "I love thee" (*Wildfell*, p. 276) and "I longed for thee" (*Jane*, p. 447) also make it possible to classify the meaning of *THOU* as "love" or "affection," and the phrase "I'll hate thee" (*N and S*, p. 154) clearly indicates "hatred." The results are shown in Table 2.6 according to the power relationship.

As the table shows, when *THOU* is chosen on a particular occasion by a speaker who does not regularly employ the form, it is used to express an intense emotion or tone either in a positive direction or a negative direction. In regards to Shakespeare's works, Barber (1981: 177) notes that *YOU* is the normal, unmarked form among the upper classes and that *THOU* is the marked form, used for particular emotional effects or as an indicator of difference of social status. Likewise, in our 19th-century novels, where *YOU* is the norm, it is expected that *THOU* is basically used as an emotional marker if used at all. The table also reveals that the nature of emotion *THOU* conveys slightly differs depending on power relation. As for the strong-to-weak relationship, both positive and negative emotions are conveyed. This is only the case with the human-to-human relationship (i.e., the senior-to-junior relationship and the male-to-female relationship). In the positive direction, the human speakers in power often use *THOU* to express love, affection and pity towards the less powerful addressee as well as to attract attention in teaching something to them. On the other hand, various negative emotions like anger, hatred, mockery and contempt are also expressed in their utterance of *THOU*. In either case, the speakers in power seem to use *THOU* as if its use is their privilege. With respect to the relationship between a nonhuman entity and a character and that between a narrator and a character, positive emotion is commonly found. An absolute power gap between two sides enables the speaker to give advice to the addressee. In the equal-power relationship, *THOU* is uttered with negative emotions more often than positive ones. When the speaker and the hearer are of the same sex, only persuasion is observed as positive emotion. Affection and love are hardly conveyed with *THOU* between men, nor between women. In the utterance of *THOU* from the weak to the strong, emotions are expressed in either direction. Negative emotions are usually expressed there, which is reasonable because the utterance of *THOU* by a person in less power is itself contrary to its ordinary use. Even in the positive emotions such as appeal and request, desperate and serious feelings are sensed.

A major difference in usage between social *THOU* and emotional *THOU* is that the former is customary and the latter temporary. In regard to emotional

THOU, the connotation of THOU is largely affected by the mood of the speaker. Examples (26) and (27) are uttered by Nicholas towards his two daughters. While he expresses affection when addressing his elder daughter, Bessy, as *thou*, anger is felt in the same pronoun in reference to his younger daughter, Mary. The reason he addresses each daughter as THOU with different emotions is not that he loves one daughter and dislikes the other. It is merely temporary emotion that makes him utter different kinds of THOU. He loves both daughters, but in (30) he turns in anger towards Mary, who has informed him of her sister's death. These two examples illustrate that the use of THOU greatly depends on the speaker's momentary feelings.

(29) 'The blessing of God be upon *thee*, my child!'
       <Nicholas → Bessy: his elder daughter>   (N and S, p. 40)
(30) 'Get *thee* gone! — get *thee* gone!' he cried, striking wildly and blindly at her. 'What do I care for *thee*?' <Nicholas → Mary: his younger daughter>
                                                                       (N and S, p. 219)

In the next example from *North and South*, two male characters express completely different feelings in addressing each other as THOU. Two mill-workers, John Boucher and Nicholas Higgins, are arguing in a tense mood. They usually address each other as the dialectal form *yo*. Agitation, however, apparently makes them use THOU in this scene. The first portion is uttered by John and the next by Nicholas.

(31) '... An' look *thee*, lad, I'll hate *thee*, and th' whole pack o' th' Union. Ay, an' chase yo' through heaven wi' my hatred, — I will, lad! I will, — if yo're leading me astray i' this matter. *Thou* saidist, Nicholas, on Wednesday sennight — and it's now Tuesday i' th' second week — that afore a fortnight we'd ha' the masters coming a-begging to us to take back our work, at our own wage — and time's nearly up, — and there's our lile Jack lying a-bed, too weak to cry, but just every now and then sobbing up his heart for want o' food, — our lile Jack, I tell *thee*, lad! ...'
Here the deep sobs choked the poor man, and Nicholas looked up, with eyes brimful of tears, to Margaret, before he could gain courage to speak.
'Hou'd up, man. *Thy* lile Jack shall na' clem. I ha' getten brass, and we'll go buy the chap a sup o' milk an' a good four-pounder this very minute. What's mine's *thine*, sure enough, i' *thou*'st i' want... .'
<John Boucher, Millworker vs. Nicholas Higgins, Millworker>
                                                                       (N and S, pp. 154–155)

John and Nicholas are members of the Union of a mill under a strike. Hard-pressed Boucher is shouting at Nicholas to blame him for planning it. His utterance "I'll hate thee" suggests that John bears hatred towards Nicholas. His negative emotion here supposedly came from his fear or uneasiness towards the future. Nicholas, who understands his feelings perfectly, is not offended at all by his severe words. Rather, he sobs after John's accusation and tries to soothe him, addressing him as *THOU*. These two men thus chose the same pronoun with emotions in the opposite directions. It is obvious that their use of *THOU* does not arise from constant intimacy or solidarity. John's *THOU* expresses temporary wrath towards Nicholas, and in the face of his friend's hostile attitude, Nicholas is trying to express friendship to prevent their feelings from going apart. The exchange of *THOU* forms in opposite tones between two men in a particular scene in Shakespeare is pointed out in Jucker and Taavitsainen (2013: 123–125): In the third act of *Romeo and Juliet*, Tybalt, Juliet's cousin, chooses the insulting form *THOU* to address Romeo, while Romeo, ignoring his insult, uses the same pronoun to show him affection because he is secretly married to Juliet and wants to avoid a fight with her relative.

Bruti's axis of emotional attitude (2000: 35), which was designed to screen Shakespeare's use of *THOU/YOU*, is just as helpful to divide strong emotions expressed by the marked *THOU* in our texts into two opposite directions, positive and negative. It sometimes happens that one person employs different tones of *THOU* to the same person or that two people address each other as *THOU* with opposite attitudes. With these complex instances included, the behavior of the form *THOU* in our 19th-century corpus could be occasionally traced back to the Elizabethan period.

2.1.1.5 Summary

The second person singular personal pronoun *THOU* is extremely limited in use in our 19th-century texts. The form tends to appear in the works with religious or dramatic scenes and those set in the northern part of England. It is clear that the archaic singular form was no longer in general use in the daily life of England at that time, though it was still the norm in Christian prayers. It is possible that dialectal factors are involved in the use of *THOU*, but what should be emphasized here is that, in our 19th-century novels, the old form was preserved better in the North-based texts as a pragmatic marker than as a dialectal marker. It would be only natural that the authors living in the regions where the form itself had been better preserved in dialectal speech should retain its pragmatic function all the better. Hence, as far as our corpus is concerned, the pronoun *THOU* is chosen by most speakers as a pragmatic marker to express some particular feeling to the hearers on particular occasions.

All in all, in the use of *THOU* in our corpus sample, "power" and "emotion" are two significant elements. This archaic form is more likely to be employed from the speaker in power to the addressee in less power, but earnest emotions sometimes yield the exceptional use. To sum up, the specific emotional value conveyed by *THOU* greatly depends on the speakers' temporary attitudes as well as on the speaker-to-addressee relationship. Hence it follows that the usage of *THOU* in our 19th-century novels is quite similar to that in the upper class of Elizabethan society, in both of which *YOU* is used as the standard form and *THOU* as an emotional marker.

2.1.2 *Ye*

2.1.2.1 Overview

The second person pronoun *ye* derives from the nominative second person plural pronoun (cf. OE *ge*, ME *ye*). Referring to the usage of *ye* in Early Modern English, Barber (1976) writes:

> By the 17th century, however, *ye* is just as likely to be used for the accusative as for the nominative, but is much rarer than *you* in both functions, and during the century becomes increasingly archaic and literary... . In some examples of *ye*, however, it is possible that this is not the old nominative, but an unstressed form of *you*, representing the pronunciation [jə]. (p. 205)

In the following examples, *ye* is used in similar syntactic situations. At a glance, however, it is difficult to tell which the form stands for, the old nominative plural *ye* or the unstressed form for *you*.

a. "Farewell, *ye* tempers!" (*Wildfell*, p. 180)
b. 'Novy youself, *ye* Scrabble-towners! ...' (*Captains*, p. 87)

The usage of *ye* in Late Modern English is only partially referred to as regional dialect in literature (Wright 1905; Hosoe 1956; Hirooka 1965; Blake 1981) or colloquial language (Wyld 1920: 330) and/or treated as individual authors' language (Hosoe 1935; Brook 1970: 86, 120, 124; Phillipps 1970: 167; Clark 1975: 83–86; Phillipps 1978: 144). Little attention has been paid to the overall behavior of the pronoun *ye* in this period. In the following sections, I would like to investigate the distribution of *ye* and clarify its complex behavior in our 19th-century texts from sociolinguistic, syntactic and stylistic perspectives and suggest how to distinguish one from the other.

2.1.2.2 Data

To begin with, let us look at the distribution of variants of the second person pronoun *you* and its variants in our 19th-century texts. The following table shows the variants and their frequency (absolute number and percentage) in the twenty texts.

Table 2.7: Distribution of the second person pronoun *you* and its variants

	you	ye	yo	yah	Total
abn. (%)	35878 (97.7%)	418 (1.1%)	373 (1.0%)	44 (0.1%)	36713 (100%)

abn.: absolute number. *You*: you; your; yours; yourself; yourselves. *Ye*: ye; 'ee; yer; yerself; yerseln. *Yo*: yo'; yo; yo'r; yor; yo'rs; yo'rsel.

Table 2.8: Distribution of nonstandard second person pronouns

Text		ye			yo			yah	
	abn	fp. 10,000	n. sps	abn	fp. 10,000	n. sps	abn	fp. 10,000	n. sps
Pride									
Frankenstein	5	0.67	(1)						
N and S	12	0.66	(4)	373	20.37	(7)			
Vanity	34	1.12	(11)						
Great	35	1.89	(5)						
Barchester	9	0.45	(7)						
Jane	12	0.64	(2)						
Wuthering	39	3.34	(3)				44	3.77	(2)
Silas	2	0.28	(1)						
Water	8	1.17	(4)						
Wildfell	3	0.18	(2)						
Alice	7	1.25	(4)						
Jude	76	5.23	(21)						
Treasure	5	0.73	(1)						
Dorian									
Satan	6	0.37	(1)						
Ryecroft									
Scarlet	6	1.38	(2)						
Captains	113	21.16	(10)						
Invisible	13	2.66	(8)						
Total	385	1.6	(87)	373	1.55	(7)	44	0.18	(2)

abn: absolute number; fp. 10,000: frequency per 10,000 words; n. sps: number of speakers

The extremely limited occurrence of variants *ye* as well as *yo* and *yah* shows that the form *you* is the default. In order to obtain a clearer view, the occurrence of the nonstandard variants and the number of speakers who use each variant per text are given in Table 2.8. The examples found in mere quotations of passages from poems and the Scriptures are excluded, since they are not regarded as the usage of the authors of our 19th-century texts. As a result, the total number of the examples of *ye* is reduced from 418 in Table 2.7 to 385. According to Table 2.8, while *ye* is found throughout the texts, *yo* and *yah* are limited to two texts with the former in *North and South* and the latter in *Wuthering Heights*. The number of speakers of *ye* is greater than those of the other two, and the numbers of speakers of *yo* and *yah* are very few in spite of their relatively high frequencies. This means only a limited number of characters use the variants *yo* and *yah* repeatedly.

2.1.2.3 Complex behavior of *ye*

Since in *North and South* and *Wuthering Heights* the pronoun *ye* is found with other local variants, it would be better to observe its behavior in these two texts separately and see how *ye* is related to such local variants. We then will examine the use of *ye* in the rest of the texts.

2.1.2.3.1 Examples in *North and South*

In *North and South* the seven characters who use *yo* /jo/ are local people in Milton, a town modeled on Manchester in the Northwest of England. Out of its 373 examples, as many as 348 are used by a mill worker named Nicholas Higgins (221 exx.) and his two daughters, Bessy (117 exx.) and Mary (10 exx.). The remaining 25 examples are used by other mill workers and their families. This evidently indicates that *yo* belongs to a dialect of the place where the speakers live. According to the *Oxford English Dictionary* (2nd edition, CD-Rom Version 3.1) (*OED*), *yo* is historically an obsolete form of *you*, and in modern use it represents dialectal pronunciation of *you* and *your* (s.v. *yo*). This may have generally become obsolete today but in the 19th century, when this text was written, it was not necessarily so in Northern England,[9] as seen in the fact that the users of *yo* include two young women aged 19 and 17. The nonstandard variants of *you* seen in *North and South* are shown by case in Table 2.9.

Table 2.9: Case variation of *yo/ye* in *North and South*

	you nom.	obj.	voc.	*your* poss.	*yours* poss.	*yourself* ref.	Total
yo/yo'	231	101	2				334
ye	11	1					12
yor/yo'r				36			36
yo'rs					1		1
yo'rsel						2	2
Total	242	102	2	36	1	2	385

Twelve examples of *ye* are found in this text, where its frequency is much lower than that of *yo*. The variant *yo* is used both for the nominative and objective whereas *ye* is almost exclusively used for the nominative. In terms of sentence structure, the nominative *ye* appears not in the declarative but in the interrogative and imperative. In other words, all the instances of *ye* occur in the post-verbal order. Because of this order the pronoun *ye* is probably pronounced unemphatically as follows:

(32) 'what have *ye* gained by striking? ...' <Bessy> (p. 133)
(33) 'Sit *ye* down, sit *ye* down... .' <Nicholas> (p. 290)

In contrast, the nominative *yo* appears in the post-verbal position only 31 times out of the 231. It is then assumed that for the characters who use both *yo* and *ye*, *ye* is the unstressed variant /jə/ of *yo*. What complicates this issue is that there are two characters who do not use *yo* but utter *ye* just once: Mr. Bell and Mr. Thornton. These two gentlemen belong to the upper middle class and do not speak in the local dialect. Hence, the pronoun *ye*, which Mr. Bell and Mr. Thornton use in speech, would be an unstressed variant /jə/ of *you*. Let us look at the circumstances under which they utter *ye*.

(34) 'Your what *d'ye* call him? What's the right name for a cousin-in-law's brother?' <Mr. Bell → Margaret> (p. 375)
(35) 'You'd better go and try them, then, and see whether they'll give you work. I've turned off upwards of a hundred of my best hands, for no other fault than following you and such as you; and *d'ye* think I'll take you on? I might as well put a firebrand into the midst of the cotton-waste.' <Mr. Thornton → Nicholas> (p. 319)

Both Mr. Bell and Mr. Thornton use *ye* just once in the text and both use the same contracted form *d'ye* for "do you." In example (34), Mr. Bell is talking to his god-daughter Margaret. Seeing her speedily hiding letters away, he seems to feel like teasing her. Their familiar relationship probably makes him utter *d'ye* in a carefree and witty mood. In (35), Mr. Thornton is indignantly refusing an unreasonable request from Nicholas Higgins, who is responsible for a recent strike, and his agitation possibly produced the shortened form. It is not rare that even the educated unintentionally choose shorter and easier terms either in familiar or emotional talk (e.g., Nakayama 2009: 14–15; 2011a: 71).

2.1.2.3.2 Examples in *Wuthering Heights*

In *Wuthering Heights* two variants of the second person pronoun, *yah* and *ye*, are found. As mentioned above, the variant *yah* /ja:/ is limited to this text and used by two characters: Joseph and a nameless housekeeper working for an established family at Wuthering Heights. Though most examples of *yah* are uttered by Joseph, the housekeeper's language is quite the same as his. Joseph (and perhaps the housekeeper as well) was modeled on an old female servant employed by the Brontës, who spoke in the local dialect (Blake 1981: 147). We have two characters who do not use *yah* but use *ye* on certain occasions: Zillah, another housekeeper, and Hareton, the son of the family. There are a total of 83 examples of *yah* and *ye* in this text, 79 of which are uttered by Joseph. He uses *yah* and *ye* for *you*, *yer* for *your* and *yerseln* for *yourself*. The distribution of the nonstandard second person pronoun by case is shown in Table 2.10.

Table 2.10: Case variation of *yah/ye* in *Wuthering Heights*

	you nom.	voc.	obj.	your poss.	yours poss.	yourself ref.	Total
yah	39	1	4				44
ye	12	1	14			1	28
yer				10			10
yerseln						1	1
Total	51	2	18	10		2	83

Joseph uses *yah* to address anyone from his coworkers to the master and his children and tenants. Grammatically he distinguishes one from the other forms. He always uses *yah* in the singular. On the other hand, he uses *ye* as the second person plural nominative pronoun, as Blake (1981: 150) points out. Although *ye* is originally a nominative case (OE *ge*), by Shakespeare's time both *ye* and *you* could be used as either nominative or accusative (Barber 1993: 186). If this is the case, Joseph's restricted use of *ye* as nominative plural could afford evidence of the preservation of the earlier pronoun system in local dialects. The following are examples of *yah* in the singular and *ye* (/jiː/ or /ji/) in the plural. In example (39) the word *childer* (an older term for "children" in a Yorkshire dialect) illustrates that *ye* is used in the plural.

Yah for the second person singular
(36) Bud *yah*'re a nowt, and it's noa use talking — *yah*'ll niver mend uh yer ill ways; <Joseph → Mrs. Heathcliff> (p. 11)
(37) "But Maister Hareton nivir ate nowt else, when he wer a little un: und what wer gooid enough fur him's gooid enough fur *yah*, Aw's rayther think!" <Joseph → Heathcliff> (p. 184)
(38) "*Yah* gooid fur nowt, slatternly witch! Nip up und bolt intuh th' hahs, t' minute *yah* heard t' maister's horse fit clatter up t' road."
<Joseph → Catherine> (p. 77)

Ye for the old nominative second person plural
(39) '... sit *ye* dahn, ill childer! they's good books eneugh if *ye*'ll read 'em; sit *ye* dahn, and think uh yer sowls!'<Joseph → Catherine and Heathcliff>
(p. 17)

Our data also show that Joseph sometimes uses *ye* for the second person singular as well. Specifically, he uses the variant for the nominative (6 exx.) and the vocative (1 ex.) and the objective (3 exx.) as shown below:

(40) "... Hah can Aw tell whet *ye* say?" <Joseph → Isabella> (p. 121)
(41) Whear the hell, wold *ye* gang? *ye* marred, wearisome nowt!
      <Joseph → Isabella> (p.127)
(42) "he's swopped wi' *ye*, maister, an' yon's his lass!" <Joseph → Heathcliff>
      (p. 182)

Hirooka (1965: 336) says that *yah* and *ye* are both used for *you* in Yorkshire and that *yah* is more stressed than *ye*. His statement could help to explain why Joseph uses *ye* for the singular nominative as well. Although the spelling is the same, the variant *ye* here is uttered by Joseph in an unemphatic way just as seen in the use of *ye* as an unstressed form of *yo* in *North and South*. In order to understand Joseph's use of *ye*, let us look at the speech of Hareton, who provides two examples of *ye* and none of *yah*.

(43) '... Begone, wi' *ye* both!' <Hareton → Linton and Catherine> (p. 221)
(44) 'Get off wi' *ye*!' <Hareton → Catherine> (p. 278)

Though Hareton speaks with "frightful Yorkshire pronunciation" (*Wuthering*, p. 194), he does not use *yah*; he always uses *you* for the nominative and in most occasions for the objective. As seen in (43) and (44), he employs *ye* as the object of the preposition *with* for either plural or singular in quite a similar situation; he is trying to chase off the addressee(s) in anger, and in either case *ye* is presumed to be pronounced /jə/ after the stressed words "Begone" and "Get off." Then in example (42) above by Joseph, *ye* as the object of the preposition *wi'* is likely to be uttered unstressed. Similarly, when used as a subject, *ye* is less stressed in the post-verbal position as seen in Nicholas's language above. Note the following example, where Joseph uses both *yah* and *ye* for the nominative singular in the same line. Here the *ye* plainly stands for an unstressed variant /jə/ of *yah*.

(45) Bud, Aw'm mista'en if *yah* shew yer sperrit lang. Will Hathecliff bide
      sich bonny ways, think *ye*? <Joseph> (p.127)

Zillah, a housekeeper, uses the objective *ye* for the reflexive pronoun. It is not uncommon for the objective case of the simple second person pronoun to be used with a reflexive function in North Country speech (Wright 1905: 276).[10] The pronoun *ye* in (46) by Zillah therefore could be regarded as dialectal speech in Yorkshire.

(46) Wisht, wisht! you munn't go on so — come in, and I'll cure that. There now, hold *ye* still." <Zillah> (p. 14)

To sum up the usage of the variants *yah* and *ye* in *Wuthering Heights*, *yah* is used for the second person singular pronoun; as for *ye*, on the one hand it is considered the old nominative plural (/jíː/ or /ji/), and on the other it stands for an unstressed variant /jə/ of *yah* as well as *you*, either for the nominative or objective case.

2.1.2.3.3 *Ye* in the other texts

This section focuses on the usage of the variant *ye* in the remaining fifteen texts by examining the contexts in which it is used. There are a total of 334 relevant examples with 80 people using it. In our corpus, as shown in Table 2.8, three texts have no example of *ye*: *Pride and Prejudice*, *The Picture of Dorian Gray* (henceforth referred to as *Dorian Gray*) and *Henry Ryecroft*. What is commonly said of these texts is that they are basically written in standard English. In *Pride and Prejudice* and *Dorian Gray*, the main characters belong to either the upper or middle class and *Henry Ryecroft* presents a diary written by a retired writer named Henry Ryecroft. This indicates that *ye* was used as some kind of dialectal marker, either regional or social, at that time.[11]

The old nominative plural *ye*

As we have seen in the usage of Joseph in *Wuthering Heights*, in some texts the older second person plural *ye* has survived as regional dialect, noticeably in the northern part of England and Ireland. In *Jane Eyre*, Hannah, an old housekeeper living with St. John and his sisters, uses *ye* in reference to more than one person. When she first meets them, the narrator, Jane Eyre herself, describes the housekeeper and the sisters as follows: "They [two girls] could not be the daughters of the elderly person at the table; for she looked like a rustic, and they were all delicacy and cultivation." Her narration suggests that Hannah speaks a regional dialect heard in Yorkshire at that time, as given in (47). Here again, the archaic "childer" is used in reference to the two girls.

(47) Ah, childer! that's t' last o' t' old stock — for *ye* and Mr. St. John is like of a different soart to them 'at's gone; <Hannah> (*Jane*, p. 334)

Characters from Ireland use *ye* as well. P. W. Joyce (1910: 88) says "They [the Irish] always use *ye* in the plural wherever possible: both as a nominative and as an objective." In *The Water Babies*, Dennis, who is assumed to be an old

Irish servant working for the narrator's family, uses the form to address his master's son. The term "your honour's" suggests that the old plural *ye* is used as a mark of deference.

(48) 'Shure thin, and your honour's the thrue fisherman, and understands it all like a book. Why, *ye* spake as if *ye*'d known the wather a thousand years! ...' <Dennis> (*Water*, p. 73)

The old nominative plural *ye* sometimes occurs in poetic and archaic contexts. Such instances are found in *Frankenstein* (4 exx.), *The Sorrows of Satan* (2 exx.) and *The Water Babies* (5 exx.). In *Frankenstein*, the scientist Frankenstein, who creates the monster, uses *ye* to address a group of people such as a crew, a family, "wandering spirits" and "stars and clouds, and winds" as in (49). Similarly, in (50) Lucio in *The Sorrows of Satan* addresses devils as *ye* because of their plurality. On the other hand, in (51) from an old tale narrated in *The Water Babies*, a noble old dame and tenant of Sir John in the North Country addresses him as *ye* after she "curtsied very low" (*Water*, p. 44). The pronoun signifies her respect towards him.[12] These examples illustrate that in Gothic novels and fantasies, in which nonhuman entities appear and supernatural events happen, the old nominative plural *ye* tends to be effectively used to produce a glorious and solemn atmosphere suitable to the story.

(49) 'Oh! stars and clouds, and winds, *ye* are all about to mock me: if *ye* really pity me, crush sensation and memory; ...' <Frankenstein>
 (*Frankenstein*, pp. 148–149)
(50) 'Back, *ye* devils of the sea and wind! — *ye* which are not God's elements but My servants, the unrepenting souls of men! ...' <Lucio> (*Satan*, p. 367)
(51) 'Oh, Harthover, Harthover,' says she, '*ye* were always a just man and a merciful; and *ye*'ll no harm the poor little lad if I give you tidings of him?' <Old dame> (*Water*, p. 44)

This tendency is particularly the case with the vocative, yielding seven examples out of the twelve: *The Sorrow of Satan* (4 exx.), *Vanity Fair* (1 ex.), *Frankenstein* (1 ex.) and *Wildfell Hall* (1 ex.). In all these examples except one, the addressees are nonhuman entities such as devils, heavens, nature, gods and tempers. The remaining five examples of *ye* in the vocative are all uttered by the crew of a fishing vessel in *Captains Courageous*. These examples indicate that in the vocative, *ye* could represent two different variants which are the same in form but different in pronunciation. To take specific examples, in (52) and (53), where noble men are addressing supernatural beings in a religious atmosphere, *ye* is considered the old plural /jiː/ while in (54), in which a young fisherman is calling addressees "Scrabble-towners," a derogatory term for opportunist landsmen,[13] it is an unstressed variant /jə/ of *you* (here we have the answer to the question presented in §2.1.2.1).

Unstressed archaic form *ye*
(52) 'Back, *ye* devils of the sea and wind! ...' <Lucio>   (*Satan*, p. 367)
(53) "Farewell, *ye* tempers!" <Mr. Lowborough>   (*Wildfell*, p. 180)

Unstressed recent form *ye* of *you*
(54) 'Novy yourself, *ye* Scrabble-towners! *Ye* Chatham wreckers! ...' <Dan>
   (*Captains*, p. 87)

The unstressed variant *ye* of *you* as a dialectal marker
Although the old nominative plural *ye* ("old *ye*") is only found in speech in the North, the unstressed recent *ye* of *you* and its dialectal variants ("recent *ye*") is found almost everywhere. Since the recent *ye* is so widely used, it is difficult to determine whether it belongs to a local or social dialect. Let us examine the situation surrounding the recent *ye* used in the relevant texts.

In *Jude the Obscure* there are 76 examples of *ye* used by as many as 21 people living in Wessex in the Southeast of England. The number of the speakers in this text is much greater than in any of our other texts. Many of the users of *ye* are local working-class people who play only minor roles, such as a mason, a farmer, a shepherd, a grave digger and a washerwoman. In this text, therefore, *ye* could be regarded as both a local and social dialect. One point to be mentioned here is that, unlike Nicholas in *North and South* and Joseph in *Wuthering Heights*, all the speakers of *ye* here use it for the standard *you*. The following example by a local blacksmith in *Jude the Obscure* illustrates that the same person uses an unstressed *ye* /jə/ along with a stressed *you*.

(55) 'Bring on that water, will *ye*, *you* idle young harlican!'   (*Jude*, p. 5)

Similar usage of *ye* is found in other texts as follows:

(56) '... A door onbust is always open to bustin', but *ye* can't onbust a door once *you*'ve busted en.'   (*Invisible*, p. 32)
(57) "Who d'*ye* live with — supposin' *you*'re kindly let to live, which I han't made up my mind about?"   (*Great*, p. 5)
(58) 'though how *you* come to know it, Heaven only knows. *Ye* see, when I got up to the door, it was so still and so lonesome, that I thought I'd be none the worse for some one with me... .'   (*Scarlet*, p. 38)
(59) 'This is a hard road for a gradely foot like that. Will *ye* up, lass, and ride

behind me?' ... '*You* may please yourself,' (*Water*, p. 10)

It occasionally happens that people in the same community have a similar usage of language if it is not a regional one. Out of a total of 334 examples of *ye*, 113 examples belong to *Captains Courageous* alone and the number of the speakers is 10. It is to be noted that all these speakers of *ye* are fishermen of the schooner named *We're Here*, which is based in Gloucester, Massachusetts, in America. This suggests that American people used the unstressed variant *ye* for *you* quite frequently at that time. The most frequent user of *ye* is Dan Troop, the son of the captain of the schooner (44 exx.). His father, Disko Troop, uses the variant quite often as well (15 exx.). Among the crew there are some who come from other countries. An Irish fisherman named Long Jack, who is the second most frequent user of *ye*, utters the variant 23 times. His usage is just the same as the Troops. Another foreigner is a Portuguese fisherman called Manuel, who says *you* but never *ye*. Supposedly, American and Irish people similarly use the unstressed form *ye* of *you*.[14] The following example by Uncle Salters clearly shows that *ye* is an unstressed variant of *you* since the word "did" is italicized for emphasis before *ye*. He otherwise uses the standard forms *you* and *your* in a line of his speech.

(60) '*You* an' *your* nervis dyspepsy be drowned in the Whalehole,' roared Uncle Salters, a fat and tubby little man. '*You*'re comin' down on me agin. *Did ye* say forty-two or forty-five?' (Italicized "Did" in the original)

(*Captains*, p. 24)

Ye is also employed as a reflexive for *yourself*, as seen in instance (61). The usage is the same as that by Zillah in *Wuthering Heights* (cf. example [46]).

(61) 'Seat *ye*! Seat *ye*!' a voice Harvey had not heard called from the foc's'le.

(*Captains*, p. 25)

Since seamen's language tends to be rough, it is no surprise that the crew of *We're Here* use the casual form *ye* habitually. It would be safe to say that *ye* used in this text is a social marker existing in seamen's communities in the Northeast of the United States at that time.

Regional difference may possibly be found with the usage of the weakened variant *'ee* (pronounced /i:/ or /i/). There are 84 examples of this variant both for the nominative (27 exx.) and the objective (57 exx.). Except for one, all the examples are used by 25 characters living in Southern England: fifteen characters in *Jude the Obscure*, four in *Great Expectations*, three in *Barchester Towers*, two in *Vanity Fair* and one in *The Invisible Man*. The speakers generally belong to the lower class but Sir Pitt in *Vanity Fair* and Miss Thorn in *Barchester Towers* are from the nobility. The nobles who mingle with local people acquire dialectal speech more easily, especially in informal speech. Old Sir Pitt sometimes talks "in the coarsest and vulgarest Hampshire accent" (*Vanity*, p. 84) and though Miss Thorn's language is generally standard, Clark (1975: 83–84) suggests that the weakened variant *'ee* is heard among local people in Barsetshire, an imaginary region in the South of England. Furthermore, in both cases, combined with familiarity with dialectal speech, their psychological conditions may also help them utter *'ee*. In example (62), Sir Pitt is speaking to his daughter-in-law in a friendly manner while in (63) Miss Thorn, who is having a party with local tenants, is "so distressed" on seeing Mr. Arabin:

(62) 'I'm gittin very old, and have been cruel bad this year with the lumbago. I shan't be here now for long; but I'm glad *ee*'ve come, daughter-in-law... .' <Sir Pitt: Ballonet> (*Vanity*, p. 502)

(63) 'That is the very reason why you should lose no more time. Come, I'll make room for you. Thank*'ee*, my dear,' <Miss Thorn: Landowner>

(*Barchester*, II, p. 127)

Brook (1970: 120) maintains that in Dickens' works some regional features of phonology, accidence and syntax are paralleled in the speech of low-life London characters and change of lightly-stressed /juː/ to /i/ or /ə/ as in *thankee* is among them. This means that the form *'ee* can be regarded as both a local and social dialect and well explains why a well-bred lady like Miss Thorn and Magwitch the convict share the same term *thank'ee* as seen in (63) and (64).

(64) "Thank*'ee* dear boy, thank*'ee*. God bless you! You've never deserted me, dear boy." <Magwitch: Convict> (*Great*, p. 454)

There would perhaps be another element to be considered in the utterance of *thank'ee* by educated Miss Thorn. Colloquial use of *ye* in fixed phrases such as *thank ye/thank'ee* and *How d'ye do?* is more likely found across society, probably because of its idiomatic use. There are 24 examples of *thank ye/thank'ee* and seven of *How d'ye do?*, which are employed by twelve and seven characters respectively. When analyzed in terms of social class, these phrases are used more frequently by characters with a good upbringing than by those without by a ratio of 12 : 7. In example (65) from *Barchester Towers*, the clergyman Slope says *thank ye* to the lady bishop, and example (66) from *Alice's Adventures* illustrates that the phrase *How d'ye do?* is fixed in form.

(65) "Pray be seated, Mr. Slope," said the lady bishop.
"*Thank ye, thank ye,*" said Mr. Slope, and walking round to the fire, he threw himself into one of the arm-chairs that graced the hearth-rug.

(*Barchester*, II, p. 254)

(66) 'It would never do to say "*How d'ye do?*" *now,*' she said to herself: 'we seem to have got beyond that, somehow!'

(*Alice*, p. 161) (Italicized "now" in the original)

Barber (1976: 205) cites *d'ye* as a typical example of an unstressed form of *ye* and in our texts the contracted from *d'ye* is in common use.[15] As we have observed so far, the variant *ye* in *d'ye* would be better treated as an unstressed variant of *you* in our 19th-century texts. The educated people occasionally use this contraction. Remember that in *North and South* the two gentlemen, Mr. Thornton and Mr. Bell, use the unstressed *ye* in this form (see examples [34] and [35]). The examples of these educated men and Alice, a well-bred girl, lead us to assume that *d'ye* was used in a variety of regions and by people from various ranks.

Another fixed phrase including the unstressed *ye* is *look ye* and its variants, whose treatment might be a little tricky. Busse (2002: 292), who studied the distribution of *thou* and *ye* in Shakespeare's English, says that "[a]part from exclamations, *ye* is syntactically frequent in imperatives, that is to say in postverbal position with verbs to summon attention such as *hark ye* and *look ye.*" In this discussion, he argues that *ye* started to be replaced by *you* in the postverbal position in the 14th century and that the syntactic position, pronunciation in the unstressed position, and analogy with *thee* could have been associated with the change from *ye* to *you*. He obviously treats *ye* in *hark ye* as well as *look ye* in Shakespeare's English as the old nominative plural. Laurel J. Brinton (2008: 199) indicates that "[t]he now rather archaic *hark* bears a striking resemblance to *look* in that it occurs as an attention-getting pragmatic marker in conjunction with the second-person pronoun, *you, ye,* or *thee* ..." She, however, does not refer to the difference between the old *ye* and the recent *ye*. Which variant of *ye*, then, is used in *look ye* and *hark ye* in our 19th-century texts?

There are a total of 22 examples of *look ye* and its variants found in three texts: *Great Expectations* (19 exx.), *The Invisible Man* (2 exx.) and *Wildfell Hall* (1 ex.). Except for one example, the form *look ye* comes in the contracted form, including combined terms such as *looky* and *lookee* without an apostrophe. Interestingly enough, the sole example of the full form *look ye* is found in Northern speech (*Wildfell Hall*) while contracted forms such as *looky* (2 exx.), *look'ee* (12 exx.) and *lookee* (7 exx.) occur in Southern speech (*Great Expectations* and *The Invisible Man*). Although no example of *look ye* is found in either *North and South* or *Wuthering Heights*, which are rich in Northern dialectal terms, one example of *look thee* by a local millworker is attested in the former. It is probable that *look ye* and *look thee* belong to the Northern dialect and that the variant *ye* in the full form *look ye* at issue is the old nominative plural. Note that in example (67) the term "look ye sir" is uttered by a coachman to his passenger, possibly with respect, while millworker John Boucher uses "look thee, lad" to attract attention from his coworker in the next example. Imahayashi (2007a), who researched the use of *look* forms in the 19th century, also suggests that both *look ye* and *look thou/thee* are survival forms in Northern dialects.[16]

(67) 'Ahem! — I should think she'll marry none but a nobleman, myself. *Look ye* sir,' <a coachman> (*Wildfell*, p. 456)
Cf. An' *look thee*, lad, I'll hate thee, and th' whole pack o' th' Union.
(*N and S*, p. 154)

According to the OED (s.v. *look*, *v*. 4a), *look you* is in modern colloquial use in representations of vulgar speech written *look'ee*. All the 21 examples of the contracted *look* form belong to the speech of four lower-class characters including Cockney speakers, Magwitch the convict and Joe the blacksmith. Regarding the 19 examples found in *Great Expectations*, the relevant form is spelled out either as *look'ee* or *lookee* and both are followed by *here*, making a set phrase, *look'ee here/lookee here*. The most shortened spelling *looky* is found in the latest text, *The Invisible Man*. These examples seem to follow the process of grammaticalization of *lookee* in this century.[17]

(68) "*Look'ee* here, Pip. I'm your second father. You're my son — more to me nor any son... ." <Magwitch> (*Great*, p. 315)
(69) Suddenly an old woman, peering under the arm of the big navvy, screamed sharply. '*Looky* there!' she said, and thrust out a wrinkled finger. <Old woman> (*Invisible*, p. 152)

The two instances of the phrase *hark ye* are both found in *Vanity Fair*, one of the earlier texts. The speakers, Captain Dobbin and Lady Crawley, belong to the upper class. Both are addressing people in the lower class to seek to gain their attention. The lady's expression "with great graciousness" in (71) indicates the difference in social rank. In these contexts, *ye* in *hark ye* would be regarded as the old nominative plural as seen in Shakespeare's texts.

(70) '*Hark ye*, John, I have friends still, and persons of rank and reputation, too.' <Captain Dobbin> (*Vanity*, p. 241)

(71) 'and *hark ye*, Bowls,' she added, with great graciousness, 'you will have the goodness to pay Mr. James's bill.' <Lady Crawley>   (*Vanity*, p. 424)

There is no example of *hark you* in the fifteen texts under discussion but one in *Wuthering Heights*, which is used by the master of the novel's titular lands. Since the term *hark* itself is archaic, the usages of *hark ye* as well as *hark you* would have become obsolete in this century. Brinton (2008: 200) writes that a phonologically reduced form *harkee* (*hark'ee*, *harky*, *harkye*), which is not attested in our texts, is common in the 18th century and occurs sporadically even into the 19th century.[18] Even in such a "fused/coalesced form" with *hark*, the second person pronoun is more likely to be considered as the old *ye*, because unlike the *look* form, the *hark* form is disappearing in the 19th century (*OED*: s.v. *hark v.* 2c). Thus, as for the two similar imperative markers, it is assumed that *ye* in the full form (*look ye*, *hark ye*) is regarded as the old *ye* while the pronoun blended in *look'ee/looky* is regarded as the recent *ye*.

Syntactic analysis

This section deals with the usage of *ye* from a syntactic point of view. I would first like to see the distribution of the old nominative plural *ye*, either stressed or unstressed, and the unstressed recent *ye* of *you* in relation to case variation.

Table 2.11: Case variation of *ye* in the 15 texts concerned

	nom.	voc.	obj.	poss.	ref.	Total
ye	144 (18)	12 (7)	72		2	230 (25)
'ee	27		57			84
yer	6		2	10		18
yerself					2	2
Total	177 (18)	12 (7)	131	10	4	334 (25)

Note: The bracketed figures stand for the tokens of the archaic plural *ye*.

The above table shows that the old *ye* is limited to the nominative and vocative, which faithfully reflects that the second person plural *ye* is originally a nominative case. Since the old *ye* occurs in either the nominative or vocative, I would like to focus on the usage of *ye* in these two cases. In the case of the vocative, more than half of the examples are used as the old *ye* in poetic or religious contexts. On the other hand, the recent *ye* and its variants (*'ee*, *yer*) are employed in various cases. The variant *'ee*, though found either in the nominative or in the objective, is more frequently found in the latter.

From what we have observed above, it is hinted that the recent *ye* is inclined to occur in the post-verbal position. Let us find out if there is any disparity in the nominative between the old *ye* and the recent variants *ye/'ee/yer*.

Table 2.12: Position of the pronoun *ye/'ee/yer* in the nominative

		Pre-verbal	Post-verbal	Total
Old nominative plural	*ye*	14	4	18
Recent variants	*ye*	58	68	126
	'ee	1	26	27
	yer		6	6

Table 2.12 demonstrates that the recent *ye* appears in the post-verbal position more often than the old *ye*. Three examples of the old *ye* occur in the imperative, which are those of *look ye* and *hark ye* discussed above, and one in the inverted declarative as below. In each example, the pronoun *ye* is pronounced /ji/.

(72) '... O wicked souls of men and women! — is there no touch of grace or thought of God left in you! — and will *ye* make my sorrows eternal!'

(*Satan*, p. 291)

Compare the above example with (73), in which a recent *ye* /jə/ is used in apparently the same construction *will ye*, but *you* is chosen for the vocative.

(73) 'Bring on that water, *will ye*, you idle young harlican!'
<Drusilla Fawley>   (*Jude*, p. 5)

2.1.2.4 Distribution of two types of *ye* and how to tell the difference

The analyses conducted above will finally enable us to obtain a map of distribution of the two different types of *ye*, as shown in the table below.

Table 2.13: Distribution of old/recent variants *ye*

	Old nominative plural		Unstressed variant of *you*		Unstressed variant of *yo/yah*	
	abs n.	n. of speakers	abs n.	n. of speakers	abs n.	n. of speakers
ye	29	11	210	55	31	3
ee			84	26		
yer			28	9		
yerself/-seln			3	3		
Total	29 (7.5%)	11	325 (84.4%)	93	31 (8.1%)	3

It is found that the pronoun *ye* is mostly used as the unstressed variant *ye* of *you* as well as its dialectal variants *yo* and *yah* in our 19th-century novels with 92.5 percent of the total instances, whereas the old nominative plural *ye*, whether stressed or unstressed, accounts for only 7.5 percent. The ratio of the numbers of speakers of these two is 96 : 11, presenting a similar difference in disparity between them. From these data as well as the discussion given in the previous sections, the following criteria for distinguishing the two different kinds of *ye* can be drawn.

1. Regionally, the old *ye* is found in the northern part of England and Ireland while the recent *ye* is found across England as well as America.
2. *Ye* in fixed terms, such as *How d'ye you do?*, *thank ye/thank'ee* and the contracted *look'ee/looky*, is mostly the recent *ye*, but in the cases of the archaic phrases *look ye* and *hark ye*, the old *ye* is the norm.
3. Syntactically, the old *ye* is limited to the nominative and vocative, but the recent *ye* comes out in the objective as well.
4. In the nominative, the recent *ye* shows preference to the post-verbal position, but this is not always the case with the old *ye*.
5. Textual contexts are important, especially when *ye* appears in the vocative. The old *ye* is often uttered solemnly in poetic or religious atmospheres, while the recent *ye* is spoken in casual dialogue.

2.1.2.5 Summary

The second person pronoun *ye* shows such complex behavior in 19th-century novels that it is difficult to decide which variant is used in a particular example at a glance: *ye* stands for the old nominative plural (pronounced /jiː/ or /ji/) in some cases, either to refer to more than one person or to express respect to the addressee, but in others it is used as an unstressed variant (pronounced /jə/) of the standard *you* as well as dialectal variants *yo* and *yah*. Its usage cannot be reduced to any simple formula, but as I have shown in the previous sections, application of multiple linguistic criteria makes the distinction much easier. In particular, clues for identifying the recent *ye*, which have rarely been provided, are as essential as those of the old *ye* in dealing with the complex behavior of *ye*.

2.2 Third Person

In Late Modern English, third person pronouns are the same as today: the nominative, objective, and possessive cases are *he*, *him*, and *his* for the singular masculine; *she*, *her*, and *her* for the singular feminine; and *they*, *them*, and *their* for the plural. However, this is not necessarily the case in dialectal or colloquial speech. This section will mainly deal with the phonetically (or morphologically in the case of speech written in the novel) and grammatically nonstandard usage of the third person pronouns.

2.2.1 Third person singular

2.2.1.1 Nonstandard forms for *he*

The third person singular masculine (*he*, *him*, *his*) has considerable variation in dialects. According to Wright (1905: 272), for the nominative case the stressed form is generally /h)ī/, and rarely /h)ei/, and the unstressed form is generally /i/ or /ə/, and for the objective case the stressed form is /h)im/ and the unstressed form /im/. But in some south regions, /ən/, which is generally written as *en*, *un* (<OE, *hine*), is the regular unstressed form for /im/.

There are a total of 71 examples of the relevant pronoun found in five texts, which are divided in nine different nonstandard variants as shown in Table 2.14.

Table 2.14: Nonstandard variants for the third person singular male pronoun

	he		*him*				*his**		*his***	Total
	'e	*a*	*en*	*'n*	*'im*	*un*	*'is*	*uz*	*his'n*	
N and S									1	1
Vanity				2		3				5
Jude		3		7		25				35
Treasure									1	1
Invisible	9		11	4	2		1	2		29

*his: possessive adjective ***his*: possessive pronoun

According to the OED, the variant form *a* dates back to *ha* in Middle English and *he* in Old English (s.v. *he, pers. pro.* A). Both *a* and *'e* are obsolete and only used in dialect today (s.v. *a, pron.*; *e*). The objective form *him* had displaced *hine* in the North and the Midlands by 1150, and had become the common literary form before 1400, while *hin* and *hen* had been retained by some Southwestern writers of the 15th century. These archaic forms are still used in the Southern dialect in the forms *en*, *un* and *'n* (s.v. *him, pers. pron.*). Table 2.14 shows that *The Invisible Man* has the largest variation of this pronoun, and *Jude the Obscure* is the highest in absolute frequency. Since the relevant variants are used by those living in certain villages in the South of England, they are assumed to reflect the local dialect there.

Let us see how the variants are used in each text. In *The Invisible Man*, 29 examples are uttered by thirteen people living in a village named Aping in West Sussex. It is interesting that in this area the dialectal forms for *he* and *him* are used not only for a man but also for an animal and even for an inanimate object. In the nominative, eight examples of *'e* for *he* refer to the invisible man and one is used for the dog "who" bit the man, as seen in examples (74) and (75).

(74) "If *'e* ent there,' he said, 'his close are. And what's *'e* doin' without his

close, then? ...' ('*e* = *he*: the invisible man)　　　(*Invisible*, p. 30)
(75)　'What '*e* bite'n for then?' ('*e* = *he*: a dog)　　　(*Invisible*, p. 14)

In the objective, a similar usage is attested: the variant *en* for *him* is used for a man (7 exx.), a dog (2 exx.), a door (1 ex.) and sperrits "spirits" (1 ex.) while four instances of '*n* and two of '*im* are all for men. In dialects of the South of England, the objective case of the third person singular masculine (*im*, *en*, *an*) is also used of an inanimate object, though never of a woman (Wright 1905: 272). In the following examples, different kinds of objects are used, either as an objective of a verb or as a preposition.

(76)　'You just missed *en* — ' (*en* = *him*: the invisible man)　　　(*Invisible*, p. 37)
(77)　'Don't you leave go of *en*,' (*en* = *him*: the invisible man)　(*Invisible*, p. 151)
(78)　There is a clergyman and a medical gent witnesses, — saw '*im* all right and proper — or leastways, didn't see '*im*. ('*im* = *him*: the invisible man)
　　　　　　　　　　　　　　　　　　　　　　　　　　　　(*Invisible*, p. 67)
(79)　'I'd shoot *en*, that's what I'd do,' (*en* = *him*: a dog)　　(*Invisible*, p. 15)
(80)　'... A door onbust is always open to bustin', but ye can't onbust a door once you've busted *en*.' (*en* = *him*: a door)　　　(*Invisible*, p. 32)
(81)　'I know 'tas sperrits. I've read in papers of *en*... .' (*en* = *him*: sperrits)
　　　　　　　　　　　　　　　　　　　　　　　　　　　　(*Invisible*, p. 31)

Concerning the possessive, the three examples of the dialectal variants ('*is*, *uz*) are all referred to the invisible man as follows:

(82)　'Fetched off '*is* wrappin's, 'e did — ' ('*is* = *his*: the invisible man)
　　　　　　　　　　　　　　　　　　　　　　　　　　　　(*Invisible*, p. 37)
(83)　Back he comes with a knife in *uz* hand and a loaf; (*uz* = *his*: the invisible man)　　　　　　　　　　　　　　　　　　　　(*Invisible*, p. 37)

It may not be particularly characteristic to use the third person singular masculine for a dog and a spirit, since personal pronouns are sometimes used in reference to an animal and a supernatural being in the standard usage as well. Nevertheless, the examples of the objective *en* and possibly those of the nominative '*e* for an inanimate object seem to illustrate the broader usage of the third person singular masculine in this region. In the following sentence, quoted from the narration by the omniscient narrator and written in standard English, the dog which bit the invisible man is referred to as *it*. This suggests that the nonstandard variants of *he/him* are used for a dog in dialectal speech.

No sooner had Fearenside's dog caught sight of him, however, than *it* began to bristle and growl savagely, and when he rushed down the step *it* gave an undecided hop, and then sprang straight at his hand

(*Invisible*, p. 13).

Although the local variants of *he, him,* and *his* are habitually uttered by those in Southern England, standard forms are also found in their repertoire. Mr. Hall, an innkeeper, who uses the local forms most frequently (9 exx.), may show how to distinguish in use between Southern and standard forms.

(84) a. ''*E*'s not in uz room, '*e* ent.' (*Invisible*, p. 30)
     b. '*He* wuz bit,' (*Invisible*, p. 14)
(85) a. 'I heerd '*n*,' (*Invisible*, p. 57)
     b. 'That's *him*!' (*Invisible*, p. 37)

His examples indicate that in contrast with the dialectal forms, the standard *he* and *him* are uttered more emphatically; while Mr. Hall and perhaps those in this region as well usually employ the local variants, they choose the standard form when stressing the pronoun. In examples (84a) and (84b), emphasis is placed on *not* in the former and *he* in the latter; in examples (85a) and (85b), the terms *I heerd* are stressed in the former and *him* in the latter.

Let us next discuss how the variants for *he* and *him* are used in *Jude the Obscure*. The story is mainly developed in a village in the southern part of Wessex. Eight villagers (five females and three males) provide us with 35 examples: the nominative variant *a* (3 exx.) and the objective variants *un* (25 exx.) and '*n* (7 exx.). According to the *OED*, *a* is used for *he, she, it* (for *he*), and *they* (s.v. *a, pron.*). Note that the variant *a* is used for different personal pronouns — standard *she, he* and *they* respectively — in the following three examples:

(86) They'd try to coax her out again. But '*a* wouldn't come.'
     (*'a = he > she*: Sue) (*Jude*, p. 106)
(87) No doubt that's how he that the tale is told of came to do what '*a* did — if he *were* one of your family.'
     (Italicized "were" in the original) (*'a = he*: a gibbeted man) (*Jude*, p. 272)
(88) Weddings be funerals '*a* b'lieve nowadays. (*'a = he > they*) (*Jude*, p. 386)

The objective *un* also seems to be used not only for male persons but for animals, as in the following examples:

(89) 'Do ye love *un*?' (*un = him*: Mr. Phillotson; Schoolmaster) (*Jude*, p. 183)
(90) 'Every good butcher keeps *un* bleeding long. (*un =him > it*: a pig)
     (*Jude*, p. 58)

CHAPTER 2 DIALECTAL VARIATION OF PERSONAL PRONOUNS 55

It is noteworthy that the nominative variant *'a* is used by the two old women, Jude's great-aunt, Drusilla Fawley, and her nurse, Mrs. Edlin, while the objective variant *un* is employed by a greater variety of characters. Given that female teenagers who use the latter do not use the nominative variant *'a*, this variant can be considered more obsolete. Another point to be mentioned is that the villagers in this text use the standard pronoun (*he, his, him*) as well, usually when stress is placed on it. In example (91), in which Arabella uses *un*, *him* and *'n* in reference to Jude, her local variants are weakened after the verb *get* and the preposition *for*, while the standard forms *he* at the beginning and *him* after *let* are pronounced with an emphasis. Her utterance here illustrates that she wants to be alone with him in her house without being disturbed. She is planning to seduce Jude there. The sentence "I shall let him slip through my fingers" including the stressed *him* conveys her fearfulness of losing him.

(91) '... *He*'s shy; and I can't get *un* to come in when you are here. I shall let *him* slip through my fingers if I don't mind, much as I care for *'n*!'
<Arabella> (*Jude*, p. 49)

In *Vanity Fair*, there are five examples of the variants *'n* and *un* used for *him*; *'n* is used by a butler and a porter once each and *un* is used by Sir Pitt the baronet three times. The "noble" baronet uses local variants just as many other local people do. Miss Rebecca Sharp, who works as governess for the family of Sir Pitt, writes in her letter to her friend, "He [Sir Pitt] speaks with a country accent" (*Vanity*, p. 89). Since his country is in Hampshire, located on the coast of Southern England, he must have a Southern accent. His usage, though limited in sample, is similar to the villagers' in *Jude the Obscure*. The following example comes from Mr. Horrocks, who is Sir Pitt's friend and butler.

(92) 'He *be* a bad 'n, sure enough,' Mr. Horrocks remarked; 'and his man Flethers is wuss, ... but I think Miss Sharp's a match for *'n*, Sir Pitt,' he added, after a pause. (Italicized "be" in the original) (*Vanity*, p. 130)

Two examples of the absolute possessive *his'n* for *his* belong to *North and South* (1 ex.) and *Treasure Island* (1 ex.). According to the OED, this form is attested in the Midlands, eastern and southern parts of England (s.v. *hisn, his'n*). Our data suggest that the variant is used in the northern part as well. Similar variants in a different person, *theirin* for *theirs* and *our'n* for *ours*, are used by a woman in a village in the Midlands in *Silas Marner*.

2.2.1.2 Nonstandard forms for *she*
There are not many dialectal variants of the third person singular feminine. Its

stressed nominative form is generally /ʃɪ/, rarely /ʃei/, but in some of the North-Midland dialects it is /ʃu/. The objective form is generally /h)ɔ̄(r/ or /h)ə(r/ (Wright 1905: 272–273). According to Hirooka (1965: 334), *shoo* /ʃu:/ can be mistaken as the remnant of OE sēo, but since North ME /o:/ became /iu/, not /u:/, the pronoun written as *shoo* should be treated as a dialectal pronunciation of *she*. In our texts, there are two nonstandard nominative variants, *shoo* and *hoo*, exclusively found in *Wuthering Heights* and *North and South*, respectively.

2.2.1.2.1 Shoo

In *Wuthering Heights*, two local servants habitually use the variant *shoo* for *she*. They use some other dialectal personal pronouns besides *shoo* such as *Aw* for *I* and *yah* and *ye* for *you*. Out of the eleven instances of *shoo*, nine belong to a local servant, Joseph, who uses many dialectal forms such as *Aw, yah, ye* and *shoo*, as follows:

(93)   "... and Miss Nelly, *shoo*'s a fine lass! *shoo* sits watching for ye i' t'kitchen; and as yah're in at one door, he's aht at t'other ..." <Joseph>

(*Wuthering*, p. 77)

(94)   "Aw mun hev my wage, and Aw mun goa! Aw *hed* aimed tuh dee, wheare Aw'd sarved fur sixty year; un' Aw thowt Aw'd lug my books up intuh t' garret, un' all my bits uh stuff, un' they sud hev t' kitchen tuh theirseln; fur t' sake uh quietness. It wur hard to gie up my awn hearthstun, bud Aw thowt Aw *could* do that! Bud nah, shoo's taan my garden frough me, un' by th' heart! Maister, Aw cannot stand it! Yah muh bend tuh th' yoak, an ye will — *Aw'm* noan used to't, and an ow'd man doesn't sooin get used tuh new barthens — Aw'd rayther arn my bite, an' my sup, wi' a hammer in th' road!" (Italics in the original) <Joseph>

(*Wuthering*, p. 283)

2.2.1.2.2 Hoo

The variant *hoo* is found only in *North and South*. As for the third person feminine pronoun, Brook (1963: 104–105) states that "[t]he Old English equivalent was *heo*, and this has survived in many Northern and North-Midland dialects as [u] or [u:], usually spelt *hoo*." However, the specific area where the variant was used is unknown (Blake 1981: 152). The variant *hoo*, which derives from Old English and is seen in *North and South*, is not found in Yorkshire dialect. It is accordingly not attested in *Wuthering Heights* nor in any work of the Brontë sisters in our corpus. There are 45 relevant examples, which are used by four characters: Nicholas Higgins (33 exx.), John Boucher (7 exx.), his female neighbor (4 ex.) and Nicholas's daughter, Bessy (1 ex.). The speakers are all from local working class families in Milton, an imaginary village in Lancashire.

The speakers using *hoo* are all local people, but most users of the variant are elderly, except for Bessy, who uses it only once to indicate her younger sister, Mary. Mary always uses *she* in reference to her elder sister. This suggests that *hoo* is chosen when a speaker refers to a female junior in his or her intimate circle. For instance, the variant is used by Nicholas for his daughters, by Mr. Boucher for his wife and by Bessy for her younger sister, as follows:

(95) 'I'm none ashamed o' my name. It's Nocholas Higgins. *Hoo*'s called Bessy Higgins. Whatten yo' asking for?' <Nicholas>   (*N and S*, p. 73)
(96) *Hoo*'s never looked up sin' he were born, and *hoo* loves him as if he were her very life, <Mr. Boucher>   (*N and S*, p. 154)
(97) 'I wonder if there are many folk like her [Margaret] down South. *She*'s like a breath of country air, somehow.... I wonder how she'll sin. All on us must sin.... And Mary even. It's not often *hoo*'s stirred up to notice much.'<Bessy>   (*N and S*, p. 138)

The use of *hoo* from senior to junior can be contrastively illustrated in the following example, in which Nicholas refers to Mrs. Boucher as *she* and his daughter Bessy as *hoo*.[19]

(98) I were fetched to Boucher's wife afore seven this morning. *She*'s bedfast, but *she* were raving and raging to know where her dunder-headed brute of a chap was, as if I'd to keep him — as if he were fit to be ruled by me.... And I were sore-hearted, too, which is worse than sore-footed; and if I did see a friend who ossed to treat me, I never knew *hoo* lay a-dying here. <Nicholas>   (*N and S*, p. 221)

While Bessy and Mary use the standard *she* in referring to Margaret, who is their mutual friend, Nicholas refers to her as *hoo*. In examples (99) to (101), Nicholas uses *hoo* in reference to Margaret not only because she is his daughters' age but probably because he holds some affection towards her. Let us closely examine each situation. Example (99) illustrates the scene in which he meets her for the first time, when walking with his daughter, Bessy. Finding his daughter wishing to make friends with her, he has a similarly friendly emotion towards the girl. Likewise, in example (100), Nicholas tells Mr. Hale, Margaret's father and a parson, how he likes his daughter. He likes her because she understands very well about millworkers' difficult situation, notwithstanding their different social positions. Example (101) is found in a serious scene in the latter part of the text. After a five-hour wait, Nicholas meets the master

Thornton, trying to clear up his misunderstanding about Margaret. He cannot bear to see him mistake her because he likes Margaret. It is thus assumed that his use of *hoo* for Margaret is a manifestation of some warmth or affection towards her.

(99) 'Aye, aye,' said the father, impatiently, '*hoo*'ll come. *Hoo*'s a bit set up now, because *hoo* thinks I might ha' spoken more civilly; but *hoo*'ll think better on it, and come... .' <Nicholas> (*N and S*, p. 74)

(100) 'I like her,' said Higgins, suddenly. '*Hoo* speaks plain out what's in her mind. *Hoo* doesn't comprehend th' Union for all that. It's a great power: it's our only power... .' <Nicholas> (*N and S*, p. 293)

(101) 'I hear, sir. I would na ha' troubled yo', but that I were bid to come, by one as seemed to think yo'd getten some soft place in yo'r heart. *Hoo* were mistook, and I were misled. But I'm not the first man as is misled by a woman.' <Nicholas> (*N and S*, p. 321)

The following example is an interesting one, in which Nicholas uses *hoo* for his daughter Mary but then in the same line shifts the local variant to the standard *she*. In talking to Mr. Hale, Nicholas flatly refuses his financial offer to Mary. Nicholas first uses *hoo* to refer to Mary, and then uses *she* for the same daughter, but under the hypothetical condition of her having received the money. His shift from *hoo* to *she* could indicate that he would no longer feel affection to her if she should accept money against his advice.

(102) 'If *hoo* takes it, I'll turn her out o' doors. I'll bide inside these four walls, and *she*'ll bide out. Thai's a'.' <Nicholas> (*N and S*, p. 290)

Elizabeth Gaskell, the novel's author, intensively uses *hoo* by putting the variant in the mouth of Nicholas Higgins. This variant, however, is also found in *Ruth* (1853), in which the variant is used by an elderly female servant twice to refer to a young woman, Ruth. In this scene, the warm sympathy the servant expresses towards this hapless girl is conveyed via the dialectal *hoo*:

> "Who's yon?"
> Mr Benson was silent, and walked a step onwards. Miss Benson said boldly out,
> "The lady I named in my note, Sally — Mrs Denbigh, a distant relation."
> "Aye, but you said *hoo* was a widow. Is this chit a widow?"
> "Yes, this is Mrs Denbigh," answered Miss Benson.
> "If I'd been her mother, I'd ha' given her a lollypop instead of a hus-

band. *Hoo* looks fitter for it." (*Ruth*, pp. 134–135)

Local variants sometimes possess subtle connotations which standard language cannot communicate. The variant *hoo* would be a case in point.

2.2.1.3 Nonstandard forms for *it*
The variation of dialectal forms of the third person singular neuter is limited. The stressed form is generally /it/ but in some regions /hit/, and the unstressed form is generally /it/ or /ət/ (Wright 1905: 273). In our corpus, the nonstandard form *ut* is intensively used in one text and the shortened form *'t* for *it* (e.g., *'tis* for *it is*; *o't* for *of it*) is found in thirteen texts.

2.2.1.3.1 Ut
The variant *ut* appers only in *Captains Courageous*. It is used only by Long Jack, a crewman on a fishing vessel. Long Jack's speech is different from the other members of the crew because he is Irish American. He employs this variant 25 times (four times as nominative and 21 times as objective). Since *ut* is an unstressed variant of *it*, it is rarely used at the beginning of utterances. When it functions as nominative, it occurs either in the post-verbal order or after a conjunction (see examples [103] to [106]). In examples (107) and (108), Long Jack uses the standard form *it* as nominative. In each case the pronoun is stressed.

(103) '... How is *ut*, Salters?' (*Captains*, p. 94)
(104) 'What is *ut*?' (*Captains*, p. 113)
(105) 'They hauled *ut* up, bein' just about in that state when *ut* seemed right an' reasonable, an' sat down on the deck countin' the knots, an' gettin' her snarled up hijjus... .' (*Captains*, p. 83)
(106) They tuk their satisfaction out av that, an' *ut* all came av not keepin' the crew an' the rum sep'rate in the first place; (*Captains*, p. 84)

(107) When they're lousy *it*'s a sign they've all been herdin' together by the thousand, an' when they take the bait thet way they're hungry.
(*Captains*. pp. 46–47)
(108) '... Guess we'll run aout aour trawl to-night. Harder on the back, this, than from the dory, ain't *it*?' (*Captains*, p. 47)

In the objective case, the unstressed variant *ut* is always chosen as follows:

(109) ... , I gave *ut* to the priest, an' he hung *ut* up forninst the altar.
(*Captains*, p. 52)
(110) 'I feel as if she'd made a cathedral av *ut* all.' (*Captains*, p. 132)

Although Wright (1898–1905: s.v. *it*) suggests that *ut* is used only in Britain, Long Jack's *ut* for *it* may be regarded as Irish English.[20] Given that none of the American crew members on the vessel in the text use the third person singular pronoun in such a way, it is assumed that Rudyard Kipling, the novel's author, illustrated Long Jack's Irish background by *ut* along with other Irish dialectal forms.

2.2.1.3.2 *'Tis* for *it is*

The form *'i* for *it* (e.g., *'tis*, *'twas*) is found across our 19th-century corpus. The form *'tis* is an abbreviation of *it is* and *'twas* is that of *it was*. These shortened forms were formerly common in prose, but are now poetic, archaic, dialectal or colloquial (*OED* s.v. *'tis*; *'twas*). The earliest examples listed in the *OED* for these terms are from c. 1450 and 1604, respectively, and are continuously attested in the 19th century. The fact that there are quite a few examples in our corpus suggests that the usage was common in the century. Along with *'tis* and *'twas*, other variant forms such as *'twere* and *'twill* are found. There are a total of 168 instances of the *'t* form in fourteen different forms.[21] A list of variations of the *'t* form per text is shown in Table 2.15.[22]

The forms *'tis* and *'twas* overwhelm the other variants in frequency. Though these variants occur across the century and across the texts, their examples are mostly restricted to the affirmative forms (*'tis*, *'twas*, *'twould*) in the older texts.[23] Moreover, it is noticed that the negative forms (*'tisn't*, *'twasn't*, etc.) are likely to be used in the more recent texts. This is probably because of the contracted negator *n't*, which came into use at a more recent time.

According to Jespersen (1909–49:V, §23.1.5), the forms in *n't* appear in writing about 1660. The examples of the relevant negative forms in our texts

Table 2.15: Variation of the *'t* form in the nominative case according to text

	it is	it was						it were		it will	it would			it ain't	Total
	'tis	'tisn't	'twas	'tas	'twuz	'twasn't	'tasn't	'twer(e)	'tweren't	'twill	'twon't	'twould	'twoudn't	'tain't	
Pride	3														3
Frankenstein															
N and S										1					1
Vanity	6	4													10
Great		1												1	2
Barchester	3	23					1								27
Jane															
Wuthering															
Silas															
Water		1													1
Wildfell															
Alice	3	3													6
Jude	25	2	9		1		1			3	1	6	1		49
Treasure	1												4		5
Dorian															
Satan	3	1													4
Ryecroft	1	1													2
Scarlet															
Captains	7	2	7	7	1					5		4	7	8	48
Invisible	3		1	4			1				1				10
Total	55	4	50	4	7	3	1	2		5	4	5	14	1	13	168

Note: The variant *'twere* includes *'twer* in *Jude the Obscure*. The variant *'tain't* includes *'tan't* in *Great Expectations*.

and their frequencies are *'tisn't* (4 exx.), *'twasn't* (3 exx.), *'tweren't* (5 exx.), *'twon't* (5 exx.), *'twoundn't* (1 ex.) and *'tain't* (13 exx.). In textual terms, a wider variation of the *'t* form is attested in the two texts, *Jude the Obscure* and *Captains Courageous*. Since the *'t* form is found both in written and spoken languages, I will examine how register is related to the use of the variants. In addition, it would be useful to find out how the contracted form *n't* affects the distribution of the *'t* form.

Table 2.16: Distribution of the *'t* form combined/not combined with *n't* in spoken/written language

	With *n't*	Without *n't*	Total
Spoken	31	99	130
Written		38	38

Note: Written language consists of narrative, verse, letter and diary.

Table 2.16 shows the occurrence of the *'t* form combined with *n't* or not combined with *n't* in spoken and written contexts. All the 31 examples of the form *n't* occur in dialogue and not a single example is found in written language. The variants of the *'t* form attested in writing are *'tis* (8 exx.) and *'twas* (30 exx.). I will find out how the *'t* form is actually used in specific linguistic contexts by taking up individual instances.

The forms *'tis* and *'twas* used in writing are of literary style. Poetic use of *'tis* and *'twas* is found in the four instances in a verse for Queen Alice in *Through the Looking-Glass* in example (111).

(111) *'Tis an honour to see me, a favour to hear:*
       'Tis a privilege high to have dinner and tea
       (Italics original, underlines mine)   (*Alice*, p. 233)

Example (112) is a letter from a schoolmistress to a noble lady. Example (113) is from a diary of a retired writer, Ryecroft. In the latter, although the sentence ending with an exclamation mark gives the line a flavor of conversation, the *'t* form is not to be labeled as substandard since his diary is thoroughly written in literary context.

(112) *'Tis* most gratifying to one in my most arduous position to find that my maternal cares have elicited a responsive affection;
       <Miss Pinkerton: Schoolmistress>   (*Vanity*, pp. 116–117)
(113) *'Tis* all very well to like vegetables and fruits up to a certain point; but to breakfast on apples! <Ryecroft: Writer>   (*Ryecroft*, p. 86)

Twenty-eight examples of the form *'tis/'twas* are found in narrative in three texts: *Barchester Towers* (26 exx.), *Vanity Fair* (1 ex.) and *Great Expectations* (1 ex.). The narrator of *Barchester Towers* uses these forms most frequently; he alone uses *'tis* (3 exx.) and *'twas* (23 exx.). In his use, the form followed by *thus* is found thirteen times as a fixed phrase in the narrative. Given that the users of *'tis/'twas* in writing are all educated, it is assumed that the shortened *'t* for *it* was of standard use in English at that time.

(114)   *'Twas thus* she played the second act in that day's melodrame.
        <Narrator>   (*Barchester*, II, p. 149)

Let us next move onto the *'t* form used in dialogue. The relevant 130 examples are employed by various kinds of characters in thirteen texts. I would like to find out how this form is used in specific examples. It would also be interesting to examine how the *'t* form with the contracted negator *n't*, which is limited to speech, is used and by which kind of people. There are forty-seven users of the *'t* form in total, including twelve who employ the form with *n't* and two who employ the form followed by the uncontracted negator *not*. These characters are categorized according to their social status in Table 2.17.

A striking difference can be seen in the use of the *'t* form with *n't*: those in the upper and middle classes never employ the form combined with *n't*, while lower-class people and Americans use the *'t* form both without and with *n't*. Let us have a look at how the individual characters actually employ the form in their speech according to social class.

Table 2.17: Number of characters who use the *'t* form (with *n't/not*) classified according to social class

	't form	*'t* form with *n't*	*'t* form with *not*
U	8		
M	6		(1)
L	21	(5)	(1)
American	10	(7)	
Total	45	(12)	(2)

U: upper class, M: middle class, L: lower class (The same applies hereinafter)
Note: Two people whose social status cannot be identified are omitted.

The following examples are utterances by some characters from the upper class: Mr. and Mrs. Bennet and their eldest daughter, Jane, in *Pride and Prejudice*, Mr. Arabin (a young clergyman) in *Barchester Towers*, a Duchess in *Alice*, Dr. Livesey (a physician) in *Treasure Island*, and Lucio (a prince and Satan) in *The Sorrows of Satan*.

(115)   '*'Tis* an etiquette I despise,' said he. 'If he wants our society, let him seek
        it. He knows where we live. I will not spend *my* hours in running after

CHAPTER 2 DIALECTAL VARIATION OF PERSONAL PRONOUNS 63

my neighbours every time they go away, and come back again.' (Italicized "my" in the original) <Mr. Bennet: Gentleman>   (*Pride*, p. 253)
(116) '*'Tis* too much!' she added, 'by far too much. I do not deserve it. Oh! why is not every body as happy?' <Jane: Gentleman's daughter>
(*Pride*, p. 264)
(117) 'My dearest child,' she cried, 'I can think of nothing else! Ten thousand a year, and very likely more! *'Tis* as good as a Lord! And a special licence... .' <Mrs. Bennet: Gentleman's wife>   (*Pride*, p. 290)
(118) 'I have esteemed, do esteem you, as I never yet esteemed any woman. Think well of you! I never thought to think so well, so much of any human creature. Speak calumny of you! Insult you! Wilfully injure you! I wish it were my privilege to shield you from calumny, insult, and injury. Calumny! ah, me. *'Twere* almost better that it were so. Better than to worship with a sinful worship; sinful and vain also.'
<Mr. Arabin: Clergyman>   (*Barchester*, II, p. 36)

People in the higher rank have something in common in the usage of *'t* form: they use the form with heightened emotions, as seen in examples (115) to (118). This can be said of all the examples from *Pride and Prejudice*: In example (115), Mr. Bennet, who is usually a mild gentleman, is exceptionally irritated at the troublesome custom those days; in (116), Jane is in the happiest mood because her love for Bingley has finally come to fruition; and in (117), Mrs. Bennet is just as happy in discovering the match between her second daughter Elizabeth and Mr. Darcy. Similar emotion-related usage is also seen in example (118), in which the exclamation mark is lavishly used; Mr. Arabin is eager to propose marriage to Eleanor though he cannot bring himself to do so properly.

A similar tendency is found in the examples taken from characters belonging to the middle class. In (119), emphasis is indicated by exclamation marks and in (120) and (121), by emphatic terms like "too much" and "more genteel," respectively. These examples illustrate that those in the higher social ranks utter the *'t* form in an elated or agitated mood.

(119) "Nay!" said I, "*'tis* I should cry Murder! — for if ever an arresting hand held a murderer, mine holds one now! Your system of slaying is worse than that of the midnight assassin, for the assassin can but kill the body — *you* strive to kill the soul. You cannot succeed, *'tis* true, but the mere attempt is devilish... . down you go!" (Italicized "you" in the original) <Geoffrey: Writer>   (*Satan*, p. 84)
(120) And with her unconquerable aversion to myself as a husband, even though she may like me as a friend, *'tis* too much to bear longer. She has conscientiously struggled against it, but to no purpose. I cannot beat it

— I cannot! <Mr. Phillotson: Schoolmaster> (*Jude*, p. 221)
(121) 'Say a bouquet, sister Jemima, *'tis* more genteel.'
<Miss Pinkerton: Schoolmistress> (*Vanity*, p. 4)

There are a total of 21 lower-class users of the *'t* form, of which as many as fourteen belong to *Jude the Obscure*. The greater number of the speakers and the greater variation of the *'t* form in this novel suggest that the *'t* form is part of a local dialect in Southern England. As shown in Table 2.15, this text alone yields 49 examples of the *'t* form in nine different types: *'tis* (25 exx.), *'tisn't* (2 exx.), *'twas* (9 exx.), *'twasn't* (1 ex.), *'twer* (1 ex.), *'twill* (3 exx.), *'twon't* (1 ex.), *'twould* (6 exx.) and *'twouldn't* (1 ex.). The two female lower-class characters use the *'t* form with *n't*. The *'t* form is occasionally used emotionally as seen in (122) to (127), where various relevant forms are uttered with exclamation marks.

(122) '' *Tis* clear she don't!' <Anny: a village girl> (*Jude*, p. 44)
(123) '... ' *Tis* done o' purpose! — *'tis* — *'tis*!' <Arabella's boy> (*Jude*, p. 323)
(124) '... *'Twon't* fetch so much by a shilling a score!'
<Arabella: Pig-breeder's daughter> (*Jude*, p. 60)
(125) 'Perhaps *'twouldn't* have happened then! But of course I didn't wish to take him away from your wife,' <Arabella: Inkeeper's wife> (*Jude*, p. 336)
(126) 'I shall have to keep 'ee entirely, — that's what *'twill* come to! ...'
<Arabella: Mason's wife> (*Jude*, p. 373)
(127) 'I told 'ee how *'twould* be!' <Mrs. Edlin: Old nurse> (*Jude*, p. 382)

In the following instances also, heightened emotions such as irritation and lamentation are conveyed in the use of the *'t* form.

(128) '... Jude my child, don't *you* ever marry. *'Tisn't* for the Fawleys to take that step any more. She, their only one, was like a child o' my own, Belinda, till the split come, Ah, that a little maid should know such changes!' (Italicized "you" in the original) <Drusilla Fawley: Baker> (*Jude*, p. 8)
(129) '... Ah well: he must walk about with somebody I s'pose. Young men don't mean much now-a-days. *'Tis* a sip here and a sip there with 'em. *'Twas* different in my time.' <Arabella's neighbour > (*Jude*, p. 49)

In *The Invisible Man*, in which the form appears either without or with *n't*, the ten examples of the *'t* form are used by three local villagers.

(130) '... *'Tas* a most curious basness.' <Mr. Hall: Landlord> (*Invisible*, p. 30)
(131) ''*Tasn't* right *have* such dargs';

(Italicized "have" in the original) <a villager>   (*Invisible*, p. 14)

The remaining four lower-class characters who employ the *'t* form are: Mr. Grimes the Chimney-sweep in *The Water Babies*, Orlick the Journeyman in *Great Expectations*, Silver the buccaneer in *Treasure Island*, and Nicholas the millworker in *North and South*. As their occupations reveal, the users of the negator *n't* belong to the lowest class of society at that time. This indicates that the relevant form is regarded as substandard, at least in their region. Note that *tan't* in (133) and *'taint* in (134) are shortened forms of the nonstandard forms *it an't* and *it ain't*, respectively. In *Treasure Island*, Dr. Liversey also uses the *'t* form. However, unlike his lower-class counterparts, he uses only the *'t* form without *n't*, as seen in (135).

(132) *'Twasn't* for cleanliness I did it, but for coolness.
 <Mr. Grimes: Chimney-sweep>   (*Water*, p. 12)
(133) "Two can go up-town. *Tan't* only one wot can go up-town."
 <Orlick: Journeyman>   (*Great*, p. 111)
(134) '... But what sort of a way is that for bones to lie? *'Tain't* in natur'.'
 <Silver: Buccaneer>   (*Treasure*, p. 173)
(135) 'Heaven forgive them,' said the doctor; "*'tis* the mutineers!'
 <Dr. Livesey: Physician>   (*Treasure*, p. 188)

From the contexts of the utterances of the three lower-class characters above, it is presumed that they use the *'t* form with some kind of exclamation just as the doctor does in his utterance. If so, the negative *'t* form here works as an emotional marker as well as a substandard marker.

From a regional standpoint, as far as England is concerned, our data show that the *'t* form is more likely to be used in Southern England. Various kinds of the *'t* form are used in the texts with a Southern area as a main stage, including *Jude the Obscure* and *The Invisible Man*, while the form hardly ever occurs in Northern language or Midland language — with the exception of Nicholas in *North and South*, who uses the *'t* form only once, no one uses the *'t* form in the three texts by the Brontës or in *Silas Marner*.

Lastly, I will deal with the American usage portrayed in *Captains Courageous*, in which 48 examples of the *'t* form are used by ten people. It should be noted that out of these ten characters, seven use both forms (i.e., with and without *n't*). The variation of the *'t* form found in this text is as follows: *tis* (7 exx.), *'tisn't* (2 exx.), *'twas* (7 exx.), *'twaz* (7 exx.), *'twasn't* (1 ex.), *'tweren't* (5 exx.), *'twon't* (4 exx.), *'twould* (7 exx.) and *'tain't* (8 exx.). The frequency of the *'t* form and the number of its speakers are close to those in *Jude the Obscure*. Some variant forms are demonstrated below.

(136) *'Tweren't* the women neither thet tarred and feathered him —
       <Disko: Skipper>   (*Captains*, p. 56)
(137) 'I knew haow *'twould* be,' <Disko: Skipper>   (*Captains*, p. 87)
(138) 'I should very much, indeed. *'Twon't* hurt you, mama, and you'll be able to see for yourself.' <Mr. Cheyne: Railway magnate>

                                                                                                     (*Captains*, p. 129)

(139) *"Twasn't* a calm,' said Harvey sulkily.
       <Harvey: Railway Magnate's son>   (*Captains*, p. 8)
(140) *"Tisn't* bad,' said Milsom modestly. <Milsom: Secretary>

                                                                              (*Captains*, p. 119)

(141) 'We lose one hundred a year from Gloucester only, Mr Cheyne,' she said — 'one hundred boys an' men; and I've come so's to hate the sea as if *'twuz* alive an' listenin'... .' <Mrs. Troop: Skipper's wife>

                                                                               (*Captains*, p. 135)

The characteristic use of the *'t* form in *Captains Courageous* is that characters' social status has little to do with its occurrence. Mr. Cheyne, a wealthy railroad magnate, and his son use the negative *'t* form just as casually as fishermen, as shown in (138) and (139). The negator *n't*, therefore, does not directly reflect nonstandard usage in the new land. Moreover, among the variations of the *'t* form, the nonstandard variant *'tain't*, which does not occur in *Jude the Obscure*, is found in this text. Interestingly, the form *'tain't*, which is used only once by a buccaneer in England, is uttered by the skipper's son seven times. In all these respects, it may be concluded that the usage of the negative *'t* form was slightly more acceptable in America than in Southern England at that time; in *Captains Courageous*, many of the relevant instances can be regarded as colloquial rather than substandard.

2.2.1.3.3 O't for *of it*

The third person singular objective *it* is sometimes shortened in the post-prepositional position (e.g., *o't* for *of it*, *wi't* for *with it*) as well as in the post-verbal position (e.g., *see't* for *see it*). Our corpus gives only nineteen instances in total occurring in six different forms, as shown in Table 2.18.

Table 2.18: Variation of 't form in the objective case according to text

	on't	o't	to't	wi't	see't	oppen't	Total
N and S	1						1
Great	1		1				2
Wuthering	5		1	2		1	9
Silas					1		1
Jude		4					4
Treasure	1						1
Ryecroft	1						1
Total	9	4	2	2	1	1	19

The prepositions and verbs placed before 't have either a vowel or a nasal at the end. Note that, unlike the nominative case, the shortened objective 't is used in Northern speech, with nine examples in *Wuthering Heights* and one in *North and South*. Its Northern feature is also suggested by the fact that neither the villagers in *The Invisible Man* nor the American seamen in *Captains Courageous* use this form. All these examples are used in local dialects except for one used by Ryecroft the writer. As for the form *on't*, *on* is used for *of* in eight examples out of the nine. The *OED* says, "In senses now expressed by OF. In *on't* and the like, common in literary use to c1750 but now *dial.* or *vulgar*" (s.v. *on, prep.* III. 27). Of these eight, one example of literary use is found in *Ryecroft*, six examples of dialectal use are seen in *Wuthering Heights* and *North and South*, and one example of vulgar use, belonging to 19th-century Cockney speech, is attested in *Great Expectations*.[24]

(142) The flower simply a flower, and there an end *on't*? <Ryecroft: Writer>
(*Ryecroft*, p. 111)

(143) 'Their bookstuff goes in at one ear and out at t'other. I can make nought *on't*... .' <Nicholas: Millworker> (*N and S*, p. 229)

(144) "Why, where the devil is the use *on't*?" <Hareton: Landowner's son>
(*Wuthering*, p. 194)

(145) "They must ha' thought better *on't* for some reason or another," said the Jack, "and gone down." <Jack: a grizzled male creature>
(*Great*, p. 435)

Let us examine the other variations of objective case 't forms. All four examples of *o't* are uttered by three villagers in *Jude the Obscure*, probably as dialectal speech in the southern English region of Wessex. As in example (146) below, the preposition *of* is regularly shortened in this region, which results in production of *o't* for *of it*. The examples of *to't* belong to Magwitch in *Great Expectations* and Joseph in *Wuthering Heights*, which indicates that the form is used in both social and regional dialects.

(146) '...Nobody thought o' being afeard o' matrimony in my time, nor of much else but a cannon-ball or empty cupboard. Why when I and my poor man were married we thought no more *o't* than of a game o' dibs.' <Mrs. Edlin: Old nurse>   (*Jude*, p. 277)

(147) "Darn Me if I couldn't eat 'em," said the man, with a threatening shake of his head, "and if I han't half a mind *to't*!" <Magwitch: Convict>

(*Great*, p. 5)

The form *wi't* is only used by Joseph twice in *Wuthering Heights* while a similar variant *wi' it* has six examples found in *Jude the Obscure, North and South* and *Silas Marner* as shown below. Due to the limited sample, I should refrain from deciding that *wi't* is part of Yorkshire dialect. It is safe to say, however, that the form *wi' it*, not seen in *Wuthering Heights*, is commoner than *wi't*.

(148) "Nor-ne me! Aw'll hae noa hend *wi't*," <Joseph: Servant>

(*Wuthering*, p. 6)

Cf. If salvation, and life to come, and what not, was true — not in men's words, but in men's hearts' core — dun yo' not think they'd din us *wi' it* as they do wi' political 'conomy? <Nicholas: Millworker>

(*N and S*, p. 226)

The following are examples of *see't* and *oppen't*. There is only one example of each form. It seems that the pronoun *it* is not often used in the contracted form combined with a preceding verb even in dialectal speech.

(149) they'll find you fifty reasons straight off, and all the while the real reason's winking at 'em in the corner, and they niver *see't*.
<Mr. Macey: Parish Clerk>   (*Silas*, p. 47)

(150) "They's nobbut t' missis; and shoo'll not *oppen't* an ye mak yer flaysome dins till neeght." <Joseph: Servant>   (*Wuthering*, p. 6)

2.2.1.4 Summary

There are quite a few dialectal variants for the third person singular pronouns in our 19th-century texts. As for the third person singular masculine, a variety of dialectal forms of Southern England are found, such as *'e, a* for *he*; *en, 'n, 'im* for *him*; and *'s* and *uz* for *his*. The local variants of *he* and *him* are used in reference not only to a male person but also to an animal as well as an inanimate object. The standard form (*he, his, him*) is used for an emphatic effect in the local area where the unstressed nonstandard form is the norm. The third person singular feminine has two regional variants, *shoo* and *hoo*, in Northern

England. The variant *hoo* in *North and South* tends to be used by a senior in reference to a female junior, often with a tone of affection or pity. As for the third person singular neuter *it*, the unstressed variant *ut* is used presumably as Irish English. The shortened *'t* form (e.g., *'tis, 'twas*) is found across the texts. In speech of the upper and middle classes, it is used in emotional tones. The *'t* form used by lower-class people occasionally includes the contracted negator *n't*. The other shortened *'t* form in the post-verbal or the post-prepositional positions (e.g., *on't, o't*) occurs in either literary or dialectal contexts. It is attested both in the North and in the South.

2.2.2 Third person plural *'em* for *them*

For the third person plural pronouns, Old English used *hīe, hiera, him*, but Scandinavian *they, their* and *them* were borrowed in the Middle English period, perhaps in order to avoid confusion with singular forms (<OE *hē, his, him*, <ME *he, his, him*) (e.g., Baugh and Cable 2002: 102). Although both *they* and *them* are pronounced in slightly different ways from region to region, the difference in pronunciation is rarely reflected in spelling. The unstressed objective /əm/, written as *em* or *'em*, is the variant found in fictional speech.

2.2.2.1 Overview
It is generally considered that *'em* is a remnant of the unstressed form of *hem* in Middle English (<OE *heom*). The history of the form *'em* is stated in the OED as follows:

> Originally the unstressed form of HEM, dative and accusative 3rd person plural. The emphatic form of the pronoun was early superseded by THEM, but the unstressed form continued to be used, being regarded as an abbreviation of *them*. In literature it is now *obsolete* or archaic, but is still common in familiar speech. (s.v. *'em, pron.*)

Blake (1981: 96) observes that the variant *'em* is common from the Elizabethan period onwards in plays and novels where it is used by characters of all ranks. Regionally, this unstressed form *'em* is used in all the dialects of Ireland and England in the 19th century (Wright 1905: 274). Although most historical linguists state that the form *'em* seen in Modern English literature also derives from *hem*, there are some who cast doubt on the theory. Takanobu Otsuka (1970: 759) comments that it is not quite certain whether *'em* in present-day colloquial English is the descendant of ME *hem* or a reduced form of *them*. In *Thomas Hardy's Use of Dialect*, Hirooka refers to the passage from Shakespeare where "both *them* and *'em* are used side by side in the same context":

> They shall have none, I swear, but these my joints;
> Which if they have as I will leave *'em them,*
> Shall yield them little, tell the constable. (*Henry V.*, IV. iii. 123–125)
>
> (Hirooka 1983:68)

Prior to this argument, Hirooka (1965: 120–121) notes that *th* / ð / in *than, these, that* and *with* sometimes drops in Southwestern dialect. Moreover, the *OED* states that "in north midland dialects *'em* may have arisen from *them*: cf. South Yorkshire *'at* for *that*." (s.v. *'em, pron.*). Wyld (1920: 327–338), who himself supports the "distinct" origin of *'em* in the Modern English period, presents an interesting observation about the absence of the variant in the 16th century and its reappearance in the 17th, when the apostrophe (as in *'em*) shows that already it was thought to be a weakened form of *them*.

2.2.2.2 Data

It is not difficult to find users of the unstressed *'em* in our 19th-century novels. A total of 403 examples of *'em* are found in fourteen texts. In most instances, *'em* appears as objective but in five it is used as nominative, as shown below. The dialectal form *'em* for *them* in the nominative position is only found in *Jude the Obscure* (3 exx.) and *North and South* (2 exx.), both of which are rich in dialectal variants. In regional dialects the objective case is often used as a subject. Example (151) shows that *'em* is used both as nominative and as objective, and example (152) indicates that both *they* and *'em* are employed as nominative, but that the unstressed nominative form *'em* is chosen in the post-verbal position while *they* is preferred in the pre-verbal position.

(151) *'Em* lives on a lofty level; there's no gainsaying it, though I myself med not think much of *'em*. <a carter> (*Jude*, p. 19)

(152) And what is *'em* to do? It's little blame to them if *they* do go into th' gin-shop for to make their blood flow quicker, and more lively, and see things *they* never see at no other time — pictures, and looking-glass, and such like. <Bessy: Millworker's daughter> (*N and S*, p. 136)

In 398 cases, *'em* is used for the objective *them*. Their distribution is shown in table 2.19. While six texts have no relevant example, the absence of the variant does not indicate that it is old-fashioned. In contrast, relatively high proportions of *'em* are seen in the more recent texts such as *Captains Courageous* and *The Invisible Man*, which suggests that the form was attested throughout the 19th century. The average frequency of the variant as a percentage of overall third person plural pronoun use is 6.6 percent in the twenty texts. Among the fourteen texts in which *'em* is found, the highest proportions relative to *them* are found in *Captains Courageous* (34.8%), followed by *Silas Marner* (33.2%), *Treasure Island* (17.7%), *Great Expectations* (11.3%), *The Invisible Man* (11.0%), *North and South* (10.6%) and *Jude the Obscure* (9.5%). This demonstrates that the form occurs in various regions across England and possibly in some other countries. On the other hand, *'em* is not used either in texts such as *Pride and Prejudice* and *Dorian Gray*, where most dialogue is limited to the upper and middle classes, or in *Henry Ryecroft*, which mostly consists of written language. All this suggests that *'em* is restricted to dialectal or informal speech, even though it is widely attested.

Table 2.19 Distribution of *'em* and *them* in the objective position according to text

	'em		*them*		Total
Pride		0%	435	100%	435
Frankenstein		0%	127	100%	127
N and S	54	10.6%	454	89.4%	508
Vanity	44	7.3%	573	92.7%	617
Great	47	11.3%	368	88.7%	415
Barchester	5	1.2%	397	98.8%	402
Jane	2	0.5%	395	99.5%	397
Wuthering	16	6.5%	232	93.5%	248
Silas	69	33.2%	139	66.8%	208
Water		0%	416	100%	416
Wildfell	5	1.2%	420	98.8%	425
Alice	8	4.3%	177	95.7%	185
Jude	32	9.5%	304	90.5%	336
Treasure	31	17.7%	144	82.3%	175
Dorian		0%	203	100%	203
Satan	1	0.3%	311	99.7%	312
Ryecroft		0%	144	100%	144
Scarlet		0%	142	100%	142
Captains	74	34.8%	137	65.2%	211
Invisible	10	11.0%	81	89.0%	91
Total	398	6.6%	5599	93.4%	5997

2.2.2.3 Sociolinguistic analysis

Since the variant *'em* is only found in speech, it will be worthwhile to investigate how the pronoun *'em* is used and by what kinds of people. Out of the 105 speakers who use *'em*, I will focus on the 99 who can be identified by social class and sex.

Table 2.20: Number of characters who use *'em* classified according to social class and sex

	Male	Female	Child	Total
U	11	2		13
M	18	2		20
L	36	17	3	56
American	6	2	2	10
Total	71	23	5	99

As shown in Table 2.20, the variant is used by what Blake calls "characters from all ranks." In terms of social class, the highest figure goes to the lower class, but the number of the upper- and middle-class users is not small. Americans in *Captains Courageous* are included in the table as well. The characters who employ *'em* more than ten times are: Dan (28 exx.), a young American fisherman, and Mr. Cheyne (11 exx.), an American railway tycoon, in *Captains Courageous*; Nicholas (24 exx.), a millworker, and his daughter Bessy (20 exx.) in *North and South*; Dolly (22 exx.), a wheelwright's wife, and Mr. Macy (12 exx.), a tailor and parish-clerk, in *Silas Marner*; Magwitch (16 exx.), a convict, in *Great Expectations*; Joseph (13 exx.), a servant, in *Wuthering Heights*; Arabella (13 exx.), a pig breeder's daughter, in *Jude the Obscure*; Silver (14 exx.), a buccaneer, in *Treasure Island*; and baronet Sir Pitt (11 exx.) in *Vanity Fair*. The variant *'em* is used in many regions and is more likely to be used by those in lower ranks as shown below.

(153) 'Jest look at *'em*!' <Dan: Fisherman>   (*Captains*, p. 24)
(154) I'd tell *'em* my mind. <Nicholas: Millworker>   (*N and S*, p.151)
(155) 'Well, to be sure, you can read *'em* off,' <Dolly: Wheelwright's wife>
     (*Silas*, p. 79)
(156) 'Well, let *'em* come, lad — let *'em* come,' <Silver: Buccaneer>
     (*Treasure*, p. 157)
(157) 'I don't want to hear about *'em*! They bore me.'
     <Arabella: Mason's wife>   (*Jude*, p. 381)
(158) "yon dainty chap says he cannut ate *'em*... ." <Joseph: Servant>
     (*Wuthering*, p. 184)

People in the middle and upper classes are not hesitant to use the form, either. The usage of *'em* could be colloquial rather than substandard. This may be supported by examples of a few noble or educated characters who rarely provide us with examples of nonstandard speech.

(159) 'They all can,' said the Duchess; 'and most of *'em* do.' <Duchess>
     (*Alice*, p. 53)
(160) And tell *'em* to get my horse saddled. <Mr. Cass: Squire>   (*Silas*, p. 71)

Yet, the use of this variant is not common among noble ladies. Among female characters, it is basically reserved for the lower class, as clearly illustrated in the following example, where the clergyman's wife, Mrs. Crawley, is condemning a kitchen maid for trying with a bunch of keys at old Sir Pitt's cabinet, in which he had locked jewels. The kitchen maid, who dropped the keys in alarm, utters *'em* while the clergyman's wife uses *them*.

(161) 'He gave *'em* me; he gave *'em* me!" she cried.
'Gave *them* you, you abandoned creature!' screamed Mrs. Bute.
<Miss Horrocks: Kitchen maid vs. Mrs. Bute Crawley: Clergyman's
wife> (*Vanity*, p. 506)

2.2.2.4 Syntactic and phonological analyses

In this section I would like to investigate whether internal linguistic (i.e., syntactic and phonological) factors are relevant to the occurrence of *'em*. Out of the 398 examples in which *'em* is used as objective, 263 occur as the object of a verb and 135 as the object of a preposition. Let us examine which kinds of verbs or prepositions appear with *'em*.

The words preceding the objective *'em* vary to a great degree. There are 152 verb forms and twenty different prepositions. In this classification, grammatically different forms of a verb are counted separately: *have*, *has*, and *having*, for instance, are considered three different verb forms, but standard and nonstandard variants ending with the same sound, such as *have* and *hev*, are combined. This is because some phonological factors could be involved in the linkage of two words, and if so, the ending sound of the word before *'em* would be significant. Tables 2.21a and 2.21b show the verbs and prepositions preceding *'em* and their absolute frequencies, respectively.

As observed in these two tables, the form *'em* is apparently used in regional dialects; the words co-occurring with *'em* include dialectal variants such as *cotched* 'caught,' *hev* 'have,' *layin'* 'laying,' *letten* 'let,' *p'inting* 'pointing,' *sarve* 'serve,' *swallered* 'swallowed,' *tech* 'take' and *zee* 'see,' and nonstandard prepositions such as *on* 'of,' *agin'/agean* 'against' and *frum* 'from.' We cannot deny the possibility that *'em* is the norm in some dialectal speech.

Table 2.21a: Verbs preceding 'em

Verb	Token	Verb	Token	Verb	Token	Verb	Token
let	13	has	2	dig	1	pitch	1
lets	1	have	2	driving	1	praise	1
letten	1	hev	1	examine	1	prick	1
put	10	heave	1	feed	1	retail	1
help	9	having	1	fight	1	rise	1
see	9	heaving	1	flog	1	rub	1
zee	2	catch	1	follow	1	sarve	1
saw	3	caught	1	forced	1	saying	1
seen	3	cotched	1	grudge	1	sell	1
tell	9	hear	2	handle	1	send	1
told	2	heard	1	harden	1	sent	1
make	7	leave	2	hawk	1	set	1
mak'	1	leaving	1	head	1	sets	1
making	1	beat	2	hide	1	sizes	1
made	1	beats	1	hist	1	slip	1
give	6	bust	2	hit	1	sowed	1
gave	4	cost	2	hurt	1	spend	1
gives	2	do	2	hurts	1	spent	1
read /rɛd/	5	fends	2	judge	1	strike	1
read /ríːd/	1	tie	2	killed	1	strikes	1
keep	5	slat	2	know	1	swab	1
bring	4	use	2	laced	1	swallered	1
brought	2	want	2	laid	1	talk	1
buy	1	abide	1	layin'	1	taught	1
bought	2	answer	1	lead	1	teach	1
find	4	asked	1	lick	1	tech	1
found	1	avoid	1	lighted	1	throw	1
get	4	back	1	like	1	thwart	1
got	1	bid	1	liked	1	took	1
lay	4	bless	1	losing	1	transport	1
take	4	chucked	1	marry	1	trick	1
eat	3	coax	1	meet	1	troubled	1
ate	1	commit	1	melt	1	uses	1
calls	2	cut	1	mowing	1	wants	1
call'	2	cutting	1	nail	1	warn	1
calling	1	daddle	1	paralyse	1	wear	1
show	3	damn	1	pass	1	win	1
had	2	defy	1	p'inting	1	wish	1
Total							263

CHAPTER 2 DIALECTAL VARIATION OF PERSONAL PRONOUNS

Table 2.21b: Prepositions preceding 'em

Preposition	Token	Preposition	Token
of (o')	46 (1)	before	3
on	29	agin' (agean)	3 (1)
upon	1	after	1
with (wi')	11 (1)	among	1
for	8	behind	1
to	8	between	1
in	7	by	1
into	1	frum	1
at	6	round	1
about	4	like	1
Total			135

In order to discover particular features in the relevant linkages, I will examine how often *'em* is used with these individual words by comparing the shortened form *'em* with its full form *them* in frequency. For the sake of convenience and statistical accuracy, the words which yield three or more instances of *'em* will be considered. There are twenty verbs and ten prepositions that satisfy this condition. Moreover, since the form *'em* is only found in dialogue, let us see the distribution of these two variants in spoken language.

Table 2.22a: Distribution of 20 verbs preceding *'em/them* in the dialogue of the 14 texts concerned

	'em	them	Ratio ('em : them)
help*	9		1 : 0.0
lay	4		1 : 0.0
make	8		1 : 0.0
saw	3	1	1 : 0.3
read /rεd/	5	2	1 : 0.4
gave	4	4	1 : 1.0
put	10	10	1 : 1.0
eat	3	4	1 : 1.3
seen	3	4	1 : 1.3
take	4	6	1 : 1.5
let	13	21	1 : 1.6
give	6	10	1 : 1.7
show	3	5	1 : 1.7
bring	4	8	1 : 2.0
tell	9	18	1 : 2.0
find	4	9	1 : 2.3
get	4	9	1 : 2.3
keep	5	12	1 : 2.4
see	11	28	1 : 2.5
have/hev	3	18	1 : 6.0

*Nine examples of *help* are used in the phrase "God help 'em" by two characters.

Table 2.22b: Distribution of 10 perpositions preceding 'em/them in the dialogue of the 14 texts concerned

	'em	them	Ratio ('em : them)
on*	29	14	1 : 0.5
before	3	4	1 : 1.3
agin'/agean	3	4	1 : 1.3
at	6	14	1 : 2.3
in	7	17	1 : 2.4
of	46	163	1 : 3.5
about	4	15	1 : 3.8
with	11	45	1 : 4.1
for	8	44	1 : 5.5
to	8	74	1 : 9.3

*In 27 examples the preposition *on* is used for *of* in dialect.

Table 2.22a shows that some verbs (*help, make, lay, saw, read* /rɛd/) show a higher frequency of the nonstandard *'em* to the standard *them*. With regard to the prepositions, as indicated in Table 2.22b, *on* is the only preposition that occurs with *'em* more often than *them*. Moreover, with the exception of one example, *on* is used for *of*, as seen in example (168). Out of the 29 examples of this *on*, seventeen are found in *North and South* and ten in *Wuthering Heights*, which indicates that *on 'em* is uttered as a set phrase in dialectal speech.

(162) 'God *help 'em*! North an' South have each getten their own troubles... .'
(*N and S*, p. 307)
(163) 'How d'you *make 'em* tell you everything without opening your head?'
(*Captains*, p. 139)
(164) 'There's lots o' loose stones about, some *of 'em* not big, and we might *lay 'em* atop of one another, and make a wall... .' (*Silas*, p. 143)
(165) And you *read 'em*; don't you? (*Great*, p. 316)
(166) '... I *saw 'em* now.' (*Jude*, p. 282)
(167) "Hearken, hearken, shoo's cursing *on 'em*!" (*Wuthering*, p.13)
(168) Why, most *on 'em* aboard here, and glad to get the duff — been begging before that, some *on 'em*. (*Treasure*, p. 57)
(169) 'For it'll look bad when Justice Malam hears as respectable men like us had a information laid *before 'em* and took no steps.' (*Silas*, p. 56)

As observed in the set phrase *on 'em*, the occurrence of *'em* is evidently connected to its preceding sound. It would be helpful to examine the occurrence of *'em* under such circumstances from a phonological standpoint, i.e., the kinds of sounds that are likely to occur in conjunction with *'em*. The final sounds of the twenty verbs and ten prepositions preceding *'em* will be examined.

Table 2.23a: Distribution of 20 verbs preceding *'em/them* according to final sound

	'em	*them*	Ratio (*'em* : *them*)
Plosive	69	81	1 : 1.2
Nasal	3	4	1 : 1.3
Vowel	21	34	1 : 1.6
Lateral	9	18	1 : 2.0
Fricative	13	32	1 : 2.5

Table 2.23b: Distribution of 10 prepositions preceding *'em/them* according to final sound

	'em	*them*	Ratio (*'em* : *them*)
Nasal	39	35	1 : 0.9
Plosive	10	29	1 : 2.9
Fricative	57	208	1 : 3.6
Vowel	19	122	1 : 6.4

The tables show that, as for verbs, plosive consonants, such as /p/ /t/ /k/ /d/ /g/, are the commonest sounds to be linked with *'em*, followed by nasals and vowels, and that, as for prepositions, nasal consonants are the commonest, followed by plosives and fricatives. These results can be explained in terms of "progressive assimilation" to a certain extent, as Peter Roach (1991: 125) states (C^i stands for an initial consonant and C^f stands for a final consonant):

> In one particular case we find progressive assimilation of manner, when a word-initial ð follows a plosive or nasal at the end of a preceding word: it is very common to find that the C^i becomes identical in manner to the C^f but with dental place of articulation.

Following this rule, *get them* /get ðəm/ becomes /gettəm/ and *on them* becomes /ɔnnəm/. If this is the case, the form *'em* in our texts are written in accordance with their pronunciation, virtually representing a weakened form of *them*. The following examples show how some characters differentiate *them* from *'em*:

Smollett: Captain in *Treasure Island*
(170) a. 'Silver, sir,' returned the captain; 'he's as anxious as you and I to smother things up. This is a tiff; he'd soon talk *'em* out of it if he had the chance, and what I propose to do is to give him the chance. Let's allow the men an afternoon ashore. If they all go, why we'll fight the ship. If they none of *them* go, well then, we hold the cabin, and God defend the right. If some go, you mark my words, sir, Silver'll bring *'em* aboard again as mild as lambs.' (p. 70)
 b. 'Out, lads, out, and fight *'em* in the open! Cutlasses!' cried the captain. (p. 112)

Bessy: Millworker's daughter in *North and South*
(171) a. so it's but a few of th' masters as will put *'em* up; and I've heard tell o' men who didn't like working in places where there was a wheel, because they said as how it made *'em* hungry, at after they'd been long used to swallowing fluff, to go without it, and that their wage ought to be raised if they were to work in such places. (p. 102)
   b. They say it winds round the lungs, and tightens *them* up. (p. 102)

Mr. Marvel: Street loafer in *The Invisible Man*
(172) I've been cadging boots — in particular — for days. Because I was sick of *them*. They're sound enough, of course. But a gentleman on tramp sees such a thundering lot of his boots. And if you'll believe me, I've raised nothing in the whole blessed county, try as I would, but **THEM**. Look at *'em*! (Italicized "them" and bold-faced "THEM" in the original) (p.44)

Mr. Cheyne: Railway magnate in *Captains Courageous*
(173) a. I can break *them* to little pieces — yes — but I can't get back at *'em* to hurt *'em* where they live. (p. 143)
   b. 'They think we're on the war-path. Tell *'em* we don't feel like fighting, just now, Milsom. Tell *'em* what we're going for ... Tell *'em* the truth — for once.' (p. 120)

Example (170) shows that while he employs *them* after *of*, which ends with a fricative, Captain Smollett in *Treasure Island* utters *'em* after the terms *talk*, *bring* and *fight*, which end with a plosive consonant (albeit /k/ in the ending of *talk*, and /g/ in the ending of *bring* are not alveolar stops). Similarly, in example (171), Bessy in *North and South* uses *'em* after *put* and *made*, both ending with a plosive, but *them* after *tightens* ending with a fricative; and in (172), Mr. Marvel in *The Invisible Man* utters *'em* after *at* but *them* after *of*. These examples indicate that *'em* is more likely to occur after a plosive, regardless of its place of articulation, at least in the authors' perception. Examples (173a) and (173b), which belong to Mr. Cheyne, an American railway king in *Captains Courageous*, are slightly different. In (173a), he first uses *them* and then utters *'em* twice though both *them* and *'em* come just after a plosive. The shift from *them* to *'em* in this case is caused by his heightened mood; in this scene, Mr. Cheyne, who is not a university graduate himself, is passionately talking to his son about the importance of higher education. In example (173b), unlike the previous example, Mr. Cheyne utters *'em* three times after *tell*, the final consonant of which is neither a plosive nor a nasal, in an obviously rapid speech. Then, here as well, it would be practical to consider that he uses the weakened form *'em* for *them* rather than the archaic variant of *hem*. This sort of utterance is commonly found in novels in the next century as well. For example, in *The Great Gatsby* (1925), Daisy, an American girl, is unable to articulate *them* properly because of drunkenness:

> "Take *'em* down-stairs and give *'em* back to whoever they belong to. Tell *'em* all Daisy's change' her mine. Say: 'Daisy's change' her mine!'"
>
> (*The Great Gatsby*, p. 61)

The intoxicated Daisy's speech suggests that /ð/ cannot be clearly pronounced not only after a plosive but also after a lateral (/l/ in *tell*) and a fricative (/v/ in *give*) under certain psychological or physical circumstances. In relation to the progressive assimilation of /ð/, Roach (1991: 125) notes that the phoneme /ð/ seems to frequently occur with no discernible friction noise.

In *Jude the Obscure*, the villagers in Wessex occasionally utter *'em* even when its preceding sound is not a plosive or a nasal. Hirooka (1983: 68) states that the phenomenon of dropping /ð/ is often observed in dialects, as in *more'n* 'more than,' *rather'n* 'rather than,' *whe'r* 'whether,' and *smorning* 'this morning.' If the expression of "the phenomenon of dropping /ð/" could be translated as "the phoneme /ð/ with no discernible friction noise," as Roach suggests, there might be no need to argue whether /ð/ can be dropped or not. It is assumed that people utter *'em* instead of *them* simply because it is easier to say than its full form.

With all the above examples taken, the form *'em* which our characters utter instead of *them* can be generally regarded as a weakened form of *them*. This might also be true of the use of *'em* in Early Modern English. And more importantly, this assumption might properly explain what Wyld (1920: 327–328) called "the absence of such forms as *hem* or *'em* in the 16th century and their reappearance in the 17th century." There should be a time lag in occurrence between the archaic variant *'em* of *hem* and the weakened form *'em* of *them* in literature in the Modern English period and today.

However, we cannot completely deny the possibility that the archaic variant *'em* of ME *hem* survives in dialectal speech in 19th-century novels. Remember example (151) by a carter in *Jude the Obscure*, in which *'em* is used in the nominative function: "*'Em* lives on a lofty level; there's no gainsaying it, though I myself med not think much of *'em*." The first *'em* does not have any preceding sound which could cause assimilation. Besides, as far as his speech is concerned, the carter regularly employs *'em* in either the nominative or objective function; he utters *'em* four times but never uses *them* or *they*. It is possible that this "elderly" man living in a village in Wessex preserves the archaic weakened form *'em*. In comparison, other local people, including a village girl,

Arabella, use standard *them* and *they* along with *'em* in their dialectal speech: "What can *'em* do otherwise?" (p. 54); "I don't want to hear about *'em*! *They* bore me." (p. 381); "But whatever profit there is in public-house keeping goes to *them* that brew the liquors, and not to *them* that retail *'em*... ." (p. 300). It is interesting to notice that her usage of *'em* more or less follows the rule of progressive assimilation.

2.2.2.5 Summary

The unstressed form of the third person plural *'em* is widely found in the casual speech of literally all ranks of people in our 19th-century English novels. While the frequent speakers of *'em* are those in the lower class and/or in rural areas, upper- and middle-class characters also utter the form occasionally. The form *'em* seems to be casually used by American characters as well.

Syntactic and phonological factors are greatly involved in the production of the weakened form *'em*. Under the rule of progressive assimilation, the weakened form *'em* is likely to occur after words ending with a plosive or a nasal. This suggests that the authors used *'em* in place of *them* to express a lost or indiscernible fricative sound /ð/. In the field of historical linguistics, the form *'em* has been generally treated as the descendant of *hem*, even in Modern English. However, it would be more reasonable to consider *'em* as representing a weakened form of *them* in our 19th-century texts, though we cannot completely deny the possibility that the old variant *'em* survived in dialectal speech at that time.

2.3 Reflexive pronouns

2.3.1 Overview

The standard usage of reflexive pronouns is virtually the same in the 19th century as today except that *thyself* is out of use in Present-day English. Referring to the use of reflexive pronouns, Cobbett (1819: 39) writes:

> the words *self* and *selves* are sometimes added to the personal pronouns; as, *myself, thyself, himself*; but, as these compounded words are liable to no variations that can possibly lead to error, it will be useless to do any further than just to notice them.

In our 19th-century texts, however, there are some nonstandard variants for the reflexive pronoun just as for the simple personal pronoun. According to Wright (1905: 276), in dialectal speech the reflexive pronouns are generally

CHAPTER 2 DIALECTAL VARIATION OF PERSONAL PRONOUNS 81

Table 2.24: Variation of nonstandard reflexive pronouns according to text

	-seln, -sen	-sel'	hisself etc.	yerself, 'emselves	Total
N and S		mysel' (16), oursel' (1), yo'sel' (2), yoursel' (1), himsel' (6), hissel' (1), hersel' (1)		'emselves (1)	29
Barchester			hisself (1), theyself (1)		2
Wuthering	yourseln (2), yerseln (1), hisseln (7), theirseln (1), itsseln (2)				13
Silas	mysen (2), himsen (1)		theirselves (1)		4
Wildfell			hisself (1)		1
Jude			hisself (1)		1
Treasure			hisself (3)		3
Scarlet			hisself (1)		1
Captains			meself (1)	yerself (2), 'emselves (1)	4
Total	16	28	10	4	58

formed by adding *self, sel, sen,* or *seln* for the singular, and *selves, sels, sens* (rarely *sen*) for the plural, to the conjunctive possessive pronouns, usually the unstressed forms. In the case of the first and second persons, the reflexive is formed by means of the objective case of the personal pronoun joined to *self/ selves* (e.g., *usselves, ussens, theeself*).

2.3.2 Data and observation

Let us first have a look at the overall distribution of nonstandard reflexive variants in our texts. A total of 58 relevant examples are found in nine texts.

The examples are grouped according to their formation as follows: (1) the form *seln/sen* is used instead of *self* (*yourseln, yerseln, hisseln, itsseln, mysen, himsen*); (2) the final *f* is omitted (*itsel', mysel', oursel', yo'sel', yoursel', himsel', hissel', hersel'*); (3) a nonstandard case of the personal pronoun appears before *–self* (*meself, hisself, theyselves, theirselves*); and (4) weakened forms of the standard case are used (*yerself, 'emselves*). Some variants such as *itsseln* and *hissel'* have more than one dialectal feature. The higher absolute frequency and the larger variation are enjoyed by *North and South* and *Wuthering Heights,* which both contain an abundance of the Northern dialect, as we have seen in the previous sections. Out of the total of 58 instances, 29 are found in the former, thirteen in the latter, and the remaining sixteen belong to seven other texts, which provide no more than four instances each. All the nonstandard variants for the singular in the *–sel'* form appear in *North and South,* those in the *–seln* form in *Wuthering Heights,* and those in the *–sen* form in

Silas Marner. Wright notes that *–sel* is the only form that occurs in Northern England, with some exceptions (1892: 122–24), while the endings *sen, seln, sens* are chiefly confined to the North-Midland dialects (1905: 276). The *–sel'* and *–seln* forms in our texts hence reflect Northern features, with *–sel'* in South Lancashire and *–seln* in Yorkshire. The variant *hisself* occurs with a relatively high frequency; it has seven examples in five texts. Let us see how these nonstandard reflexive variants are used and by what kind of people according to the texts: firstly the *–sel'* type in *North and South*, secondly the *–seln/–sen* type in *Wuthering Heights* and *Silas Marner*, and then the other variants in the remaining texts.

2.3.2.1 The *–sel'* type

North and South provides us with quite a few instances of nonstandard reflexive variants. In this text, the users of the *–sel'* type are all local people: millworker Nicholas Higgins (19 exx.) and his daughter Bessy (6 exx.), and millworker Boucher (1 ex.) and his wife (2 exx.). The variant *'emselves* for *themselves* is also used by Nicholas, the most frequent user of the regional variants. All these variants are considered to be used in dialectal speech. On the other hand, both Nicholas and Bessy use the standard reflexive pronoun as well; the former uses *ourselves, himself, itself* and *themselves* once each, and the latter *myself* twice. The following are nonstandard examples and some standard examples, listed under their standard counterparts:

Myself
(174) a. '... I'm but an ailing creature *mysel'* — I've been ailing this long time.' <Mrs. Boucher: Millworker's wife> (p. 296)
b. '... I thank yo' for *mysel'*, as much as for Boucher, for it just makes my heart warm to yo' more and more.'
<Bessy: Millworker's daughter → Margaret: Parson's daughter>
(p. 156)
c. I wish I'd letten *myself* be choked first. <Bessy → Margaret> (p. 136)

Ourselves
(175) a. Yo're not to think we'd ha' letten 'em clem, for all we're a bit pressed *oursel'*; <Bessy → Margaret> (p. 156)
b. and it's ours to stand up and fight hard, — not for *ourselves* alone, but for them round about us — for justice and fair play.
<Nicholas: Millworker → Margaret> (p. 135)

Himself
(176) a. He ne'er showed *himsel'* abroad for a day or two.

<Nicholas→Mr. Hale: Parson> (p. 293)
b. 'Him as went and drownded *himself*, poor chap! ...'
<Nicholas→Mr. Hale> (p. 305)
c. 'Why, the mayor *hissel'* dines there; and the members of Parliament and all.' <Bessy → Margaret> (p. 148)

Herself

(177) Hoo's just sinking away — not for want o' meat *hersel'* — but because hoo cannot stand th' sight o' the little ones clemming.
<Mr. Boucher: Millworker> (p. 154)

Itself

(178) 'Poor wench — poor old wench, — I'm loth to vex thee, I am; but a man mun speak out for the truth, and when I see the world going all wrong at this time o' day, bothering *itself* wi' things it knows nought about, and leaving undone all the things that lie in disorder close at its hand ...'
<Nicholas> (p. 91)

Nicholas uses both standard and nonstandard variants when he talks to Mr. Hale, a retired parson, as in (176a) and (176b). This is also the case with Bessy when she talks to Margaret, Mr. Hale's daughter, as in examples (174b), (174c) and (176c). What then makes them choose the standard form one time and the nonstandard one another? One plausible explanation is that the standard form is chosen to give emphasis, as often observed in dialectal speech (Hirooka 1965). Graveness and seriousness are more effectively delivered in the full form, which is usually pronounced more clearly and therefore more impressively than its dialectal short and weak form. In Bessy's (174c) and Nicholas's (176b) examples, the standard variants *myself* and *himself* seem to be uttered more fervently; the exclamation marks in (174d) and (176b) and the terms "I wish" in (174c) illustrate that these variants are stressed, but no such signs are found when the nonstandard variants are used. Another intriguing point is that in example (176a), Nicholas utters *himsel'* for *himself*, while his daughter says *hissel'* in example (176c). These two forms are different in grammatical function: Nicholas uses *himsel'* as an objective while Bessy uses *hissel'* as an emphasizing pronoun. Nicholas's usage of *himsel'* is the same in all his six examples. Reflexive pronouns are sometimes used as emphatic adjuncts to nouns without reflexive use (Kruisinga 1932: §1024), and can be used to emphasize surprise, delight, awe or even fear (Simpson 2001: 41). Bessy's *hissel'*, which refers to "the mayor," expresses the delight and awe she feels towards him. Because of the limited sample size, no firm conclusion can be drawn at this stage, but it is possible that emphatic tone is embedded in *hissel'*.

Although there is no example of *themsel'*, Nicholas alone uses both *'emselves* in (179a) and *themselves* in (179b). As he is talking to two different persons, it is possible that he differentiates these variants according to the addressees. Still, it is not plausible that Nicholas should choose the standard form *themselves* for politeness while talking with a parson's daughter, yet not do the same for her father. As for Nicholas, the difference in his usage of *'emselves* and *themselves* is similar to that in his usage of *'em* and *them*. Since he uses *'em* more frequently than *them*, it is natural that he would employ *'emselves* more often than *themselves*. When he chooses the full form *themselves*, he probably utters it in an emphatic way. In example (179a), Nicholas, who is now out of work after a strike, tells Mr. Hale how difficult working at a mill is. In the course of his speech, he grows irritated, which is gathered not only from his speech but also from the author's use of the term "scornfully." On the other hand, in example (179b), which takes place before the strike, Nicholas is explaining to Margaret what he is striking for. Here, he employs the full form *themselves* in a calmer and confident tone. His choice of these two variants, therefore, depends on his mood.

(179) a. 'Now yo've got it. Yo've hit the bull's eye. Hamper's — that's where I worked — makes their men pledge *'emselves* they'll not give a penny to helf th' Union or keep turnouts fro' clemming. They may pledge and make pledge,' continued he, scornfully; 'they nobbut make liars and hypocrites... .' <Nicholas→Mr. Hale>   (pp. 291–292)

b. 'Why, yo' see, there's five or six masters who have set *themselves* again paying the wages they've been paying these two years past, and flourishing upon, and getting richer upon. <Nicholas→Margaret>

(p. 134)

In the following example, Nicholas shifts the second person reflexive from *yoursel'* to *yo'rsel'* while talking to Mr. Hale. Beginning with the utterance "Yo' needn't trouble yoursel', sir," he makes quite a long speech, covering twenty lines. The repeated use of *yo'* might possibly cause him to use *yo'rsel'* instead of *yoursel'*.

(180) 'Yo' needn't trouble *yoursel'*, sir,' said Nicholas. 'Their bookstuff goes in at one ear and out at t'other... . ; and in yo'r preaching, did yo' stop every now and then, and say, half to them and half to *yo'rsel'*, <Nicholas→Mr. Hale>   (p. 229)

2.3.2.2 The *–seln/–sen* type
In another northern text, *Wuthering Heights*, thirteen examples of nonstandard

reflexive variants are used by three characters: Joseph (9 exx.), Zillah (3 exx.) and Hareton (1 ex.). Zillah and Hareton speak Yorkshire dialect though their accent is not as strong as Joseph's. They commonly use the possessive case with *–seln*, such as *yourseln*, *yerseln*, *hisseln* and *itsseln*.

(181) "... It's empty; yah muh hev it all tuh *yerseln*, un' Him as allas maks a third, i' sich ill company!" <Joseph> (p. 127)
(182) "un' it 'ull be mitch if yah find 'em agean; soa, yah muh plase *yourseln*!" <Joseph> (p. 280)
(183) He's patience *itsseln* wi' sich careless, offald craters — patience *itsseln* he is! <Joseph> (p. 74)
(184) un' Aw thowt Aw'd lug my books up intuh t' garret, un' all my bits uh stuff, un' they sud hev t' kitchen tuh *theirseln*; fur t' sake uh quietness. <Joseph> (p. 283)
(185) "And I never knew such a faint-hearted creature," added the woman; "nor one so careful of *hisseln*... ." <Zillah> (p. 186)

Joseph uses *yerseln* in example (181) and *yourseln* in (182). Both variants are in the *–seln* form but the latter contains the standard *your*. *Yerseln* is the weakened form of *yourseln*. The variant *yourseln* with the standard form of the second person possessive is followed by an exclamation mark, which demonstrates that stress is laid on the reflexive.

Although the form *–sen* usually belongs to the North, all the examples of this form are found in the Midland dialect of *Silas Marner*: *mysen* (2 exx.) and *himsen* (1 ex.). These examples are all found in the speech of Mr. Macey, a tailor and parish-clerk:

(186) And so I says to *mysen*, (*Silas*, p. 49)
(187) there's the 'pinion a man has of *himsen*. (*Silas*, p. 46)

The *–sen* form is rarely attested in the Southern dialect. Since only one character, Mr. Macey, uses this form and those living in the village set in Warwickshire, including the tailor himself, use the standard reflexives *myself* and *himself*, it would be safe to say that the examples of the *–sen* form in this text do not illustrate a feature of the Midland dialect.

2.3.2.3 The *hisself* type and others
The remaining thirteen examples of the nonstandard reflexive are *yerself* (2 exx.), *'emselves* (1 ex.), *meself* (1 ex.), *hisself* (7 exx.) *theyselves* (1 ex.) and *theirselves* (1 ex.). The nonstandard reflexive of the greatest frequency is *hisself*. This variant is used in five texts, but no example is found in either *North*

and South or *Wuthering Heights*. Among the characters from the North, a coachman in *Wildfell Hall* employs *hisself*. In this example, the pronoun is separated by a hyphen, as in (188). In terms of syntactic function, the variant is used as an objective or an emphatic adjunct. *Hisself* is also used as an object in *Jude the Obscure, Barchester Towers* and *A Study in Scarlet*.

(188)   she'd a rare long purse, and Mr. Hargrave wanted it all to *his-self*; <a coachman>   (*Wildfell*, p. 451)
(189)   The maid-servant recognized Jude, and whispered her surprise to her mistress in the background, that he, the student 'who kept *hisself* up so particular,' should have suddenly descended so low as to keep company with Arabella. <Maid-servant>   (*Jude*, p. 41)
(190)   'In fact he couldn't stir, or you may be certain on such a day he would not have absented *hisself*.' <Mrs. Lookaloft: Tenant farmer>
(*Barchester*, II, p. 97)
(191)   'He'd ha' found *hisself* in the station if we hadn't been so took up.' <John Rance: Police officer>   (*Scarlet*, p. 39)

In *Treasure Island*, the same variant is employed for an emphatic purpose in all its three examples.

(192)   Your doctor *hisself* said one glass wouldn't hurt me. <Billy: Buccaneer>
(*Treasure*, p. 13)
(193)   Well, he's dead now *hisself*; <Israel: Seaman>   (*Treasure*, p. 61)
(194)   '... Gunn is a good man (you'll say), and he puts a precious sight more confidence — a precious sight, mind that — in a gen'leman born than in these gen'leman of fortune, having been one *hisself*.' <Ben Gunn: Buccaneer>   (*Treasure*, pp. 82–83)

The examples (188) to (194) indicate that *hisself* is witnessed not only in Northern England but also in Southern England, which agrees with Wright's observation (1905: 276) that the standard forms *himself* and *themselves* are seldom used in genuine dialect speech in England. Moreover, our data show that *hisself* is used by buccaneers and seamen in *Treasure Island* and a low-rank police officer in *A Study in Scarlet* whose speech is framed with nonstandard usage. Thus the variant *hisself* belongs to social dialect. It seems that the "wrong" case of personal pronouns in the reflexive form is not limited to local dialect, unlike regional dialectal endings such as *–seln* and *–sel'*.

As Wright indicates (1905: 276), nonstandard variants for *themselves* are supposedly common in dialectal speech, but the frequency of *themselves* itself is low: there are only two examples.[25] The variant *theirselves* appears in the

Midland-based *Silas Marner*, while *theyselves* appears in the Southern-based *Barchester Towers*.

(195) 'Hush, lad, hush; that's the way the ladies dress *theirselves*, that is,' <Mr. Winthrop: Wheelwright> (*Silas*, p. 101)
(196) 'Likening *theyselves* to the quality, as though they was estated folk, or the like o' that!' <Mrs. Guffern: Tenant farmer> (*Barcherster*, II, p. 135)

In *Captains Courageous*, *meself* is used instead of *myself*. The speaker is the Irish-born Long Jack. The variant *meself* can be considered one of the features of Irish English brought to the United States (Filppula 1999: 83). As seen in (197), Long Jack's utterance is full of dialectal features.

(197) 'I'm murderin' *meself* to fill your pockuts. Slate ut for a bad catch. The Portugee has bate me.' <Long Jack: Fisherman> (*Captains*, p. 23)

In (198), the unstressed form *yerself* occurs in *Captains Courageous*, where many examples of the unstressed forms *ye* for *you* and *'em* for *them* are attested. The speakers of these variants are fishermen. Just as *ye* and *'em*, *yerself* and *'emselves* would be often used in casual talk by various people in society.

(198) 'Fix *yerself* an' go on deck... .' <Dan: Skipper's son> (*Captains*, p. 8)
(199) 'The boys they make believe all the time till they've cheated *'emselves* into bein' men, an' so till they die — pretendin' an' pretendin' ...' <Tom Platt: Fisherman> (*Captains*, p. 70)

2.3.3 Summary

Northern variants in *–sel'* or *–seln* take up around three-fourths of our sample of nonstandard reflexive pronouns. The users are all local residents. The *–sel'* form is found in South Lancashire's dialect and *–seln* in Yorkshire's. Some local people employ standard forms for emphatic use as well. The variants with nonstandard case of personal pronoun in *–self* or *–selves* (e.g., *hisself*, *meself*) are regionally more widely dispersed, and therefore may be regarded as social dialect. Finally, there are cases in which *hisself* is used as an emphatic pronoun.

Notes
1 Johnson uses thirty-three comedies and fourteen works of fiction of the 17th century to determine the social usage of the era. The reason she did not use Shakespeare's drama is that he did

not always employ *you* and *thou* with the utmost consistency.
2 The breakdown of *THOU* is *thou* (98 exx.), *thy* (75 exx.), *thee* (76 exx.), *thine* (16 exx.) and *thyself* (7 exx.). The tokens of the nomative *thou* include the dialectal forms *thah* (1 ex.) and *tuh* (1 ex.) seen in *Wuthering Heights*.
3 This chronological arrangement is applied throughout this work.
4 Included among spiritual beings are God and Satan. Although God is often treated as an exceptional case in the use of *THOU*, God and Satan are occasionally described as two opposite existences as seen in *The Sorrows of Satan*. For this reason I included God in this category.
5 Emphasis is added and the same hereinafter unless explained otherwise. The quotation style (i.e., double or single) observes the source.
6 Referring to the social situation of the male and the female in 1825–80, Susan Kingsley Kent (1999: 179) writes: "men possessed the capacity for reason, action, aggression, independence, and self-interest" while "women inhabited a separate, private sphere, one suitable for the so-called inherent qualities of femininity."
7 Hebrew 13:5.
8 According to Luther Allan Weigle (1963: 361–362), Bishop Westcott wrote in 1868 that "[f]rom the middle of the seventeenth century, the King's Bible has been the acknowledged Bible of the English-speaking nations throughout the world simply because it is the best."
9 According to Wright (1905: 695), *yo* /joː/ is attested in west Yorkshire, south Lancashire, south Cheshire, west Stafford and north-west Derby.
10 "North country" includes Yorkshire (except southwest and south Yorkshire).
11 *Ye* is attested in Jane Austen's other works. In *Sense and Sensibility*, the author makes Marianne Dashwood use the old nominative plural *ye* to address "trees" in her birthplace when leaving there. In other texts, such as *Emma*, *ye* is found in *How d'ye do?* (Phillipps 1970: 167).
12 According to Wyld (1920: 330), in Present-day English the plural forms already found in Middle English are used in respectful address to a single person.
13 Leonee Ormond (1995: 176): "Explanatory Notes" in *Captains Courageous*.
14 Kenzo Fujii (2004, 2006) points out the significant influence of Irishism on American English. He says that in the 19th century, many Irish people moved to America due to a severe famine at the beginning of the century and that while the Irish moved around the United States to seek work, their unique English spread among working-class immigrants who did not know how to speak English.
15 The kinds of (auxiliary) verbs used before the nominative *ye* per sentence structure are: *d'* in *d'ye(r)* (22 exx.), *do* (5 exx.), *don't* (1 ex.), *did* (11 exx.), *didn't* (1 ex.), *are* (7 exx.), *can* (1 ex.), *can't* (5 exx.), *cannot* (1 ex.), *hev* (3 exx.), *hain't/ha'n't* (4 exx.), *will* (3 exx.), *won't* (1 ex.), *would* (1 ex.), *might* (1 ex.) and *should* (1 ex.) in the interrogative, *look* (22 exx.), *hark* (2 exx.), *do* (1 ex.), *don't* (9 exx.) and *think* (1 ex.) in the imperative and *will* (1 ex.) in the declarative.
16 He presents two examples of *look ye* found in Lancashire dialect in Elizabeth Gaskell's other texts.
17 Brinton (2008: 200–202) refers to *look* forms as one of the examples of grammaticalization. In *lookee*, there is a reduction of /lʊkjiː/ to/lʊkiː/.
18 She presents one example of *harkye* from the 19th century: "Harkye, fellow, who are all these people/assembled in my antechamber (1813 Cumberland, *The False Demetrius* IV, 163–64 [ED]).
19 Also attested are a few examples in which Nicholas uses *she* for Bessy (e.g., Yo're sure and certain *she*'s dead – not in a dwam, a faint? – *she*'s been so before, often. (p. 219)).
20 A list of the English spoken in Belfast includes the following description: "lowering and

sometimes centralization of /ɪ/, /bɛt, sɛns/ or /bʌt, sʌns/ for *bit, since*" (Raymond Hickey 2004: 51; 2007: 333).
21 The examples quoted from the earlier centuries are not included.
22 The abbreviated interrogative form *is't* for *is it* is excluded because of the difference in syntactic construction. There is one example of this kind: "*Is't* the meanin' or the words as makes folks fast i' wedlock?" (*Silas*, p. 48)
23 The negator *not* is placed immediately after the *t* form in the following two examples: 'You are sure *'twas not* the undergraduate?' (*Jude*, p. 135); "*Twer not* that exactly... .' (*Jude*, p. 272).
24 Dickens used regional dialects in some works but not in *Great Expectations*. Three English regions whose dialects are represented in detail in Dickens' novels are East Anglia in *David Copperfield*, Yorkshire in *Nicholas Nickleby* and Lancashire in *Hard Times* (Brook 1970: 117).
25 Though uncommon in genuine dialect speech, *themselves* and *himself* occasionally appear in Scotland and Ireland.

CHAPTER 3
The Case Problems of Personal Pronouns

Despite the existence of a great number of prescriptive grammars in Late Modern English, a discrepancy between common usage and "correct" use as designated by grammarians has been seen for centuries as Görlach states:

> From the 15th century on, pronouns were exceptional in the nominal system since they retained some categories of case apart from the genitive. The fact created a great deal of insecurity which again reflected the contrasting trends of usage and prescriptive correctness. The problems discussed by 18th-century grammarians continued – but were not solved. (1999: 66–67)

This section will deal with several problematic choices between nominative and objective as in *It is I/me*, *younger than I/me* and *as tall as I/me* and will find out how much prescriptive correctness influenced the usage in the 19th century.

3.1 *It is I* vs. *It is me*

3.1.1 Overview

Among the case problems, one of the most frequently discussed is whether to use *It is I* or *It is me*. Brook (1958: 152) states that this type of sentence occurred in Old English in the form of *Ic hit eom* 'I it am' and survived in early Middle English. In later Middle English, the word order was changed to give a sentence like *It am I*. Since the subject of a sentence generally precedes the verb in English, the first person form *am* was changed to the third person form *is* in agreement with the grammatical subject. According to Brook, this form was still regarded by many speakers as the correct form around the middle of the 20th century though as early as the 16th century there appeared instances like

It is me. In Present-day English, *me* is generally used for the nominative when predicative (*OED*, s.v. *me, pers. pron.*). Quirk et al. (1985: 336) note that, as subjective complement, though the nominative case is stipulated by prescriptive grammarians, the objective form is generally felt more natural, in particular, in informal style. Wales (1996: 95) states that for the younger generations today a sentence like "It is *I/we/she/he/they*" appears pedantic or stilted in whatever register, spoken or written.

Before starting to discuss our 19th-century usage, it would be useful to take a look at how contemporaneous prescriptive grammarians viewed this issue. As one of the most influential grammarians in the 18th century, Lowth (1769: 78) argued that the verb *to be* has always a nominative case after *it* as in "it *was I*, and not *he* that did it" unless it is in the infinitive form as in "though you took it *to be him*." Cobbett (1819: 101) plainly stated that the pronouns following the pronoun *it* and the verb *to be* must always be in the nominative case. Brown (1884: 175) regarded the construction *It is I* as one of agreement: the attribute agrees in case with the subject. Let us find out how the normative usage is observed in our 19th-century corpus.

3.1.2 Data

The only pronouns which show a difference in case between nominative and objective after *it is* are the personal pronouns except for *you* and *it*. The construction of Type *It is I* therefore stands for "It is *we/he/she/they*" as well as "It is *I.*" Likewise, the construction of Type *It is me* stands for "It is *us/him/her/them*" as well as "It is *me.*" As variations of *it is*, constructions like *it was, it were, that is, it's, that's, it can be*, etc. are to be examined as well. Note that we also take into consideration *It is I/me* in negative, interrogative and cleft sentences (e.g., It is she who came). The following are some representative instances of the *It is I* type and the *It is me* type:

Type *It is I*
(1) *It is he* that is badly treated.   (*Barchester*, II, p. 67)
(2) '... What made you think *it was she?*'   (*Jude*, p. 252)
(3) '... But *it is not I* altogether that am to blame!'   (*Jude*, p. 212)
(4) *Is it I*, Henry Ryecroft, the harassed toiler of so many a long year?
                                                 (*Ryecroft*, p. 39)
(5) '*It may not be he* after all; ...'   (*Wildfell*, p. 319)

Type *It is me*
(6) '... *It is only me*, Charlotte!'   (*N and S*, p. 54)
(7) 'Bedad *it's him*,'   (*Vanity*, p. 349)

(8)   it's quite certain that *it was her*, and nobody but her, that set it going.
                                                                    (*Jane*, p. 427)
(9)   *It's not them* I mind;   (*Treasure*, p. 91)
(10) '*That's him*!'   (*Invisible*, p. 37)

There are a total of 133 examples of *It is I/me*, of which 90 instances (67.7%) are of the *It is I* type and 43 instances (32.3%) are of the *It is me* type; the nominative is used more than twice as often as the objective. The distributions of these two types by text are presented in Figure 3.1.

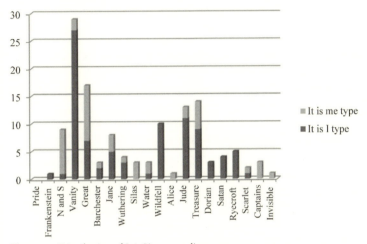

Figure 3.1: Distribution of *It is I/me* according to text

According to Dekeyser (1975: 222), who conducted statistical research on the relevant rivalry in his 19th-century sample, overall rates and percentages of predicative pronouns in equational constructions may indicate a slight diachronic shift towards objective forms; the ratios of *It is I* and *It is me* are 44 (83%) and 9 (17%), respectively, before 1850 and 80 (76.9%) and 24 (23.1%), respectively, after 1850. Although no distinct chronological change is observed in our 19th-century corpus, it is noted that not a few instances of the objective are used against grammarians' instructions at that time. In order to uncover linguistic factors involved in this transition, I will investigate in more detail where the prescriptive use is violated.

3.1.3 Analysis

As Table 3.1 shows, among the several different patterns for the construction *It is I/me*, the most frequently used is *it is/was/were*, garnering the great majority of examples (104 exx.), followed by *it's* with 20 examples and the other variants with only two or three each.

Table 3.1: Variation of *it is* in the construction *It is I/me*

	It is I	It is me	Total
it is/was/were	83	21	104
that is/was/were	1	1	2
'tis/'twas	2		2
it's	3	17	20
that's		3	3
Aux + *be*	1	1	2
Total	90 (67.7%)	43 (32.3%)	133

These figures illustrate a striking difference in the proportion of the two types in terms of style; while in the uncontracted forms *it is/was* and *that is/was*, the nominative case is preferred; in the contracted forms *it's* and *that's*, the objective case is more often employed. Since contraction tends to occur in colloquial language, it is assumed that the objective case is used in spoken language.

It may be helpful to examine which type appears in which kind of register. As Table 3.2 shows, the examples of *It is I/me* are found in four registers: dialogue, letter, diary and narrative. According to the table, Type *It is me* is mostly limited to dialogue while Type *It is I* is used both in dialogue and in written language such as letter, diary and narrative. It is also revealed that while more than half of the examples of *It is I* are used in written context, both the nominative and objective cases are equally employed in spoken context. This requires us to examine who observes the grammarians' instruction and who does not among a variety of characters in our corpus. The characters who use Type *It is I* and those who use Type *It is me* are classified by social class and sex in Tables 3.3a and 3.3b respectively.

Table 3.2: Distribution of *It is I/me* according to register

	It is I	It is me	Total
Dialogue	42	42	84
Letter	2		2
Diary	9		9
Narrative	37	1	38

Table 3.3a: Number of characters who use Type *It is I* classified according to social class and sex

	Male	Female	Child	Total
U	5	8		13 (42%)
M	10	3		13 (42%)
L	1	2	1	4 (13%)
Unknown	1			1 (3%)
Total	17	13	1	31

Table 3.3b: Number of characters who use Type *It is me* classified according to social class and sex

	Male	Female	Child	Total
U	3	3		6 (19%)
M	5	1		6 (19%)
L	13	3	1	17 (55%)
American	1		1	2 (6%)
Total	22	7	2	31

According to Tables 3.3a and 3.3b, most users of Type *It is I* belong to the upper or middle classes while Type *It is me* is more frequently employed by characters of the lower class. The ratio of male and female for Type *It is I* is 17 : 13 and that for Type *It is me* is 22 : 7. Since it is generally known that women tend to use standard forms (e.g., Trudgill 2000; Holmes 2008), the lower rate of Type *It is me* by the female characters would suggest that the objective form was marked as nonstandard at that time. Expressions of this type are most frequently put in the mouths of the working-class males. At the same time, the sporadic use of *It is me* employed by females or members of the middle and upper classes could be a sign that the use of the objective form has spread from the lower to the upper and from the male to the female to earn a "grammatical" status such as it holds today. Two Americans, a railway magnate's son and a fisherman, both use the objective form, which may suggest different usage in American English. The following are some examples of these two types used by characters differing in class and sex.

(11) The bishop, or I should rather take the blame on myself, for *it was I*, — I brought him down from London to Barchester.
<Mrs. Proudie: Bishop's wife>   (*Barchester*, II, p. 112)

(12) '... *It is she* who has tumbled my hopes and all my pride down.'
<Mr. Osborne: Successful industrialist>   (*Vanity*, p. 445)

(13) I wish *it was* only *me* that got put out, Pip; <Joe: Blacksmith>
(*Great*, p. 49)

(14) 'He'd better not say again as *it was me* robbed him,' cried Jem Rodney, hastily. <Jem Rodney: Mole-catcher>   (*Silas*, p. 54)

(15) but I thought that maybe *it was him* that died o' the typhoid inspecting the drains what killed him. <Rance: Constable>   (*Scarlet*, p. 38)

The choice between the types *It is I* and *It is me* can be explained by sociolinguistic factors to a certain degree but not fully; there are several higher-class characters who use the objective form.

Let us consider the role of syntactic factors in causing the use of the objective case. Or to put it another, what syntactic elements follow the pronoun in the construction *It is I/me*? For this analysis, I will classify all the 133 examples into eight different patterns as exemplified below. The results are presented in Table 3.4.

[FINAL]: If anybody is to blame *it is I*. (*Jude*, p. 332)
[*who*]: and *it was he who* had provided a physician and a nurse.
(*Frankenstein*, p. 178)
[*that*]: Yet let me remember *it is not I that* am guilty: (*Wildfell*, p. 296)
[*as*]: if *it's me as* is deppity, I'll go back with you, (*Silas*, p. 56)
[*whom*]: *It was she whom* I had heard pecking at a piece of bark;
(*Treasure*, p. 148)
[*whose*]: *It was he whose* arrival in his capital called up all France in arms to defend him there; (*Vanity*, p. 219)
[zero¹ + VP]: *it's us must break* the treaty when the time comes; (*Treasure*, p. 166)
[zero + NP + VP]: *it is me they want*. (*N and S*, p. 175)

Table 3.4: Syntactic elements following *It is I/me* in written/spoken language

	Written		Spoken		Total
	It is I	It is me	It is I	It is me	
FINAL	11	1	18	22	52
who	23		15		38
that	10		7	9*	26
as				3	3
whom	1				1
whose	1				1
which			1		1
zero + VP	2		2	2	6
zero + NP+VP				5	5
Total	48	1	42	42	133

*The figure includes one instance of the dialectal form *wot* for *that*.

The patterns with higher frequencies are the construction *It is I/me* without a connector (or FINAL) and the construction followed by the connector *who* or *that*. These three patterns alone account for 116 examples of the total. What is more, in the cases of FINAL and *that*, the objective case is preferred to the nominative case in spoken language. Another construction in which the objective case is dominantly used is "zero + NP +VP." This pattern has no examples of the nominative case either in writing or speech. It is also noted that in the cases of *who* and *that*, the nominative form is more often used on the whole. This is especially the case of *who*, where all its examples belong to the nominative. It follows that the relative pronoun *who* works as a preventer against the use of the objective case. This is still the case with English today (Mair 2006:

142). As Biber et al. (1999: 336) argue, the nominative forms are presumably felt to be more correct since they are typically co-referential with the subject of the following subordinate clause. The connectors *whom* and *whose* are also used in a "grammatically correct" way while this is not the case with *as* as far as our limited data are concerned. The zero + VP pattern is similar to FINAL and the form with *that* in that both the nominative and objective are used. According to Biber et al. (1999: 336), objective forms are "nearly universal" in conversation today: even where cleft constructions occur in conversation, an objective form is usually found together with *that* or zero connective. In the 19th century, on the other hand, the nominative case occurs as often as the objective in speech. In the dialogue of our 19th-century texts, the nominative case still enjoys a higher frequency when followed by *that*.

The choice between the nominative and objective cases after copula *be* is apparently affected not only by register but also by the users' social status and syntactic factors. These two factors sometimes work together. Although people of higher social status more often choose the formal type (*It is I*), they also use the informal type (*It is me*). It should be interesting to investigate the relationship between social class and syntactic elements in the use of *It is I/me*. In order to avoid the interference of difference in style between written and spoken languages, I will here focus on the examples in dialogue. There are 41 and 39 relevant examples of the nominative and objective forms, respectively.

Table 3.5: Examples of *It is I/me* in dialogue categorized according to social class and syntactic element

	It is I			It is me		
	U	M	L	U	M	L
FINAL	6	6	6	9	4	7
who	6	7	2			
that	2	3	1			9
as				1	1	
which						1
zero + VP	1	1				2
zero + NP +VP				1	3	1

Note: One example of *It is I* by a creature in *The Water Babies* and three examples of *It is me* by two Americans in *Captains Courageous* are omitted from this table since they do not belong to English society.

As shown in Table 3.5, except for one (to which I will return later), the characters in the upper class use the objective case only for FINAL. A similar tendency is observed with the middle class. The lower-class members, on the other hand, use the objective case in all the syntactic patterns discussed here except for that with *who*. There are seven female characters who use Type *It is me* (cf. Table 3.3b); they exclusively use FINAL, the commonest pattern, regardless of social standing. On the other hand, the (male) characters in the lower class show a wider grammatical variation. These facts confirm our previous assumption that the transition from the nominative form to the objective form started in speech with the lower class and then has gradually spread to the higher class and females in other classes, who had first accepted the objective case for FINAL.

Grammatical factors can affect the choice of case even at the individual level. There are four characters who employ both the nominative and objective cases for the construction *It is I/me*: three females (Mrs. O'Dowd, an Irishwoman and Major's wife, in *Vanity Fair*; Margaret, a clergyman's daughter, in *North and South*; and Sue, a schoolteacher, in *Jude the Obscure*) and one child (Jim, an innkeeper's son, sea boy and narrator, in *Treasure Island*).

Mrs. O'Dowd:
(16)   a.   'If a reformed rake makes a good husband, sure *it's she* will have the fine chance with Garge,'   (p. 330)
       b.   'Bedad *it's him*,'   (p. 349)

Margaret:
(17)   a.   '... *It was I* — blame me.'   (p. 128)
       b.   'Let me in! Let me in! *It is* only *me*, Charlotte!'   (p. 54)
       c.   '... I know *it is him* — I can — I must manage it all myself.'   (p. 281)
       d.   '*It is* only *us*. Won't you let us come in?'   (p. 299)
       e.   '... all this flashed through my mind, and I said *it was not me*... .'   (p. 396)

Sue:
(18)   a.   '*Is it she?*'   (p. 253)
       b.   'What — *is it he* — so soon?'   (p. 267)
       c.   '... If anybody is to blame *it is I*.'   (p. 332)
       d.   'No — *it was I*... .'   (p. 341)
       e.   '... But *it is not I* altogether that am to blame!'   (p. 212)
       f.   'Ah; but *it was I* who incited him really, though I didn't know I was doing it! ...'   (p. 327)
       g.   '... But say *it's me*! — say *it's me*!'   (p. 236)

Jim:
(19)   a.   and now, sullen, old, serviceable servant, *it was he* that was to die. <Narrative>   (p. 94)
       b.   A moment since we were firing, under cover, at an exposed enemy; now *it was we* who lay uncovered, and could not return a blow.

<Narrative> (p. 112)
c. *It was she* whom I had heard pecking at a piece of bark; *it was she*, keeping better watch than any human being, who thus announced my arrival with her wearisome refrain. <Narrative> (p. 148)
d. Ben, in his long, lonely wanderings about the island, had found the skeleton — *it was he* that had rifled it; <Narrative> (p. 183)
e. '... and if you want to know who did it — *it was I!* ...' (p. 152)
f. '... And as for the schooner, *it was I* who cut her cable, and *it was I* that killed the men you had aboard of her, and *it was I* who brought her where you'll never see her more, not one of you... .' (p. 152)
g. But Silver, from the other boat, looked sharply over and called out to know if *that were me*; <Narrative> (p. 72)

These characters use the objective case only in FINAL. When the pronoun is followed by VP, *that*, *who* or *whom*, they choose the nominative case. As for Margaret, all her five examples are FINAL. Noticeably, she uses both the nominative and objective for the first person singular pronoun: she chooses the nominative *I* in example (17a) and the objective *me* in (17b). Otherwise, she chooses the objective case (*him*, *us*). This tendency is also seen in the language of Sue and Jim. They use the nominative for the third person singular (*she*, *he*) and the first person plural (*we*) while resorting to both cases for the first person singular (*I/me*). These speakers have something in common in their use of the first person pronoun. In the sentences (17b) and (18g), in which the objective is used, the pronoun *me* is used in a heightened mood with an exclamation mark. Mrs. O'Dowd, an Irishwoman, who does not use the objective *me*, uses *him* in her example (16b), supposedly in astonishment since the Irish interjection "bedad" expresses surprise. It is worth noting that F. Th. Visser (1963-1973: §268) refers to the emphatic use of the objective case in this type of construction.

In (19g), Jim's example "that were me" is found in his narrative, which was written in standard English some years after coming back from the Treasure Island. Hence, this usage is assumed to have been quite acceptable as standard though it may be a little coated with agitation. Here I would like to point out that this is the sole example of Type *It is me* found in written language in our texts (see Table 3.4).

3.1.4 *I!* vs. *Me!*

3.1.4.1 Data

In the use of isolated pronouns in response, the objective case is common in Present-day English. According to Visser (1963-1973: §276), this usage has been in English since the latter part of the sixteenth century; interjectional phrases like "Oh me!" and a surprised interrogation like "Me pay?" are now colloquial, if not substandard. In our 19th-century texts, however, both the nominative *I!* and objective *Me!* are attested. In this section, I will consider the examples of the relevant isolated construction in which the nominative form is grammatical. I exclude those constructions in which the objective form is required as in the following example: '... I think she regards you in the light of a rival.' '*Me?* Impossible Mr. Markham!' (*Wildfell*, p. 80).

The total number of the examples of this type is 116, which consist of 96 examples (82.8%) of the *I!* type (*I/we/he/she/they*) and 20 examples (17.2%) of the *Me!* type (*me/us/him/her/them*). Our sample here does not include interjectional phrases such as *dear me!* and *ah me!*, which will be treated later since these expressions are regarded as idioms.[2] The distribution of *I!/Me!* is shown by text in Figure 3.2.

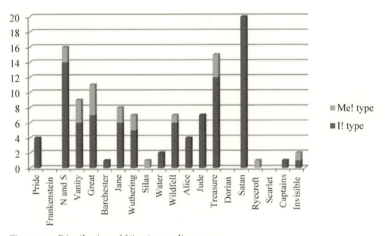

Figure 3.2: Distribution of *I!/me!* according to text

Being quite different from today's linguistic situation, the nominative case is predominant in our texts. No chronological change is observed during the 19th century. The proportion of the nominative case is even higher in *I!/Me!* than *It is I/me* (67.7%). A similar tendency is found in Dekeyser's study (1975: 225) with 84.5 percent of the nominative in *I!/Me!* and 79 percent in *It is I/me*.

3.1.4.2 Analysis

In order to find out how *I!/Me!* is used, I would first like to focus on registers in which the construction is used. Table 3.6 shows that out of the 116 examples as many as 96 belong to dialogue, demonstrating that *I!/Me!* was usually uttered in conversation but that still the nominative case was the norm at that time. Some examples of each type are presented below.

Table 3.6: Distribution of *I!/Me!* according to register

	I	*Me*	Total
Dialogue	77	19	96
Diary		1	1
Narrative	19		19
Total	96	20	116

Type *I!*
(20) "*I!* rich?" (*Jane*, p. 381)
(21) "And only *he*," (*Great*, p. 331)
(22) '*I?* I am brainsick!' (*Satan*, p. 94)
(23) "he'll touch nothing, *not he* — and, ..." (*Wuthering*, p. 51)

Type *Me!*
(24) '*Me?* No, you, Miss Sharp; ...' (*Vanity*, p. 44)
(25) "*Him?* Yes, yes! ..." (*Great*, p. 19)
(26) Kill that boy? Not *me*, mates! (*Treasure*, p. 160)
(27) *Me?* My very self? No no! (*Ryecroft*, p. 38)

In narrative, all the examples are of the *I!* type. The only example of the objective case appearing in register other than dialogue belongs to Ryecroft's diary as in example (27), in which the term "*Me?*" is uttered to the writer himself as if in monologue. *I!/Me!* is more common in spoken language than *It is I/me*, as is shown in Table 3.7.

Table 3.7: Distributions of *It is I/me* and *I!/Me!* in written/spoken language

	It is I/me	*I/Me*
Written	49 (36.8%)	20 (17.2%)
Spoken	84 (63.2%)	96 (82.8%)
Total	133	116

Why is the nominative case used more often in the construction *I!/Me!* (82.8%) (cf. §3.1.4.1) than in the construction *It is I/me* (67.7%) (cf. §3.1.3)? One major difference between these two constructions is the existence of the preceding *it is*. In Modern English, the nominative as a subject generally comes before a verb. The general use of SV order may confuse the choice of case after *be* verb; as the object comes after the verb in the construction SVO, this could lead to the use of the objective case even after *be* verb. In the isolated construction *I!/Me!*, which has no preceding syntactic element, however, the nominative case may have been less susceptible to this type of linguistic change.

I will next examine from a sociolinguistic perspective what kinds of characters use which type, *I* or *Me*. Fifty-one users of the *I* type and eighteen of the *Me* type are classified by social class and sex in Tables 3.8a and 3.8b respectively. All in all, the nominative case is used with a relatively higher frequency in the upper and middle classes although the disparity in class as well as in sex is not as distinct as in the case of *It is I/me* (see Tables 3.3a and 3.3b). It is also found that the nominative case is well preserved in the lower class, a sign that the transition from the nominative to the objective in this construction is only at an early stage if this linguistic change occurs from below.

Table 3.8a: Number of characters who use Type *I!* classified according to social class and sex

	Male	Female	Child	Total
U	13	6		19
M	9	3	1	13
L	12	5		17
American	1			1
Total	35	14	1	50

Note: Three creatures (social class unknown) are omitted from this table.

Table 3.8b: Number of characters who use Type *Me!* classified according to social class and sex

	Male	Female	Child	Total
U	2	1		3
M	3	1		4
L	4	3	1	8
Total	9	5	1	15

When we focus on individual characters, our speculation will be further justified. Pip, who is the protagonist and narrator of *Great Expectations*, uses both cases for isolated pronouns and his choice is to be systematically explained. As seen in example (28), he uses the objective case (*her*) as an orphan and the nominative case (*he, she*) as an educated gentleman and narrator in his later life.[3]

Pip in *Great Expectations*
(28) a. Therefore, I naturally pointed to Mrs. Joe, and put my mouth into the form of saying, "*her?*" [as an orphan] (p. 14)
 b. "And only *he?*" [as a gentleman] (p. 331)
 c. *She*? I looked at Joe, making the motion with my lips and eyebrows, "*She?*" [as a narrator] (p. 50)

Table 3.9: Characters who use both *I!* and *Me!*

Text	Character	Social class	I	Me
N and S	Margaret	U	Not *I*. (p. 417)	*Me!* (p. 191)
Great	Pip	L/M	And only *he?* (p. 331); *She?* (narrative) (p. 50)	*her?* (child) (p. 14)
	Joe	L	*she*. (p. 50)	*Her* (p. 48)
Jane	Jane	M	and not *I*. (child) (p. 36); Not *I*. (p. 198)	What *me!* (p. 255); *me*, who have not. (p. 255)
Wuthering	Joseph	L	nut *he!* (p. 91)	Nor-ne *me!* (p. 6); Nor nuh *me!* (p. 121)
Wildfell	Helen	U	not *she*, (p. 242)	*Me?* (p. 80)
	Mr. Huntington	U	No, not *he!* (p. 175)	not *me* (p. 148)
Treasure	Silver	L	not *I* (pp. 44, 57, 166); not *he* (p. 106)	*Me*, sir. (p. 104); not *me*, mates! (p. 160); No, not *us*. (p. 160)

Apart from Pip, there are seven characters who use both *I!* and *Me!* as shown in Table 3.9. Interesting to note is that while the characters listed there, varying in social class and sex, use various personal pronouns, members of all social classes use *me*. More specifically, the educated characters use the objective case only for the first person singular while the uneducated characters use the objective case with other forms of the personal pronouns as well. Judging from these characters' usage, it is assumed that objective *me* was already accepted in speech at that time as a harbinger of the common use of the objective in English today. Kruisinga (1932: §968) writes about the relevant usage early in 20th-century English that the nominative is the usual form in standard English for the function of the nominal predicate but that for the first person singular, *me* is the normal form. The usage of *me* in our 19th-century texts conforms to his description.

I have already referred to the emphatic use of the objective case in *It is me*. Similar usage is observed here. Three characters (Margaret in *North and South*, Jane in *Jane Eyre* and Silver in *Treasure Island*) use both *I!* and *Me!* in their speech. The fact that an exclamation mark is added only after the objective case indicates that the characters would choose the objective case for their emphatic mood. Joseph in *Wuthering Heights* uses only *me* for the first person singular. His words "Nor-ne me!" is an emphatic expression of "Not I!" in Northern dialect.[4]

Regarding the types *It is I/me*, we have found that syntactic factors affect the choice to a certain degree; the objective case tends to be avoided when the pronoun is followed by a relative clause, especially when followed by *who*. The form *I!/Me!* is rarely accompanied by a relative clause. The only grammatical element after this form is a non-restrictive relative clause beginning with *who*.

There are eight examples of this kind, out of which seven are in the nominative and one in the objective: *I* (3 exx.), *she* (3 exx.), *he* (1 ex.), and *me* (1 ex.). In examples (29) and (30), the nominative *I* and objective *me*, respectively, are used by educated female characters in similar sentences. The different choice of case could be attributed to the situation of their speech: in example (29), the pronoun *I* is in the declarative and appears in monologue, while in example (30), *me* occurs in a question to the hearer, Mr. Rochester. Though the limited data make it difficult to obtain the reason for the choice of case in these two examples, it might be due to the difference in social background between Elizabeth and Jane with the former being a gentleman's daughter and raised as such and the latter, though born to a good family, raised by a cold-hearted aunt as a repugnant orphan. Or, the different usage could have something to do with the authors' age difference; Jane Austen, the author of *Pride and Prejudice*, may have selected the nominative because she was older and accordingly more conservative in the selection of case.

(29) 'I, *who* have prided myself on my discernment! — I, *who* have valued myself on my abilities! *who* have often disdained the generous candour of my sister, and gratified my vanity, in useless or blameable distrust... .' <Elizabeth> (*Pride*, p. 159)

(30) "*me, who* have not a friend in the world but you — if you are my friend: not a shilling but what you have given me?" <Jane> (*Jane*, p. 255)

The isolated pronoun often appears in a set phrase such as *dear me*, where only the first person singular objective *me* is used. There are a total of 49 examples with six different variations: *dear me* (37 exx.), *ah me* (5 exx.), *oh dear me* (3 exx.), *dear dear me* (2 exx.), *ah dear me* (1 ex.) and *o dear me* (1 ex.). The *OED* notes that these are exclamations expressing surprise, astonishment, anxiety, distress, regret, sympathy, or other emotion and that its first quotation of "dear me" is from 1773 (s.v. *dear, a.*).[5] The idiomatic phrases accompanied by the objective *me* seem not to have a flavor of solecism. On the contrary, this kind of phrase is far more frequently used by those of higher social status. In Table 3.10, twenty-five users of the relevant phrases are classified according to their social class and sex.

Table 3.10: Number of characters who use Type *dear me* classified according to social class and sex

	Male	Female	Child
U	5	5	2
M	10	1	
L	1		1

Note: Five creatures (social class unknown) are omitted from this table.

As indicated in the table above, *dear me* and its variants are mostly used by people in the upper and middle classes. Those in the upper class include four nobles.6 By contrast, the working-class characters seldom use this phrase. Two lower-class characters who use this type are Jude in *Jude the Obscure* and Tom the sweep in *The Water Babies*: The former is an educated mason, who has learned Greek and Latin by himself, and the latter, Tom, is a sweep apprentice and the most frequent user of the phrase (7 exx.). In *The Water Babies*, besides Tom, several creatures such as a lobster and a giant resort to the phrase, along with the narrator (possibly the author himself). With all these instances taken into account, the *dear me* type seems to have been regarded as standard but slightly affected, an exaggerated phrase preferred among those of the higher rank at that time. As far as *The Water Babies* is concerned, it is assumed that the frequent use of *dear me* phrases in the work is due to the author's predilection.

3.1.5 Summary

In the foregoing sections, we have examined in 19th-century English novels the controversial case problem with a special reference to *It is I/me* and *I!/Me!*. The nominative form *It is I*, which is stipulated by traditional grammar, is dominant, while the objective form *It is me* is sometimes used in speech by lower-class speakers but hardly ever employed in written language. Upper-class characters and females prefer to use the nominative form, which indicates the solecism of its objective counterpart at that time. Among several syntactic patterns associated with *It is I/me*, people in the higher social ranks use *It is me* without any syntactic connector. When followed by the relative *who*, the objective case is avoided. As for the isolated construction *I!/Me!*, the nominative form is even more salient and is used by many more lower-class people. In both *It is I/me* and *I!/Me!*, the first person singular objective *me* seems to have been accepted earlier than the other persons (*us, him, her, them*) and is notably employed for emphatic purposes.

3.2 *Than I* vs. *than me*

3.2.1 Overview

The construction involving the element *than* has also attracted grammarians' attention since the 18th century. The 18th-century grammarians Lowth (1769: 73) and Murray (1806: 205–206) and the 19th-century grammarian Cobbett (1819: 98–99) regard *than* as a conjunction, condemning the frequently committed error of using the objective after *than* for the nominative. As an exception among 18th-century grammarians, Priestley (1769: 105–106) regarded *than* as a preposition, arguing that *greater than me* will be more grammatical than *greater than I*. Even in the 20th century, grammarians do not reach a consensus on the treatment of *than*. Jespersen (1933: § 14.2.1) states that "[*t*]*han* is (or may be) a conjunction" whereas R. W. Burchfield (1996: 769) maintains that *than* is treated both as a conjunction (*than I*) and preposition (*than me*). Burchfield adds that the objective form is much less formal than the nominative one. In constructions with *than*, three variant forms are observed: *than I am*, *than I*, and *than me*. Though there appears to be "the gradience between prepositions and conjunctions," Quirk et al. (1985: 661) argue that *than* functions as a conjunction in *than I am* and a preposition in the form *than me*, and that *than I* is not a reduction of *than I am* but is a hypercorrect form of *than me*.

3.2.2 *Younger than I* vs. *younger than me*

According to Murray (1806: 205), the normative usage of the comparison with *than* in the 18th and 19th centuries can be illustrated as follows:

a. Thou art wiser than I (am).
b. They loved him more than me.
c. He can read better than I.
d. The sentiment is well expressed by Plato, but much better by Solomon than him.
e. King Charles, and more than he, the duke and the popish faction, were at liberty to form new schemes.
f. The drift of all his sermons was, to prepare the Jews for the reception of a prophet mightier than he, and whose shoes he was not worthy to bear.

Our corpus provides nine examples where the pronoun following *than* serves as an object of a verb or a preposition. In all the instances, *than* is followed by an objective case of a pronoun:

(31) Helen she held a little longer *than me*: (*Jane*, p. 73)
(32) I thought the burden of directing and warning would be more efficiently borne by him *than me*, (*Wuthering*, p. 195)

Murray notes that when a comparison is made between subjects, the required forms are either *than I* or *than I am*. I would like to examine how much this rule is observed in our texts by shedding light on the distribution of three forms *than I am*, *than I*, and *than me*.⁷ Type *than I* stands for *than I/we/he/she/*

CHAPTER 3   THE CASE PROBLEMS OF PERSONAL PRONOUNS   107

they, Type *than I am* represents *than I am/was, than we are/were, than he is/ was, than she is/was, than they are/were*, and Type *than me, than me/us/him/ her/them*.

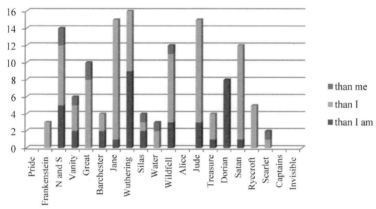

Figure 3.3: Distribution of *than I am/than I/than me* in comparison between subjects according to text

The distribution of the three types is shown by text in Figure 3.3. There are 133 examples in total with the highest proportion being *than I* (87 exx.; 65.4%) followed by *than I am* (37 exx.; 27.8%) and *than me* (9 exx.; 6.8%). The "grammatically correct" forms *than I* and *than I am* together account for 93% and *than me* is only marginally used. No chronological increase of the objective case can be observed during the century. The following are some of the examples with the nominative case ([33]-[38]) and all the nine examples with the objective case ([39]-[46]).[8]

(33) Diana was a great deal taller *than I*: she put her hand on my shoulder, and, stooping, examined my face. (*Jane*, p. 414)
(34) As a man, I love him so much, that I wish him a better wife *than I* — one as good as himself, or better — (*Wildfell*, p. 131)
(35) Ethelbert Stanhope was in some respects like his younger sister, but he was less inestimable as a man *than she* as a woman. (*Barchester*, I, p. 78)
(36) My wife is very good at it — much better, in fact, *than I am*. (*Dorian*, p. 3)
(37) 'How young she is! — younger by fourteen months *than I am*... .' (*N and S*, p. 287)
(38) and I don't b'lieve he's no more a colonel *than I am*. (*Vanity*, p. 692)

(39) He was younger *than me*, but he'd got craft, and he'd got learning, and

he overmatched me five hundred times told and no mercy.
<Magwitch: Convict> (*Great*, p. 346)

(40) "And don't *you* do it, neither; you're a deal worse than *him*!" (Italicized "you" and "him" in the original) <a sulky man in the gallery>
(*Great*, p. 251)

(41) You're stronger *than me* — that I know too well, and wiser *than me*, I know too well also. <Grimes: Chimney-sweep> (*Water*, p. 206)

(42) 'They give themselves the hairs and hupstarts of ladies, and their wages is no better *than you nor me.* <Mrs. Blenkinsop: Housekeeper>
(*Vanity*, p. 75)

(43) 'But she were younger *than me.*' <Nicholas: Millworker> (*N and S*, p. 219)

(44) I've longed for to be a man to go spreeing, even if it were only a tramp to some new place in search o' work. And father — all men — have it stronger in 'em *than me* to get tired o' sameness and work for ever. <Bessy: Millworker's daughter> (*N and S*, p. 136)

(45) But I can't leave my father, nor own anybody nearer *than him.* <Eppie: Weaver's adopted daughter> (*Silas*, p. 163)

(46) "You'll see prettier things *than them* soon," said the man confidently. <John Ferrier: Solitary traveler> (*Scarlet*, p. 72)

The examples with the objective case above belong to seven lower-class characters (four males and three females) and one man whose class cannot be identified but who is introduced as "a sulky man" in a theater in *Great Expectations*. The lower frequency of the objective form may suggest the solecism of its use. In examples (39), (41) and (42), Magwitch the convict in *Great Expectations*, Grimes the chimney sweep in *Water Babies*, and Mrs. Blenkinsop the housekeeper in *Vanity Fair* may use the objective form due to lack of education; in (42) Mrs. Blenkinsop commits another grammatical error in her use of *your nor me* instead of *yours or mine*. In (43) and (44), however, the objective form used by Nicholas and Bessy in *North and South* could be of dialectal use in their northern region. In (46), traveler John Ferrier in *A Study in Scarlet* uses the objective, possibly reflecting his American background. Moreover, in (40), the italicized *him* by the sulky man in *Great Expectations* may indicate its emphatic use. All these examples seem to indicate that the authors of those characters unanimously agreed that Type *than me* is not British Standard English at that time.

In Present-day English, even when the pronoun following *than* serves as a subject of a sentence, the objective case is common in conversation. Biber et al. (1999: 336) state that objective forms are predominant after *as/than*, especially in conversation. In the 19th-century texts under consideration here, Table 3.11 shows the distribution of the three types *than I*, *than I am*, and *than me* in terms of spoken and written contexts.

Table 3.11: Variation of the construction *than* in comparison between subjects according to register

	than I am	than I	than me	Total
Dialogue	29	34	9	72
Letter	1	3		4
Diary	1	2		3
Narrative	6	48		54
Total	37	87	9	133

As shown in Table 3.11, our 19th-century texts limit the objective form *than me* to dialogue while the nominative forms *than I am* and *than I* are found both in spoken and written languages. Worth noting is that the nominative forms are preferred even in speech. This means that regardless of register the objective form *than me* would have been considered substandard at that time. Though Quirk et al. argue that "*than I* is not reduction of *than I am* but a hypercorrect variant of *than me* (1985: 661)," this would not be the case with our 19th-century texts, in which only a few instances of *than me* are found. It would be perhaps reasonable to say that most Victorians chose the nominative form without hesitation, either *than I* or *than I am*, and that *than I* was the commonest standard form in which *be* or other verbs were omitted.

Since there are two different nominative forms following *than* (i.e., *than I am* and *than I*), I would like to clarify the difference between them. For this purpose, I will take a closer look at the seven characters who use both forms in dialogue.

Catherine Jr.: Catherine's daughter in *Wuthering Heights*
(47)   a. "He's younger *than I*," she answered, after a protracted pause of meditation, "and he ought to live the longest: he will — he must live as long as I do... ." (p. 214)
       b. "Linton is just six months younger *than I am*," she chattered, as we strolled leisurely over the swells and hollows of mossy turf, under shadow of the trees. "How delightful it will be to have him for a playfellow! ... Oh! I am happy — and papa, dear, dear papa! Come, Ellen, let us run! come run!" (p. 176)
       c. He's taller *than I am*! (p. 190)
       d. I'm older *than he is*, you know, and wiser, less childish, am I not? (p. 213)

Nelly: Servant in *Wuthering Heights*
(48)   a. She is better acquainted with his heart *than I*, or any one besides;
                (p. 91)
       b. "But there are several other handsome, rich young men in the world; handsomer, possibly, and richer *than he is* ..." (p. 69)
       c. "Be more charitable; there are worse men *than he is* yet!" (p. 152)
       d. "... There is nothing in the world less yours *than he is*!" (p. 165)
       e. "Because they are a great deal higher up *than we are*," replied I; (p. 168)

Jude: Mason in *Jude the Obscure*
(49)   a. 'you have read more *than I*,' he said with a sigh. (p. 141)
       b. Perhaps she's no worse *than I am*, after all! (p. 230)

Sue: Schoolteacher in *Jude the Obscure*
(50)   a. Do you think, Jude, that a man ought to marry a woman his own age, or one younger than himself — eighteen years — as I am *than he*? (p. 203)
       b. Please, please stay at home, Jude, and not go to her, now she's not your wife any more *than I*! (p. 254)
       c. 'My poor Jude — how you've missed everything! — you more *than I*, for I did get you! ...' (p. 328)
       d. 'Prettier *than I am*, no doubt!' (p. 159)

Mr. Bell: Landowner in *North and South*
(51)   a. The veriest idiot who obeys his own simple law of right, if it be but in wiping his shoes on a door-mat, is wiser and stronger *than I*. (p. 349)
       b. Now she is no more fit for travelling *than I am* for flying. (p. 357)

Catherine: Landowner's daughter in *Wuthering Heights*
(52)   a. Nelly, you think you are better and more fortunate *than I*; (p. 141)
       b. It would degrade me to marry Heathcliff, now; so he shall never know how I love him; and that, not because he's handsome, Nelly, but because he's more myself *than I am*. (p. 71)

Dr. Livesey: Physician in *Treasure Island*
(53)   a. No more wounded *than you or I*. The man has had a stroke, as I warned him. (p. 11)
       b. 'That man Smollett,' he said once, 'is a better man *than I am*. And when I say that it means a deal, Jim.' (p. 101)

The difference between *than I am* and *than I* might be explained by the context in which the form is used. Catherine Jr. uses similar expressions in examples (47a) and (47b) with *younger than* when referring to her cousin (and husband as well in the former). In (47b), the expression *I am* is emphatically uttered because she is filled with joy to see him for the first time and their age difference greatly interests her. In (47a), however, since she is more concerned about his ailing condition, it is assumed that she simply uses *than I*. By and large, *than I am* is used when the speaker is in a heightened emotional state or in a serious mood. Heightened emotions expressed in the use of *than I am* are often described by an exclamation mark added to the utterances as seen in (47b), (47c), (48c), (48d), (49b), (50d) and (51d). Example (52b) is a well-known line by Catherine in which she says, "I *am* Heathcliff," and *than I am* is similarly uttered emphatically. In example (53b), Dr. Livesey's words "when I say that it means a deal" demonstrate an emphatic use of *than I am*. As one generally employs non-elliptical forms to deliver important messages, it is natural that the non-elliptical *than I am* is associated with an emphatic tone.

There are quite a few examples in which *than I* is not a shortened form of *than I am*; it also stands for *than I do* or *than I have* as follows:

(54) 'You have read more *than I*,' he said with a sigh. (*Jude*, p. 141)

Various kinds of predicates are used for the first element in sentences with *than I am* or *than I*. As demonstrated in Table 3.12, while *than I am* naturally corresponds to the copula *be*, *than I* represents a greater variety of predicate. In fact, more than one third of the examples of *than I* occur with verbs other than *be* as the predicate of the main clause.

Table 3.12: Variation of predicates of the preceding subject in Types *than I am* and *than I*

	Predicates of the main clause	*than I am*	*than I*
Copula *be*	am/are/is	20	14
	was/were	4	16
	could be	2	3
	being		1
	had been		1
	shall be		1
	would be		1
	would have been		1
omit. of (*be*) verb		6	16
Total		32	54
Other verbs	had	-	6
	has	-	1
	know(s)	-	2
	knew	-	1
	expressed	-	1
	sees	-	1
	deserved	-	1
	felt	-	1
	influenced	-	1
	looked	-	1
	saw	-	1
	seemed	-	1
	spoke	-	1
	have to suffer	-	1
Aux. + verb	could know	-	2
	can eat	-	1
	could understand	-	1
	will act	-	1
	should dare to	-	1
	should show	-	1
	must have known	-	1
have + pp	has wished	-	1
	have enjoyed	-	1
	have grown	-	1
	have read	-	1
	had never laid	-	1
Total			33

In the texts under examination, the simpler form *than I* is occasionally used instead of the full forms such as *I can*, *I do* and *I had*. Since Murray regards "He can read better *than I*" as a proper example, this sort of omission may have been accepted as grammatical. Note the following examples:

(55) a. "Who can eat, or who else can hasten hereunto more *than I*?"
(*Wildfell*, p. 195)

b. 'I am so sorry Mr. Lennox is not here, — he could have done it so much better *than I can*... .'
(*N and S*, p. 434)

(56) a. you know more about such things *than I*, having much fresher experience of that kind. (*Great*, p. 408)
 b. But now I find that every man before the mast knows more *than I do*. (*Treasure*, p. 48)
(57) a. and shall anyone be more "eagerly desired" *than he*? (*Satan*, p. 240)
 b. "Any one will do better for him *than I shall*," he answered. (*Wuthering*, p. 67)

The examples of this sort are attested regardless of register; the omission is neither particularly colloquial nor characteristic to individual authors. The authors might have avoided supplying an implied verb that could make the sentence cumbersome.

3.2.3 *Than myself*

The reflexive pronouns are sometimes used after *than* without being preceded by their antecedents. The treatment of this non-reflexive *-self* varies among the scholars. Wales (1996: 97) states that the prohibition against the use of *than me* lacks a consensus amongst grammarians, which leads many people to use either a full clause, as in "Tim is taller than I am," or the reflexive in order to evade the problematic use. Burchfield (1996: 770) has a similar idea about the usage of the reflexive though he does not think that such a strategy is very successful. R. E. Zachrisson (1920) notes that the emphatic use of the reflexive pronoun without its antecedent is archaic and rarely used in Present-day English. Quirk et al. (1985: 359) treat this usage of reflexive pronouns under the category of "semi-emphatic" use, in which "the reflexive pronoun is used as a more emphatic equivalent of the first and second person personal pronouns." They also state that the "semi-emphatic" reflexive occurs after prepositions like, *than, (as...) as, but (for), except (for),* and *as for*. According to Tieken-Boon van Ostade (1994: 230; 2009: 261), in 18th-century English, the use of the non-reflexive *-self* may function as a kind of modesty device by skirting the more direct use of the pronoun *I* on the part of the speaker. She also states that this usage is more common with women than men.

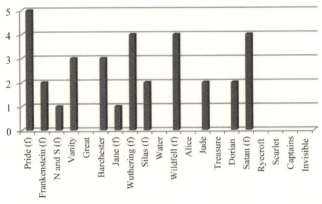

Note: The mark (f) indicates that the author is female; the same applies hereinafter.
Figure 3.4: Distribution of *than oneself* (as the subject of a clause) according to text

In the form with *than*, there are 33 relevant examples found in twelve texts. Figure 3.4 shows that the usage is not found in the four later texts. This might suggest that the usage is archaic and going out of use. However, since there is no example of the construction *than* in the two later texts (*Captains Courageous* and *The Invisible Man*), the assumption may not be sufficiently supported.

It is to be noted that the twelve authors who use constructions like *than myself* include all eight female authors. The following table statistically demonstrates that, in the construction with *than*, the female authors use the reflexive more frequently than their male counterparts.

Table 3.13: Distribution of *than I am/than I/than me* and *than myself* according to sex

	than I am/than I/than me	than myself	Total
Female authors	76 (57.1%)	57 (42.9%)	133
Male authors	29 (69.0%)	13 (31.0%)	42

As we have seen above, when the pronoun following *than* serves as the subject of a clause, the nominative form is used in our corpus except where the intentional ungrammatical choice of the objective form is made to show the uneducated or regional accents of some characters. It follows that the authors in our texts perfectly understood the grammatical use of *than I* (*am*) and *than me*. It is not plausible that they chose the reflexive pronouns instead of the personal pronouns for the evasion of possible grammatical errors. What made the female authors resort to reflexive pronouns following *than*?

Let us consider the individual examples to find out how the reflexive pronoun is actually used. In examples (58) to (60), the reflexive pronoun is used probably in order to clearly differentiate two persons (or animals) of the same sex. In example (58), where two female dogs are compared, one is referred to by *she* and the other by *herself*. In example (59), where two noble women are compared, *herself* is chosen to more clearly indicate Lady Steyne. Similarly, in (60), when *she* (Lady Catherine) asks a question of *her* (Elizabeth Bennet), *herself* is used for the latter. In each case, the reflexive pronoun helps to identify which one is referred to. In example (61), the reflexive *myself* may have been chosen to avoid an awkward repetition of *me*. The commonest feature which accounts for more than half the examples of the construction *than myself* is that, when the subject of a clause is compared with the object, the reflexive is used in reference to the former, as exemplified in (62) and (63). Example (64) is a case in which the reflexive pronoun is used without the head word simply for emphasis.

(58) and a little dog like Vick knows that Lioness is a dog too, though *she* is twenty times larger *than herself*. (*Water*, p. 110)
(59) For all *Lady Steyne* knows, this calumniated, simple, good-humoured Mrs. *Crawley* is quite innocent — even more innocent *than herself*.
(*Vanity*, p. 613)
(60) *She* asked *her* at different times, how many sisters *she* had, whether they were older or younger *than herself*, whether any of them were likely to be married, whether they were handsome, where they had been educated, what carriage *her* father kept, and what had been *her* mother's maiden name? (*Pride*, p. 126)
(61) and an impulse rose in *me* stronger than *myself*, moving me to wild and clamorous speech. (*Satan*, p. 315)
(62) *Dearest Maria* had married the man of her heart, only eight years older *than herself*, with the sweetest temper, and that blue-black hair one so seldom sees. (*N and S*, p. 15)
(63) and as *he* never associated with any gentry higher *than himself*, his opinion was not disturbed by comparison. (*Silas*, p. 66)
(64) there won't be a happier woman *than myself* in England!
(*Wuthering*, p. 281)

All these examples lead us to conclude that the reflexive pronoun is deliberately selected not for avoidance of a grammatically incorrect choice but for a good reason. Although women were often criticized for not observing grammatical rules as faithfully as men at that time due to lack of formal education, this is not the case with our female authors. The fact that they prefer to use the reflexive more frequently could rather suggest their careful and conservative attitude.

3.2.4 Summary

There are four different forms appearing in construction with *than* in our 19th-century novels: *than I, than I am, than me*, and *than myself*. The nominative form (*than I, than I am*) is absolutely the norm either in written or spoken languages. The objective (*than me*) is used to illustrate dialectal or substandard accents of the characters. While *than I* is preferred in both spoken and written contexts, *than I am* is found far more often in speech than in writing. The relatively frequent use of *than I am* in speech suggests that the full form is used for emphatic effects. The construction *than I* is often chosen to avoid cumbersome constructions like *than I* + aux. (*do, did, can, could, should, have*, etc.) regardless of register. When reflexive pronouns are chosen instead of personal pronouns, they are occasionally employed for clear contrast, and this usage is more salient in the language of the female authors.

3.3 *As I* vs. *as me*

3.3.1 Overview

The element *as* is also a conjunction used in clauses of comparison. In Present-day English, there is a strong tendency to treat *as* as a preposition and thus to use the objective form (Jespersen 1933: § 14.2.2). In formal writing, however, *as* and *than* are primarily conjunctions, and in less formal contexts, the objective form is a norm even when the pronoun serves as a subject (Kruisinga 1932: §§974–975; Quirk et al. 1985: 337; Burchfield 1996: 69; Greenbaum and Nelson 2002:150). Grammarians today do not flatly deny the use of the objective form after *as* though they generally agree that the nominative is formally correct. Eighteenth- and 19th-century grammarians regarded *as* as a conjunction without referring to colloquial use of the objective form in the relevant construction (cf. Lowth 1769: 73; Murray 1806: 205; Cobbett 1819; 98–99).

3.3.2 *As tall as I* vs. *as tall as me*

This section will discuss *as* used in clauses of comparison in our 19th-century texts. We have only four examples in the relevant construction in which objects are compared with the objective form chosen in every example.

(65) 'The Monster has given the Lion twice *as* much *as me*!' (*Alice*, p. 207)
(66) I was weeping *as* much for him *as her*: (*Wuthering*, p. 146)

CHAPTER 3 THE CASE PROBLEMS OF PERSONAL PRONOUNS

There are a total of 83 examples where the pronoun following *as* serves as the subject of a clause. As is the case with *than*, there are three types of constructions following *as*: the two nominative forms *as I am* and *as I* and the objective form *as me*. There are 30 examples (36.1%) for *as I am*, 43 examples (51.8%) for *as I*, and ten examples (12%) for *as me*, i.e., the nominative form accounts for about 88 percent of the total. The examples of the comparison construction with *as* are found in eighteen texts, out of which eleven texts have only the nominative form (*as I am, as I*), one text (*The Invisible Man*) has only the objective form (*as me*) and the remaining six texts have both forms (see Figure 3.5).

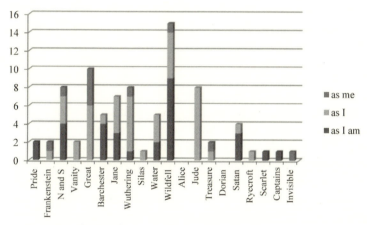

Figure 3.5: Distribution of *as I am/as I/as me* in the construction *as – as* according to text

According to Biber et al. (1999: 336), in Present-day English the objective form is predominant after *as/than*, especially in conversation. I would like to find how the construction under examination is used in our 19th-century corpus in terms of register. Table 3.14 shows that no evident imbalance is observed in the use of the nominative forms *as I am* and *as I* while the objective form *as me* mostly appears in speech. Since there are only ten examples of the objective form, I will first check who uses this type and how it is used.

Table 3.14: Distribution of *as I am/as I/as me* according to register

	as I am	as I	as me	Total
Dialogue	15	21	8	44
Letter	1	1		2
Diary	1	2		3
Narrative	13	19	2	34
Total	30	43	10	83

The eight users of the objective form are either of the lowest-status characters, such as Orlick the Journeyman, Magwitch the convict and Pip the orphan in *Great Expectations*, or working-class people living in Northern England such as Joseph in *Wuthering Heights* and Bessy in *North and South*. Pip uses the objective form as an orphan but employs the nominative as a gentleman and narrator as seen in examples (70a) and (70b). Gilbert, the narrator of *Wildfell Hall*, uses the objective form only for the first person singular *me* in the narrative and the nominative forms, including the first person singular *I*, for the remaining four examples, either in narrative or in dialogue; specifically, he uses *as me* (1 ex.), *as I* (2 exx.), *as he is* (1 ex.) and *as she was* (1 ex.). In example (71), in which the objective form is used, his speech shows a kind of agitated state of mind as illustrated with an exclamation mark. Taking these together, it is presumed that although the objective case form was generally marked as substandard at that time, the first person singular *me* was not necessarily regarded as such.

Example (72) is taken from the monster's narrative in *Frankenstein*. The monster has mastered standard English by listening to people's conversation (setting aside the question whether in reality such a case is linguistically possible or not). In this example, he uses the objective case *her* in a comparison of two women, whom he killed. It is possible that Shelly, the author, means to present him as relatively unlearned, but it would be more reasonable to assume that the pronoun *her* was chosen in order to differentiate the two different women; it would certainly sound awkward to say "*she* was not indeed as beautiful as *she*."

(67) "What'll *I* do with it! What'll *he* do with it? I'll do *as* much with it *as him*," said Orlick. (Italicized "I," "he" and "him" in the original) <Orlick: Journeyman> (*Great*, p. 111)

(68) There's others went out alonger me as has done well too, but no man has done nigh *as* well *as me*. <Magwitch: Convict> (*Great*, p. 313)

(69) 'Yo'd ha' been deaved out o' yo'r five wits, *as* well *as me*, if yo'd had one body after another coming in to ask for father, and staying to tell me each on their tale. <Bessy: Millworker's daughter> (*N and S*, p. 150)

(70) a. "Why didn't you ever go to school, Joe, when you were *as* little *as me*?" <Pip: Orphan> (*Great*, p. 45)
b. Among those few, there may be one who loves you even *as* dearly, though he has not loved you *as* long, *as I*. Take him, and I can bear it better, for your sake!" <Pip: Gentleman> (*Great*, p. 359)

(71) If this *was* the case, and if she should only discover her mistake when too late to repair it — to what a life of misery and vain regret might she be doomed *as* well *as me*! (Italicized "was" in the original)

<Narrative by Gilbert> (*Wildfell*, p. 445)
(72) A woman was sleeping on some straw; she was young: not indeed *so* beautiful *as her* whose portrait I held; but of an agreeable aspect, and blooming in the loveliness of youth and health.
<Narrative by Monster> (*Frankenstein*, p. 143)

I will next consider how the nominative forms are used and by what kind of people from a sociolinguistic standpoint. Since the nominative forms are found in written and spoken languages equally, it would be preferable to examine the distribution of the relevant examples separately. Table 3.15 below finds that the nominative forms are employed regardless of social class and sex, whether in writing or speech. While characters of the upper and middle classes use the nominative form both in written and spoken languages, the "grammatical" form is employed by six lower-class people even in speech. These lower-class speakers include Nicholas (a millworker in *North and South*), Zilla (a housekeeper in *Wuthering Heights*) and Drusilla (a baker in *Jude the Obscure*), who often use nonstandard language. It is therefore presumed that the nominative form was used across society at that time.

Table 3.15: Number of characters who use the nominative forms in the *as – as* construction classified according to social class and sex in written/spoken language

	Written				Spoken		
	Male	Female	Total		Male	Female	Total
U		2	2	U	5	5	10
M	6	1	7	M	7	2	9
L		1	1	L	2	4	6
				American	1		1
Total	6	4	10	Total	15	11	26

As to the use of the constructions *as I am* and *as I*, no major difference is found with 30 examples and 43 examples respectively (see Table 3.14). Three characters use both types. The following examples by Helen, the tenant of *Wildfell Hall*, suggest an emphatic use of the full form in the construction *as – as*; in (73a) emphasis is placed on *you* while in (73b) emphasis falls on "she is."

(73) a. 'You must know that *as* well *as I*.' (*Wildfell*, p. 385)
 b. 'Well, I think he's about *as* good *as she is*,' (*Wildfell*, p. 165)

In the construction *as I*, a *be* verb is usually omitted after the pronoun. In some examples, however, an auxiliary verb is suppressed. Out of the 43 examples of *as I*, twelve examples have an auxiliary unexpressed: *I* is used for *I did* (5 exx.), *I do* (3 exx.), *I shall/could* (2 exx.) and *I have* (2 exx.) as seen in the following examples:

(74) a. And, believe me, he soon knew nearly *as* much *as I*.' (*Jude*, p. 283)
  b. I have a deep affection for Graevius and Gronovius and the rest, and if I knew *as* much *as they did*, I should be well satisfied to rest under the young man's disdain. (*Ryecroft*, p. 33)
(75) a. But Hannah, poor woman! could not stride the drifts *so* well *as I*; (*Jane*, p. 383)
  b. '... none of them could or would attend you *as* carefully *as I shall do*.' (*Wildfell*, p. 409)

The construction *as I* in which verbs other than *be* are omitted is likely to be found in speech; out of the twelve examples, eight are found in dialogue, where shortened forms are preferred, probably for simplicity. The fact that as many as seven authors employ this type of omission indicates that this usage was common at that time.[9]

3.3.3 *Such as he* vs. *such as him*

The element *as* is used in combination with *such*, *so* and *the same*. According to Jespersen (1933: § 14.2.2), after *such as* the nominative is often used, as a verb (*am, is, are*) is easily supplied. Regarding the phrases *such – as he* etc., *so – as he* etc., H. W. Fowler (1965: 38–99) states that these phrases may be treated as declinable compound adjectives and that to ban the use of *him* in such constructions seems pedantic though *he* is always admissible. No specific description is made of the constructions with *as* by the 19th-century grammarians. The OED gives two examples of *such as I* from 1823 and 1850 and one examples of *such as them* from 1869, which indicates that both the nominative and objective were used in the 19th century.

Our 19th-century corpus yields a total of forty examples of the four types (i.e., *such as, such – as, so – as, the same – as*). As indicated in Table 3.16, the nominative case is predominant after *as*, especially for the patterns *so – as* and *the same – as*.

Table 3.16: Case variation in the construction with *as*

	I am/I	*me*
such as	6	3
such – as	12	5
so – as	9	
the same – as	4	1
Total	31 (77.5%)	9 (22.5%)

CHAPTER 3   THE CASE PROBLEMS OF PERSONAL PRONOUNS   121

The 31 examples of the nominative forms are employed both in writing and in speech while, out of the nine examples of the objective form, eight belong to speech. Moreover, some lower-class characters are included among the users of the nominative forms *as I am*/*as I*, and some educated characters among users of the objective form *as me*. Examples of the nominative and objective forms (if any) of each type are shown below. In the phrase *such as*, village girl Sarah uses the nominative and her friend Anny employs the objective in examples (76) and (77), respectively. Mr. Arabin, a clergyman, also uses the objective in (78). In the phrase *such – as*, a blacksmith uses the nominative in example (79) while a millworker and the narrator of *Vanity Fair* use the objective form in (80) and (81), respectively. As for the form *so – as*, the nominative is always chosen, as in (82) and (83). Only in the case of the phrase *the same – as*, used by convict Magwitch in (85), does the objective case suggest possible substandard usage. Thus, as far as these constructions are concerned, neither salient sociolinguistic factors nor linguistic context are involved in the use of the objective forms.

Such as

(76) 'A countryman that's honourable and serious-minded, *such as he*;
<Sarah: Village girl>   (*Jude*, p. 45)

(77) 'I knew it would with *such as him*... .' <Anny: Village girl>   (*Jude*, p. 54)

(78) Yet, surely, you would not be inclined to say that I should be wrong to do battle with *such as him*. <Mr. Arabin: Clergyman> (*Barchester*, I, p. 204)

Such – as

(79) 'You warnt horseshoes for *such* gentry *as he*.'
<Mr. Sandy Wadgers: Blacksmith>   (*Invisible*, p. 31)

(80) '*Such* a chap *as me* is not like to see the measter... .'
<Nicholas: Millworker>   (*N and S*, p. 307)

(81) Emmy defended her conduct, and showed that it was dictated only by the purest religious principles; that a woman once, &c., and to *such an* angel *as him* whom she had had the good fortune to marry, was married for ever; <Narrative>   (*Vanity*, p. 858)

So – as

(82) They wondered how one *so* charming and graceful *as he was* could have escaped the stain of an age that was at once sordid and sensual.
<Narrative>   (*Dorian*, p. 104)

(83) '... Yo' never saw a man *so* down-hearted *as he is*.'
<Bessy: Millworker's daughter>   (*N and S*, p. 199)

The same – as

(84) Have you not *the same* base passions *as I*? <Sybil: Earl Elton's daughter>

(*Satan*, p. 270)

(85) I got money left me by my master (which died, and had been *the same as me*), and got my liberty and went for myself. <Magwitch: Convict>

(*Great*, p. 317)

A syntactic consideration could lead to a better explanation of the constructions under examination. These constructions are placed in the position of subject, complement or object in sentences. The syntactic position may affect the choice of case. Table 3.17 shows that as regards the form *such as*, the objective form is used only as the object of a verb/preposition. This may explain the different choice of case by two lower class girls in *Jude the Obscure*; in examples (76) above, Sarah uses the nominative as a subject while in (77) Anny uses the objective as an object. It is to be noted that the objective form is used in the object position in the case of *such as* and *such – as* by the educated as well: see, for example, (78) and (81). The use of the objective form by the well-educated suggests that the objective form for *such* (–) *as* in this syntactic position is not necessarily labeled as substandard.

Table 3.17: Case variation in the construction with *as* in the subject/complement and object positions

	sub./comp.		obj.	
	I am/I	*me*	*I am/I*	*me*
such as	2		4	3
such – as	2	2	10	3
so – as	2		7	
the same – as	4	1		
Total	10	3	21	6

3.3.4 As myself

Reflexive pronouns are sometimes chosen instead of personal pronouns in the constructions with *as*. Table 3.18 presents the distributions of the reflexive and non-reflexive pronouns in the relevant constructions (*as tall as, so – as, such (–) as, the same – as*).

Table 3.18: Distributions of the reflexive and non-reflexive pronouns in the construction with *as*

Pronoun	*as – as*	*such (–) as*	*so – as*	*the same – as*	Total
Reflexive	36		3	9	48 (28.1%)
Non-reflexive	83	26	9	5	123 (71.9%)

The reflexive pronoun is quite frequently used; apart from the phrases with *such*, reflexive pronouns appear nearly half as often as non-reflexive pronouns. As to the phrase *the same – as*, the reflexive is more frequently used than the non-reflexive. Reflexive pronouns are mostly found in written context (41 times), and only seven are uttered in speech, by three males and three females who are all well-bred. It follows that reflexive forms are not necessarily colloquial but can be used in formal contexts as well (see Table 3.19).

Table 3.19: Distribution of the reflexive pronoun in the construction with *as* according to register

	as – as	*so – as*	*the same – as*	Total
Dialogue	6		1	7
Letter				
Diary	5		2	7
Narrative	25	3	6	34

In several examples the reflexive form is used in order to make a comparison between two persons of the same sex. In example (86), *herself* stands for a lady named Madeline Neroni. In such instances the reflexive pronoun seems to be preferred although the use of the non-reflexive pronoun is grammatical. The most frequent user of the reflexive pronoun in the relevant construction is Nelly, who uses it six times in her narrative for emphatic purpose as in example (87) below. She highlights the scene in which Miss Cathy cheerfully welcomes her father by using two reflexive pronouns in the same line. Such emphatic use of the reflexive pronoun as Nelly's is also found in some other examples.

(86) He loved Eleanor Bold, but Eleanor was not in his eye *so* beautiful *as herself*. (*Barchester*, II, p. 129)
(87) Miss Cathy shrieked, and stretched out her arms, as soon as she caught her father's face looking from the window. He descended, nearly *as* eager *as herself*; and a considerable interval elapsed ere they had a thought to spare for any but *themselves*. <Narrative by Nelly> (*Wuthering*, p. 176)

Out of the eighteen texts in which the coordinated pronouns with *as* are found, the reflexive pronoun is employed in fifteen texts, including those of all the female authors. The following table shows that the female authors employ the form *as myself* with a slightly higher frequency than the male authors do, which suggests that the emphatic use of the reflexive pronoun suits the female authors' taste.

Table 3.20: Distribution of *as I am/as I/as me* and *as myself* according to sex

	as I am/as I/as me	as myself	Total
Female authors	47 (60.3%)	31 (39.7%)	78
Male authors	36 (67.9%)	17 (32.1%)	53

Examples (88) to (91) below contain reflexive pronouns following *as–as*, *so–as* and *the same–as* used by female authors. It is also to be noted that the reflexive pronoun is uttered by the male characters as in (88), (89) and (91). This indicates that the reflexive pronoun of this kind does not necessarily imply feminine traits in itself but tends to be selected by the female authors.

(88) I demand a creature of another sex, but *as* hideous *as myself*; <Monster>
 (*Frankenstein*, p. 145)
(89) Far from desiring to publish the connection, he became *as* anxious to conceal it *as myself*. <Mr. Rochester> (*Jane*, p. 309)
(90) Had Elizabeth been at leisure to be idle, she would have remained certain that all employment was impossible to one *so* wretched *as herself*; <Narrative> (*Pride*, p. 213)
(91) and though we said nothing to each other concerning our mutual sensations, I could see that she was under *the same* cloud of depression *as myself*. <Narrative by Geoffrey> (*Satan*, p. 270)

3.3.5 Summary

In the construction *as – as I/me*, the nominative form is dominant while the objective form is quite limited, a sharp contrast with English today. The "standard" form seems to have been used across 19th-century English Society. As for the nominative forms, *as I* and *as I am* are used equally though the simpler form *as I* is used slightly more frequently in speech. Concerning the combination forms *such (–) as*, *so – as* and *the same – as*, the proportion of the objective form is higher than the form *as tall as*. As for the form *such as*, the objective case is more likely to be used as the object of a verb/preposition, regardless of the speakers' educational background. The "semi-emphatic" use of the reflexive pronoun is sporadically found in our texts, and may be somewhat more favored by female authors than by male authors.

3.4 *But, except, save*

3.4.1 Overview

Both the nominative and objective cases are used when two nouns or pronouns are joined by *but, except* or *save*. When used prepositionally, *but, except* and *save* are generally classified as simple prepositions in modern grammar books (cf. Jespersen 1933: §14.2.3, Quirk et al. 1985: 9.7, Leech and Svartvik 1994: 122, Greenbaum 1996:160).[10] Jespersen additionally comments that as the word after these prepositions is felt to be parallel with the subject of the sentence, the nominative has been in frequent use for centuries so that *but, except* and *save* must be termed conjunctions. According to Kruisinga (1932: §§ 974, 975, §977), with *but, as* and *than* the nominative is considered the correct form; in other words they primarily serve as conjunctions though in colloquial English the objective forms are also found and after *except* the objective forms are the rule. No particular instructions concerning the constructions under discussion are found in the 18th- and 19th-century grammars. According to Dekeyser (1975: 217, 221), although no consensus is found among 19th-century grammarians, the majority treat *but* as a conjunction and *save* as a preposition. *Except* is described as a conjunction in the 18th-century grammars (cf. Murray 1806: 195) but Dekeyser (1975: 220) states that in the 19th century nearly all grammarians unanimously assign it to the class of prepositions. Thus, it was not quite settled whether the three synonyms *but, except* and *save* are prepositions or conjunctions throughout the century.

3.4.2 Data and analysis

To begin with, I will examine which kinds of pronouns are placed after *but, except* and *save* in our texts. There are 22 examples in total, out of which four examples are in the objective function and eighteen examples in the nominative function as shown in Table 3.21a and 3.21b.

Table 3.21a: Pronoun type after *but, except, save* in the objective function

	I	me	myself	Total
but				0
except		2		2
save	1	1		2

(92) they had believed me to be without any friends *save them*: (*Jane*, p. 422)
(93) and Sue nervously made herself agreeable to him by talking on whatever she thought likely to interest him, *except herself*, (*Jude*, p.352)

Table 3.21b: Pronoun type after *but, except, save* in the nominative function

	I	me	myself	Total
but	5	2		7
except	1	4	4	9
save	2			2

In both functions, the reflexive pronoun is used but the nominative form is used only in the nominative function. As for *but* and *save* in the nominative function, both seem to be regarded as conjunctions since the nominative form is more likely to occur after conjunctions. On the other hand, the usage of *except* varies; its single nominative instance suggests that *except* is primarily treated as a preposition. Dekeyser's data show that *but* is used more often in objective forms with a ratio of 5 (nominative): 11 (objective). However, he also notes that "even then, it is plain that 19th century usage is divided as to the case of the pronouns collocation with *but*" (1975: 237). Our results also agree with his. The objective form in the nominative function after *but* may be due to sociolinguistic and/or syntactic factors. Regarding the form *but I/me*, two examples of the objective belong to women who do not always speak properly: Arabella in *Jude the Obscure* in (95) and Lydia in *Pride and Prejudice* in (96). The five examples of the nominative are found either in narrative (4 exx.) or speech by an educated woman (1 ex.), which suggests that the objective form after *but* would sound informal. From a syntactic point of view, it is noticed that in both (95) and (96) the objective form is used in a multiple head phrase taking a remote position from *but*. This tendency is also true with the term *except* in (98). As to the usage of multiple head phrases, I will discuss the issue in more detail below.

But

(94) He did this so that nobody *but I* saw the file; <Narrative by Pip>
(*Great*, p. 76)

(95) There's nobody in the house *but father and me*, and you can rest till you are thoroughly well. <Arabella: Pig-breeder's daughter> (*Jude*, p. 367)

(96) Not a soul knew of it, *but Col. and Mrs. Forster, and Kitty and me*, except my aunt, for we were forced to borrow one of her gowns; <Lydia: Gentleman's daughter> (*Pride*, p. 169)

Except

(97) All *except her* and his kind sister Lady Jane, whose gentle nature had tamed and won him, scared the worthy colonel; <Narrative>
(*Vanity*, p. 617)

(98) 'Yes, they all went *except you and me*....'[11] <John Ferrier: Traveler>

(*Scarlet*, p. 72)
(99) The stranger has gradually improved in health, but is very silent, and appears uneasy when any one *except myself* enters his cabin.
<Letter by Robert Watson> (*Frankenstein*, p. 27)

Save
(100) no one *save he* had given me even so much as a word of sympathy —
<Narrative by Geoffrey> (*Satan*, p. 60)

There is perhaps another syntactic factor to be considered. Quirk et al. note that after indefinite pronouns (e.g., *nobody, everyone, all*) + *but* or *except*, the usage is divided between nominative and objective cases and that there seems to be a tendency in favor of the nominative case after *but* in the "subject territory" (the preverbal subject position) and the objective case in the "object territory" (which includes all noun-phrase positions apart from that immediately preceding the verb) (1985: §6.5). Let us see whether there is a similar tendency observed with our examples in the nominative function.

Table 3.22: Distribution of *but, except, save* in the nominative function according to the subject/object territories

	Subject territory			Object territory		
	I	me	myself	I	me	myself
but	5				2	
except		2	2	1	1	2
save	2					

Note: One example of *except me* used in an isolated phrase is omitted from this table.

The above table shows that, as regards *but* and *save*, the nominative case tends to occur in the subject territory, the objective case in the object territory. With *except*, however, it is not certain. These results hint that *but* and *save* were still regarded as a conjunction while there was no consensus with respect to *except* in the 19th century. The following are some examples given according to each territory.

Subject territory
(101) Nobody *but I* even did him the kindness to call him a dirty boy,
(*Wuthering*, p. 46)
(102) All, *save I*, were at rest or in enjoyment: (*Frankenstein*, p. 136)
(103) The strangest thing of all was, that not a soul in the house, *except me*, noticed her habits, or seemed to marvel at them: (*Jane*, p. 164)
(104) All boys *except herself*; and then they'd cheer her, and then she'd say "Don't be saucy, boys," and suddenly run indoors. (*Jude*, pp. 105–106)

Object territory

(105) Not a soul knew of it, *but Col. and Mrs. Forster, and Kitty and me*, except my aunt, for we were forced to borrow one of her gowns;

(*Pride*, p. 169)

(106) Did any one indeed exist, *except I*, the creator, who would believe, unless his senses convinced him, in the existence of the living monument of presumption and rash ignorance which I had let loose upon the world?

(*Frankenstein*, p. 80)

(107) "I cannot see my prospects clearly to-night, sir; and I hardly know what thoughts I have in my head. Everything in life seems unreal."
"*Except me*: I am substantial enough: — touch me." (*Jane*, p. 279)

(108) They departed early in the morning before any one else was down, *except myself*, ... (*Wildfell*, p. 332)

Some grammarians state that the reflexive pronouns tend to be chosen after *but, except* and *save* in order to avoid the case problem entirely (Quirk et al. 1985: 339). In our texts, reflexive pronouns are quite often used, accounting for nearly one-third of the cases. This is especially so with *except*, where reflexive pronouns count for six of the eleven examples. Judging from the fact that reflexive pronouns (7 exx.) are used mostly by highly educated characters or narrators, they are employed for emphatic purposes or used as what Quirk et al. (1985: 359) call optional pronouns in "semi-emphatic" use. For instance, example (109), which is uttered by the artist who painted the picture of Dorian Gray, could be a typical emphatic use of the reflexive pronoun. Five authors (three women and two men) employ the reflexive pronoun with *except*, but insufficient data prevent any clear conclusion as to whether the use of the reflexive differs according to sex.

(109) 'If Dorian wishes it, of course you must stay. Dorian's whims are laws to everybody, *except himself*.' (*Dorian*, p. 13)

3.4.3 Summary

The usage of pronouns placed after *but, except* and *save* were examined according to nominative/objective functions. While no grammatical violation is found in the objective function, "ungrammatical" objective forms in the nominative function are sometimes employed. All our relevant examples suggest that *but* and *save* are regarded as conjunctions but uncertainty remains about *except*. It is highly possible that the choice of pronouns after *but* and *save* is affected by syntactic factors: the nominative case is likely to occur in the "subject territory" while the objective case is more likely in the "object territory." Reflexive pronouns are sometimes employed, presumably for emphasis.

3.5 *You and I* vs. *you and me*

3.5.1 Overview

Coordinated noun phrases containing pronouns are used both in the nominative and objective functions. In standard English the nominative case is used in the former and the objective case in the latter. This rule has not changed since the 18th century, though grammarians rarely comment on the usage. Cobbett (1819: 98) states that the rule is simple but he admits that the choice of case could sometimes be tricky in a long sentence:

> Take care, in using the personal pronouns, not to employ the *objective case* where you ought to employ *the nominative*; and take care also the *opposite error*. "Him strikes I: Her loves he." These offend the ear at once. But, when a number of words come in between the discordant parts, the ear does not detect the error. "It was some of those, who came hither last night, and went away this morning, who did the mischief, and not my brother and *me*." It ought to be "my brother and *I*."

Referring to the use of coordinated noun phrases in Present-day English, Quirk et al. (1985: 338) argue that "[t]he prescriptive bias in favour of subjective forms appears to account for their hypercorrect use in coordinate noun phrases in 'object territory': *between you and I, as for John and I*, etc."

3.5.2 Nominative position

Let us first consider the relevant coordinated constructions in the nominative function. I will simply use *you and I* as standard form for "NP and *I/we/he/she/they*" and "*I/we/he/she/they* and NP" and *you and me* as nonstandard form for "NP and *me/us/him/her/them*" and "*me/us/him/her/them* and NP." There are a total of 587 of these coordinated constructions in the nominative function, out of which 543 are of the standard *you and I* form (92.5%) and 44 are of the nonstandard *you and me* form (7.5%). The relevant examples are found in less than half the texts (see Figure 3.6). The absolute frequency is much higher with *Great Expectations* and *Treasure Islands*, in which various nonstandard variants are seen.

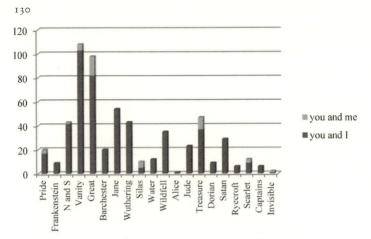

Figure 3.6: Distribution of coordinated pronouns *you and I/me* according to text

The examples of the construction *you and me* all belong to dialogue in the eight texts concerned. I would first like to examine the users of this construction from a sociolinguistic standpoint. There are 21 characters who use the form *you and me*. The characters are classified by social class and sex as shown in Table 3.23.

Table 3.23: Number of characters who use *you and me* in the nominative function classified according to social class and sex

	Male	Female	Child	Total
U	2	1		3
M	4	1		5
L	9	2		11
American	1		1	2
Total	16	4	1	21

The three examples of *you and me* in *Pride and Prejudice* are all used by Lydia Bennet, the youngest daughter of the Bennets. Though her father belongs to the gentry, to his disappointment she is frivolous and indiscreet, lacking the moral code of her society, and is one of the few characters who sometimes utter ungrammatical sentences in the novel. However, expressions like *you and me* are employed by other upper- and middle-class characters, such as Mr. Osborne in *Vanity Fair* and Captain Smollett in *Treasure Island*, as seen in examples (111) and (112). What is common among these examples is that the objective pronoun they use is the first person singular *me*. This suggests that the pronoun *me* is more acceptable than the other objective forms in the construction. Another point to be considered is the order of the pronouns. In example (110), Lydia says "Kitty and me" while Mr. Osborne says "Me and George" in (111). Quirk et al. state that a "*me*-first" phrase such as "Me and Mary" may become "even more 'reprehensible'" because it also violates the rule of politeness that the first person pronouns should occur at the end of the coordinated construction (1985: 338). Although the usage of Mr. Osborne appears to violate this politeness rule, we must take into account another politeness rule in relation to age: Kitty is Lydia's elder sister and George is Mr. Osborne's son. Thus the first person singular pronoun *I/me* can come first in the coordinate noun phrase when the speaker is senior or superior to the other(s).

(110) *Kitty and me* were to spend the day there, and Mrs. Forster promised to have a little dance in the evening;
    <Lydia Bennet: Gentleman's daughter>   (*Pride*, p. 169)
(111) 'You are a good fellow, William,' said Mr. Osborne in a softened voice; 'and *me and George* shouldn't part in anger, that is true... .'
    <Mr. Osborne: Successful merchant>   (*Vanity*, p. 278)
(112) 'You're a good boy in your line, Jim; but I don't think *you and me*'ll go to sea again... .' <Captain Smollett>   (*Treasure*, p. 185)
(113) "Which dear old Pip, old chap," said Joe, "*you and me* was ever friends... ." <Joe: Blacksmith>   (*Great*, p. 458)
(114) 'Serve him right,' said Sir Pitt; '*him and his fam'ly* has been cheating me on that farm these hundred and fifty years.' <Sir Pitt: Baronet>
                                                                                  (*Vanity*, p. 89)
(115) a. We bargained, *him and I*, and here we are: <Silver: Buccaneer>
                                                                                  (*Treasure*, p. 151)
      b. Ah, you that's young — *you and me* might have done a power of good together!' <Silver: Buccaneer>   (*Treasure*, p. 155)

In example (113), in which Joe the blacksmith in *Great Expectations* uses the form *you and me*, the copula *was* is employed instead of the grammatical *were* after the two pronouns. This illustrates substandard usage by the lower class. In example (114), Sir Pitt, a baronet, seems to use more substandard language than Joe does; he uses the objective form *him* and the singular auxiliary verb *has* for the plural subject. Rebecca, who works as a governess at his house, explained Sir Pitt's usage as follows:

> Sir Pitt might have said 'he and his family', to be sure; but rich baronets do not need to be careful about grammar, as poor governesses must be.
> (*Vanity*, p. 90)

This passage tells us how little some upper-class people care about grammar. Examples (115a) and (115b) are both uttered by Silver, a buccaneer, in

Treasure Island. He uses the nominative *I* in the combination *him and I* and the objective *me* in *you and me*. From his usage of the first person singular pronoun, we can presume that the form *you and me* has been becoming a sort of fixed phrase prior to the other combinations. Two Americans, the survivors of a pioneer party, use the phrase *you and me*. Due to the lack of data, however, it cannot be determined whether this is an Americanism.

The phrase *you and me* has various combinatory patterns both in standard and nonstandard usage (see Table 3.24). The nonstandard form has only a small variation. There are seven combinations in which both standard and nonstandard forms occur. As shown in the table, *you and me* has the highest absolute frequency (17 exx.) followed by NP *and me* (11 exx.), *him and* NP (6 exx.), and *me and* NP (6 exx.). Among these four combinations, the form *you and me* enjoys the highest relative frequency as well. The combination *you and me*, then, enjoys the highest occurrence in both absolute and relative frequency.

Table 3.24: Variation of *you and me* in standard/nonstandard forms

Standard		Nonstandard		Ratio
you and I	49	*you and me*	17	0.35
NP *and I*	176	NP *and me*	11	0.6
he and NP	121	*him and* NP	6	0.05
I and NP	29	*me and* NP	6	0.21
he and I	36	*him and me/I*	2	0.06
you and she	4	*you and her*	1	0.25
she and NP	76	*her and* NP	1	0.01
NP *and he*	8			0.00
NP *and she*	8			0.00
she and I	8			0.00
they and NP	5			0.00
he and she	4			0.00
you and he	4			0.00
he and they	3			0.00
she and he	3			0.00
we and NP	2			0.00
we and they	2			0.00
it and I	1			0.00
she and they	1			0.00
she and you	1			0.00
they and I	1			0.00
you and they	1			0.00
Total	543	Total	44	0.08

Ratio = standard form: nonstandard form

In the previous sections, we have seen a similar phenomenon in the transition from the nominative to the objective; in our 19th-century texts, the pronoun *me* appears more acceptable in constructions like *it is me, younger than me* and *as tall as me*. Although the phrase *you and me* in the subject position is still considered ungrammatical in Present-day English, no one could deny the possibility that it will attain the status of standard usage in the future.

3.5.3 *Between you and me*

In addition to appearing in the nominative position, coordinated pronominal phrases occur as the object of verbs or prepositions as well. Nonstandard combinations to be examined are "NP and *I/we/he/she/they*" and "*I/we/he/she/they* and NP," which will be represented by the *you and I* form. We have 391 examples of constructions of this kind, comprised of 102 verbal objects and 289 prepositional objects.[12] Although grammarians observe that the nominative form is sometimes mistakenly used instead of the objective form in such phrases, there is not a single instance in our corpus in which a mistake of this kind occurs. Seemingly, it is generally far more natural to choose the objective form in the object position than to choose the nominative form in the subject position.

According to Sterling Andrus Leonard (1929: 187–188), *between you and I* is almost universally used in familiar conversation despite its being ungrammatical. Burchifield (1996: 106) notes that "[t]he nation is divided in its use of *between you and me* and *between you and I.*" Dekeyser (1975: 248) quotes Gwynne, who says "Yet how often do we hear even well-educated people say 'They were coming to see my brother and I,'... 'Between you and I.'"[13] In our examination of 19th-century novels, the construction with *between* marks a high frequency: there are 178 examples of this type, nearly half the total number of coordinated noun phrases in the objective function, and the nonstandard *between you and I* type is not found.

The standard *between you and me* type (i.e., *between NP and me/us/him/her/them*; *between me/us/him/her/them and NP*) appears more often in written language than in speech, with 131 examples of the former and 47 examples of the latter. Furthermore, users of *between you and me* are mostly from the upper and middle classes, with only three lower-class characters using it (see Table 3.25).

Table 3.25: Number of characters who use *between you and me* according to social class and sex

	Male	Female	Total
U	13	12	25
M	7	2	9
L	1	2	3
Total	21	16	37

It seems that this construction sounds less colloquial and thus can be used in a formal context. The only lower-class male character using *between you and me* is Nicholas Higgins, who speaks in Lancashire dialect. The following are examples of *between* NP *and me* by Lady Sibyl in *The Sorrows of Satan* and Nicholas in *North and South*.

(116) '... Stand out of the light! — you interpose a shadow *between my god and me*!' <Lady Sibyl>   (*Satan*, p. 299)

(117) 'Yo've no business to go prying into what happened *between Boucher and me*. He's dead, and I'm sorry. That's enough.'
<Nicholas: Millworker>   (*N and S*, p. 326)

In the construction *between A and B*, reflexive pronouns are sometimes used in our texts. According to Quirk et al. (1985: 360), a reflexive pronoun (particularly a first person pronoun) is coordinated with another element, as in "Margaret and *me/myself*." With the reflexive examples included, there are 236 examples of the *between A and B* construction. Table 3.26 shows different combinations of the coordinated elements in *between A and B*. The examples are categorized according to the personal pronoun (pers.), the reflexive pronoun (ref.), the relative pronoun (rel.) and the NP. The most frequent pattern is

Table 3.26: Variation of the coordinated pronouns in *between A and B*

	Without the reflexive			With the reflexive	
pers. + NP	*him and* NP	49	pers. + ref.	*her and himself*	1
	me and NP	41		*him and ourselves*	1
	her and NP	24		*you and myself*	1
	you and NP	12	NP + ref.	NP *and herself*	8
	it and NP	8		NP *and myself*	4
	us and NP	5		NP *and himself*	3
	them and NP	5	ref. + NP	*himself and* NP	7
	him or her and NP	1		*herself and* NP	6
pers. + pers.	*you and me*	10		*myself and* NP	5
	him and her	2		*yourself and* NP	2
	her and me	2		*themselves and* NP	1
	him and me	2	ref. + pers.	*herself and him*	2
	me and him	2		*herself and me*	1
	me and them	2		*himself and her*	1
	you and them	2		*myself and them*	1
	it and him	1		*yourself and me*	1
	me and mine	1		*myself and you*	1
	you and her	1	rel. + ref.	*whom and himself*	3
	you and him	1			
NP + pers.	NP *and me*	10			
	NP *and her*	3			
	NP *and him*	1			
	NP *and you*	1			
rel. + pers.	*which and us*	1			
Total		187			49

pers.: personal pronoun, ref.: reflexive pronoun, rel.: relative pronoun pers. + NP (145 exx.) followed by pers. + pers. (26 exx.), ref. + NP (21 exx.), NP + pers. (15 exx.), ref. + NP (15 exx.), and NP + ref. (15 exx.). This indicates that the non-reflexive pronouns are far more often used than the reflexive pronouns. However, the number of examples with reflexive pronouns (49 exx.; 20.3%) is still significant.

In the foregoing sections, we have observed that reflexive pronouns are used to place emphasis upon some particular person(s). To find out whether reflexive pronouns are employed for an emphatic purpose in *between* phrases, it would be helpful to compare examples in which only non-reflexive pronouns are used with those in which equivalent reflexive pronouns are used. Consider examples (118), (119) and (120). In the case of the combination without a reflexive (e.g., *you and me, me and them, him and her*), some literal physical place is often referred to. In the combinations in which one of the objects is a reflexive pronoun (e.g., *you and myself, myself and them, himself and her*), the distance between two people, whether psychological or physical, is often emphatically illustrated. For instance, in examples (118a), (119a) and (120a), where simply physical space or position is meant by the preposition *between*, non-reflexive pairs *you and me, me and them*, and *him and her* are used, respectively. On the other hand, in examples (118c), (118d), (119b) and (120b), friendship, space and feelings between the two sides are emphasized by the reflexive pronouns seen in the combinations *myself and you, myself and them* and *himself and her*. Example (118b) might be also helpful, but in a different way: Margaret, though angry with Dixon for meddling in the business of her family, does not use the reflexive pronoun. In this case, what she is referring to is the social difference between Dixon as a servant and her mother and herself as the master's family, not that between her mother (*you*) and her (*me*) in the same family. She therefore simply uses the pronoun *me* for herself here despite her heightened mood.

(118) a. why pay an extra place? He's too big to travel bodkin *between you and me*. (*Vanity*, p. 519)
b. Don't let Dixon's fancies come any more *between you and me*, mamma. (*N and S*, p. 128)
c. I like you more than I can say; but I'll not sink into a bathos of sentiment: and with this needle of repartee I'll keep you from the edge of the gulph too; and, moreover, maintain by its pungent aid that distance *between you and myself* most conductive to our real mutual advantage. (*Jane*, p. 273)
d. And, upon the whole, our intimacy was rather a mutual predilection than a deep and solid friendship, such as has since arisen *between myself and you*, Halford, whom, in spite of your occasional

crustiness, I can liken to nothing so well as an old coat, unimpeachable in texture, but easy and loose — (*Wildfell*, p. 36)

(119) a. I was looking at the two, when there came *between me and them*, the housekeeper, with the first dish for the table. (*Great*, p. 210)
b. On a moderate computation, it was many months, that Sunday, since I had left Joe and Biddy. The space interposed *between myself and them*, partook of that expansion, and our marshes were any distance off. (*Great*, p. 183)

(120) a. She was sitting as nearly upright as she ever did, and he had brought a chair close to the sofa, so that there was only the corner of the table *between him and her*. (*Barchester*, I, p. 275)
b. Margaret had just left the room, and he was vexed at the state of feeling *between himself and her*. (*N and S*, p. 119)

In such constructions as *than myself* and *as myself*, the female authors tend to use reflexive pronouns more often than the male authors. I would like to see whether that tendency is also the case with the form *between A and B*. In terms of texts, as Figure 3.7 shows, the authors who use the *between* form consist of eleven males and eight females with all the female authors using the reflexive pronoun at least once. Nine authors use the reflexive pronoun three times or more, among whom six are women. The total statistical data demonstrate that the relative frequency in the use of the reflexive in this construction is indeed higher for the female than for the male authors. (see Table 3.27).

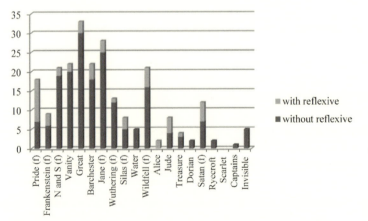

Figure 3.7: Distribution of the reflexive pronouns used in *between A and B*

Table 3.27: Distribution of *between A and B* with/without reflexive pronouns according to sex

	without the reflexive	with the reflexive	Total
Female authors	97 (74.6%)	33 (25.4%)	130
Male authors	90 (84.9%)	16 (15.1%)	106

The above figure also shows that *Pride and Prejudice*, which is the earliest text, enjoys a higher proportion of reflexive pronouns in *between A and B* while the examples with reflexive pronouns are fewer in the later texts, with the exception of *The Sorrows of Satan*. This may suggest that the use of reflexives in *between A and B* decreased during the century but that women continued it into the later period. Some examples are given below. In every instance, the reflexive pronoun is used to put emphasis on the person referred to.

(121) Mrs. Gardiner gave her the particulars also of Miss Bingley's visit in Gracechurch-street, and repeated conversations occurring at different times *between Jane and herself*, which proved that the former had, from her heart, given up the acquaintance. (*Pride*, p. 118)

(122) He felt he might have been pretty sure of his own victory if it had come to a conflict *between Phillotson and himself* for the possession of her.
(*Jude*, p. 149)

(123) Elizabeth's impatience to acquaint Jane with what had happened could no longer be overcome; ... she related to her the next morning the chief of the scene *between Mr. Darcy and herself*. (*Pride*, p. 170)

(124) 'No, my friend! If I were Satan I should probably lament! — for every lost soul would of necessity remind me of my own fall, my own despair — and set another bar *between myself and heaven*! ...' (*Satan*, p. 94)

There seem be two possible reasons to explain the choice of reflexive pronouns in *between A and B*. Firstly, when two persons of the same sex are involved in the story, the reflexive is used to make clear which one is referred to, as seen in examples (121) and (122). Secondly, reflexive pronouns are employed to make a vivid contrast between the two characters; in example (123), "the chief of the scene between Mr. Darcy and herself (Elizabeth)" indicates his proposals and her rejection of them. In (124), "another bar between myself and heaven" means a further obstacle blocking Lucio's way to heaven. In each case, the distance between two sides seems to be outlined by the reflexive pronouns.

3.5.4 Summary

In our 19th-century novels, the use of the nonstandard *you and I* in the objective position was not found. In the nominative position, the nonstandard *you and me* is primarily restricted to speech by lower-class characters, although some well-educated people use the objective form, especially for the first person singular pronoun *me*, yielding another sign of the first person singular *me* being accepted better than the objective forms of other persons. Regarding the coordinated phrases with *between*, the standard objective forms are always employed in our texts. Reflexive pronouns are sometimes chosen both in the nominative and objective positions, presumably in order to make the person referred to by the reflexive clearer or to place emphasis on the difference or the distance between the two sides. This usage is apparently preferred by the female authors though it is on the decline towards the end of the 19th century.

3.6 Overall Summary

With regard to the case problem of personal pronouns, grammatical rules are faithfully observed by our 19th-century authors on the whole. Given that lower-class characters are more likely to be responsible for the occurrence of the objective form in the position where the nominative is required, the forms currently accepted as grammatical such as *It is me, Me!, than me, as me* instead of *It is I, I!, than I (am), as I (am)*, respectively, seem to have been considered solecistic at that time. On the other hand, well-educated characters sometimes use the "ungrammatical" forms in spoken language or in specific syntactic environments. As to pronouns after *but*, *except*, and *save*, the authors' usage is divided, and again syntactic factors are involved.

Although our 19th-century corpus shows that the violation of the rules for the use of pronominal cases is quite limited, we can see signs that the grammatical change in the use of pronominal cases from the nominative to the objective had been gradually proceeding with sociolinguistic, syntactic and stylistic factors being involved. In that process, it is commonly found that the first person singular *me* was more accepted than other persons. In the form *A and B*, for instance, the phrase *you and me* in the nominative position is used among characters of all ranks in speech more frequently than other combinations.

Finally, as to reflexive pronouns chosen instead of personal pronouns in the constructions under examination, it is noteworthy that, in our 19th-century texts, this usage seems not to have been chosen for the avoidance of grammatical mistakes but for stylistic and semantic effects and is noticeably more preferred by the female authors than the male authors.

Notes

1 'Zero' stands for the absence of relative pronouns such as *who* and *that*.
2 Brown (1884: 207) regards "*Me* miserable!" from Milton as an exception as well. We have no example of this variant.
3 Linguistic change in accordance with Pip's education in London to become a gentleman is also argued in Imahayashi (2007b) and Nakayama (2009: 16).
4 Explanatory Notes in *Wuthering Heights* (p. 303).
5 Goldsm. *Stoops to Conq*. IV, Dear me! dear me! I'm sure there is nothing in my behavior to put me on a level with one of that stamp.
6 They are Lady De Courcy in *Barchester Towers*, King in *Through the Looking Glass*, Lady Agatha in *the Picture of Dorian Gray* and Lord Elton in *the Sorrows of Satan*.
7 Examples of *than I am* in which the *be* verb cannot be omitted because it expresses some specific fact or condition of the things (persons) are excluded, as when: (1) comparison is applied to the same person in different situations (e.g., He is better than he was [*Jude*, p. 301]), (2) contrast is made between a possible situation and the actual case with respect to the same person (e.g., She thinks me worse than I am. [*Silas*, p. 170]), (3) comparison is made between different persons in different situations (e.g., No woman was ever nearer to her mate than I am [*Jane*, p. 450]) and (4) special sentences such as the construction "A is no more B than C is D" (e.g., he is no more a major than I am my Lord the marquis [*Vanity*, p. 827]).
8 Example (41) has two instances of *than me*.
9 They are the Brontë sisters, Elizabeth Gaskell, Dickens, Hardy and Gissing.
10 Quirk et al. list *but* and *except* as simple prepositions and *save* as a marginal preposition.
11 In this sentence, the possibility of the collocation of *you and me* cannot be completely ignored.
12 Examples of problematic elements such as *than, but, except* are excluded from the group of prepositions here.
13 *Word to the Wise* (1879: 17–18).

CHAPTER 4
The Nonstandard Usage of Demonstrative Pronouns

In Present-day English, the demonstrative pronouns consist of two singular pronouns (*this*, *that*) and two plural pronouns (*these*, *those*). These pronouns are used as substantives as well as adjectives. As to the use of demonstrative adjectives, George O. Curme (1931: 508) writes:

> Demonstrative limiting adjectives point out persons or things either by gesture, or by the situation, or by an accompanying description. / By gesture: '*Thése* flowers bloom longer than *thóse*,' or in popular speech where there is a great fondness for excess of expression: '*These hére* flowers bloom longer'n *those thére*' (or *them there*). '*Thóse* (in popular speech often *thém*, or *them thére*) flowers are the finest,'

The demonstrative pronouns can also be modified by restrictive relative pronouns (e.g., *that which*; *those that/which/who*). In these constructions, *that* is used for a nonperson while *those* is used for both persons and nonpersons. Since the form *that which* is rare and formal, it is generally replaced by *what* (Quirk et al. 1985: §6.42). This chapter will discuss the grammatical variation of the demonstrative pronoun in our 19th-century texts by focusing on how the demonstrative *them* is used in constructions like (1) *them* + plural noun (*them books*) and (2) *them* + relative pronoun (*them that*). In the latter construction, the pronoun *they* is also used (e.g., *they who*) and will be considered as well.

4.1 *Them books* for *those books*

4.1.1 Overview

The usage of demonstrative adjectives is rather straightforward except that the pronoun *them* is occasionally used for *those*, as in *them books*. According to

Jespersen (1909-49: II, §16.13), "this word *them*, which can hardly be called a 'personal pronoun,' is used without any regard to the case of the substantive it is added to." He also indicates that the usage is not recent, referring to *A New English Dictionary's* examples as early as 1596. Poutsma (1916: 925) notes that, although the practice may be traced back to late Middle English, no instance seems to have been found in Shakespeare. Grammarians' views about *them books* are the same in the 18th and 19th centuries. Priestley (1769: 91) and Murray (1806: 150) similarly note that the "error" of this sort is not only found in conversation but also in writing.

4.1.2 Data and analysis

Ninety instances of *them books* are found scattered throughtout our texts and all these examples belong to dialogue. Figure 4.1 shows the distribution of *them books/those books* per text. The nonstandard variant is attested in the texts in which local dialects are frequently seen (i.e., *North and South, Wuthering Heights, Silas Marner, The Invisible Man* and *Jude the Obscure*) and in those in which various kinds of social dialects are attested (i.e., *Great Expectations, Treasure Island* and *Captains Courageous*). Moreover, the prevalence of this nonstandard form is even higher than that of its standard counterpart in two texts, *Treasure Island* and *Captains Courageous*.

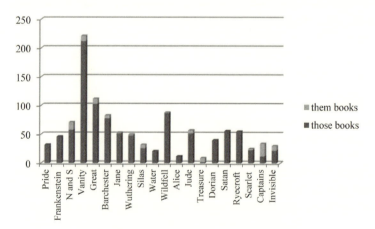

Figure 4.1: Distribution of *those books* and *them books* according to text

These findings suggest that *them books* is used primarily in certain regions and communities. Wales (1996: 100) states that the nonstandard *them books* is pervasive in many mainstream dialects including the London vernacular but that this usage is stigmatized by many "outsiders." Pervasive as the variant is in some of our texts, it is not certain whether the usage is stigmatized or not. This should be examined by consulting individual examples.

The examples of *them books* are employed by 47 characters in total. Let us consider their usage from a sociolinguistic perspective. Table 4.1 shows what kinds of characters use *them* for *those* in this construction in terms of social class and sex.

Table 4.1: Number of characters who use *them books* classified according to social class and sex

	Male	Female	Child	Total
U	2	1		3
M	7	4		11
L	17	8	1	26
American	6		1	7
Total	32	13	2	47

As far as absolute frequency is concerned, we can see that lower-class characters and working-class Americans account for 33 of the total cases, followed by middle- and upper-class speakers. The 47 users of *them books* include six seamen in *Captains Courageous* and four seamen (including buccaneers) in *Treasure Island*, which indicates that the usage is part of the language of the seamen's community. The most frequent user of *them books* is Dan in *Captains Courageous*, the skipper's son and a seaman himself. He uses the variant twelve times. The form is thus preferred among seamen. The second most frequent user is Nicholas (7 exx.) in *North and South*. In this text, where the contrast between the North and the South is illustrated in people's language and life, not only Nicholas, a millworker from the North, but also Dixon, a female servant from the South, uses the form. It follows that a certain nonstandard language is shared by working-class people from both regions. The third most frequent user is Magwitch the convict (5 exx.) in *Great Expectations*. His speech may be considered what Wales (1996:100) calls "the London vernacular." The form *them books* is also used by lower-class villagers in the South East in *Jude the Obscure*, those in the South in *The Invisible Man* and those in the Midlands in *Silas Marne*. All this suggests that the form serves as a regional marker as well as a social marker. Some examples used by lower-class characters are as follows:

(1) 'Look at *them boats* thet hev edged up sence mornin'. They're all waitin' on dad. See 'em, Harve?' <Dan: Seaman>   (*Captains*, p. 40)

(2) 'Thank yo, Miss. Bessy'll think a deal o' *them flowers*; ...'
    <Nicholas: Millworker>   (*N and S*, p. 72)

(3) There are three people I love: it's missus, Master Frederick, and her. Just *them three*. <Dixon: Servant>   (*N and S*, p. 131)

(4)   "You bring me, to-morrow morning early, that file and *them wittles*... ."
      <Magwitch: Convict>   (*Great*, p. 6)

Three upper-class users of *them books* are Mr. and Mrs. O'Dowds, an Irish born Major and his wife, and Sir Pitt in *Vanity Fair*. Middle-class users include five local tenant farmers from the southern part of England in *Barchester Towers* and a mill owner's sister in *North and South*. According to Wright (1905: 279), the standard *those* is seldom or never heard in genuine dialects in Scotland, Ireland or England. Therefore, it is not strange that the Irish couple and the five farmers should use the variant. The examples drawn from upper- and middle-class characters may illustrate that dialectal elements are stronger than social elements, since social dialects tend to be avoided by the educated while local dialects are not. An exceptional case is Baronet Sir Pitt, who frequently uses nonstandard speech without paying proper attention to grammar. He does not care about the social consequences of his vulgar speech, which is an attitude not rarely seen among the nobles (Görlach 1999: 38).[1] In example (8), the use of *them rabble* by Jane, a mill owner's sister, in *North and South*, may have been related to her agitated mood when she saw a riot break out just outside her house. It is interesting to note that Jane uses *not me* instead of *not I*, the former presumably being inappropriate usage for middle-class people at that time.

(5)   *Them husbands* are always in the way, Mrs. Osborne, my dear;
      <Mrs. O'Dowd: Major's wife>   (*Vanity*, p. 329)
(6)   'Now I likes this place better, cause I be more at home like, and don't have to pay for *them fine clothes* for the missus... .'
      <Mr. Greenacre: Tenant Farmer>   (*Barchester*, II, p. 135)
(7)   'Don't move none of *them trunks*,' he cried, pointing with a pipe which he held in his hand. <Sir Pitt: Baronet>   (*Vanity*, pp. 500–501)
(8)   'Not me, ma'am, if you please,' said Jane, shrinking back. '*Them rabble* may be all about; I don't think the cut is so deep, ma'am, as it looks.'
      <Jane: Mill owner's sister>   (*N and S*, p. 181)

According to Brook (1963: 106), forms like *them there books* and *they books* are attested especially in the South and Midlands. Our samples include two instances of *them there* NP but none of *they* NP. Forms like *them there* NP are used by two characters in *Vanity Fair* who are both from the southern part of England, though their social classes are different: one is Sir Pitt the baronet from the upper class and the other is a nameless coachman from the lower class. In example (10), the coachman omits *h* at the beginning of words as in *osses* for *horses* and *ospital* for *hospital*, which is typically observed in much of

England.²

(9)   'There's an avenue,' said Sir Pitt, 'a mile long. There's six thousand pound of timber in *them there trees*. Do you call that nothing?'
      <Sir Pitt: Baronet>   (*Vanity*, p. 89)

(10) The coachman, who grumbled that his osses should be brought out and his carriage made into an ospital for that old feller and Mrs. O., drove her with the utmost alacrity now, and trembling lest he should be superseded by Mr. Osborne's coachman, asked 'what *them there Russell Square coachmen* knew about town, and whether *they* was fit to sit on a box before a lady?' (Italicized "they" in the original) <a coachman>
                                                            (*Vanity*, p. 779)

Although Sir Pitt does not mind saying something like *them books*, the educated usually try to avoid the expression. See the examples below by Lewis Carroll. Example (11a) is from *Alice's Adventures in Wonderland* and example (11b) from his original manuscript, entitled *Alice's Adventures under Ground*.

(11) a. 'but *those* serpents! There's no pleasing them!'   (*Alice*, p. 47)
      b. "but *them* serpents! There's no pleasing 'em!"
                                              (*Alice's Adventures under Ground*)

These examples reveal that the author changed his original "them serpents" to "those serpents" in the published version. Note also that Carroll changes the shortened pronoun *'em* to the full standard form *them*.³ The correction is probably due to the author's concern about the nonstandard or incorrect usage. He would have had a chance to explain the "incorrect" usage to Alice Liddell in person if he wished. However, it would have been impossible to do so for the many more Alices who would have received the published copies. It seems likely that he took the safer course by changing the controversial part before publication for fear that children might innocently pick up the nonstandard forms. Writers of children's books are usually forced to avoid such words or clearly inform the readers about their ungrammatical nature in texts of this kind (Nakayama 2011b). Carroll's correction of the terms *them serpents* can serve as evidence to show that such usage was generally associated with the undereducated.

4.2 *Them that* for *those that*

4.2.1 Overview

While grammarians have listed the use of *them* for *those* for the demonstrative adjective as ungrammatical since the 18th century on, they are not unanimous on the modification of demonstrative pronouns by restrictive relative clauses. Jespersen (1909–49: II, §16. 372) states that "*those* is frequent before a relative clause in the indefinite sense of 'some.'" More specifically, when postmodified by restrictive relative clauses and other relative modifiers, the demonstrative pronouns are used as follows:

> *Those* who try hard deserve to succeed.
> These watches are more expensive than *those* which/that we saw in New York (cited from Quirk et al. 1985: 6.42).

Murray (1806: 150) has a different view; he criticizes the replacement of *they* with *those* in the relevant constructions though he admits that the choice between *them* and *those* in the modified object position is not easy to decide:

> We also frequently meet with *those* instead of *they*, at the beginning of a sentence, and where there is no particular reference to an antecedent; as, "*Those* that sow in tears, sometimes reap in joy." *They* that, or *they* who sow in tears.
> It is not, however, always easy to say, whether a personal pronoun or a demonstrative is preferable, in certain constructions. "We are not unacquainted with the calumny of *them* [or *those*] who openly make use of the warmest professions."

Hazlitt (1810: 119) considers *these* and *those* are better than *they* and *them* in the relevant construction, especially when used for things:

> We may use either *they* and *them*, or *these* and *those*, when a relative pronoun immediately follows; but it is in general better to make use of the latter, and particularly as applied to things. "*Those* or *they* who find fault," &c. "*Those* which are the most approved," &c.

Cobbett (1819: 111) readily supports the pronoun *those* when modified by restrictive relative pronouns. In order to explain the difference in use between *they* + rel. and *those* + rel., he cites the following examples for each usage: "They, who can write, save a great deal of bodily labour" and "Those who can write, save a great deal of bodily labour." The lack of consensus among grammarians in Late Modern English will make it all the more interesting to see how the three relevant variants (*those, they, them*) are actually used in our 19th-century texts.

4.2.2 Data and analysis

The distribution of the three forms modified by restrictive relative clauses in our corpus is shown in Figure 4.2. The commonest form is *those* + rel. (447 exx.; 89.8%), followed by *them* + rel. (44 exx.; 8.8%) and *they* + rel. (7 exx.; 1.4%). These proportions conform to Poutsuma's description of the use of these variants in Present-day English: "Much rarer is the use of *they* to replace either *these* or *those*" (1916: 925).

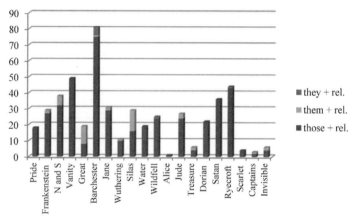

Figure 4.2: Distribution of *those/them/they* modified by restrictive relative clauses according to text

One noteworthy point is that unlike the construction *them books* observed above, the constructions *them/they* + rel. are not restricted to dialogue; they are also attested in narrative and in quotation. It is also noted that the examples found in quotation are all from the Scriptures. In other words, the constructions *them/they* + rel. were primarily used in written context in earlier times. This is especially the case with the construction *they* + rel.

Table 4.2: *Them/they* modified by restrictive relative clauses classified according to register

	them + rel.	*they* + rel.
Dialogue	42	1
Narrative	2	6
Quotation	5	4
Total	49	11

The OED lists examples of *them that* and *they that* from as early as the beginning of the 11th century. Examples (12) to (14) are of the construction *them* + rel. found in narrative and (15) is taken from a passage of the Scriptures quoted in dialogue.

(12) Would not the first of *them who* saw me wring my neck like a snipe's? <Narrative by Jim> (*Treasure*, p. 77)

(13) *they whose* suspicions had been such gall and wormwood to my soul. <Narrative by Gilbert> (*Wildfell*, p. 419)

(14) If *they who* give such laborious parties, and who endure such toil and turmoil in the vain hope of giving them successfully, really enjoyed the parties given by others, the matter could be understood. <Narrative> (*Barchester*, II, p. 93)

(15) But 'tis as Job said: "Now *they that* are younger than I have me in derision, whose fathers I would have disdained to have set with the dogs of my flock." <Job 30:1> (*Jude*, p. 11)

In example (15), the speaker (a baker) incorporates Job's words from the KJV into her daily talk, which leads us to assume that the usage was familiar to anyone regardless of social class at that time. It is noteworthy that the *New Revised Standard Version* (1989) or NRSV Bible replaces *they that* with *those who* so that the text reads: "But now they make sport of me, *those who* are younger than I, whose fathers I would have disdained to set with the dogs of my flock." Likewise, *Jane Eyre* and *The Sorrows of Satan* quote Matthew's "bless *them that* curse you; do good to *them that* hate you" (5: 44) from the KJV while the NRSV reads "pray for *those who* persecute you." These revisions illustrate that the then-standard constructions *them/they* + rel. have fallen out of use by the late 20th century. Among the characters who use the archaic constructions *them/they* + rel. are three well-educated characters: Henry Ryecroft the writer, Jane Eyre the governess and the monster in *Frankenstein*, who is self-educated. Example (16), in which Jane addresses St. John, has a religious tone in common with the Scriptures, while Rycroft uses the construction in a decree — a very literal style — in example (17).

CHAPTER 4 THE NONSTANDARD USAGE OF DEMONSTRATIVE PRONOUNS   149

(16) "I'll be preparing myself to go out as a missionary to preach liberty to *them that* are enslaved–your Harem inmates amongst the rest... ."
       <Jane: Governess>   (*Jane*, p. 269)

(17) To every man is it decreed: thou shalt live alone. Happy *they who* imagine that they have escaped the common lot; happy, whilst they imagine it. Those to whom no such happiness has ever been granted at least avoid the bitterest of disillusions. <Ryecroft: Writer>   (*Ryecroft*, p. 44)

The speakers in examples (18) and (19) are both local servants in Yorkshire. Their language has a lot of regional flavor but it should be mentioned that Joseph, an old, local religious man refers to "whet t' Scripture ses." Here he is touching on Romans 8:28 in the *KJV*: "All things work together for good to *them that* love God." The author, Emily Brontë, probably intended the *as* for *that* to reflect regional dialect in his speech. The variant *them* is revised into *those* in the *NRSV*. The form *them as* in Joseph's utterance is therefore patterned half on the Scriptures and half on dialectal use. Regarding the diarectal relative *as*, I will discuss more in detail below.

(18) Ah, childer! that's t' last o' t' old stock — for ye and Mr. St. John is like of a different soart to *them 'at's* gone; ('at's = that is)
       <Hannah: Servant>   (*Jane*, p. 334)
(19) All warks togither for gooid tuh *them as* is chozzen, and piked aht froo' th' rubbidge! Yah knaw whet t' Scripture ses — " <Joseph: Servant>
                                                                                                  (*Wuthering*, p. 76)

In the case of Joseph, the pronoun *them* is followed by the relative pronoun *as* while the same pronoun is followed by *that* in all the other five examples extracted from the *KJV* Bible. In the case of *they* + rel., the pronoun *they* is followed by *that* and *who* twice each. It might be helpful to examine the combination of *them/they* + rel. in relation to which kind of relative pronoun is placed after the demonstrative pronouns. Furthermore, since the pronoun *those* is replaced either by *them* or *they* in the subject position while replaced only by *them* in the object position, these variants will be discussed with reference to their syntactic position.

Let us first examine the use of *them/they* in the subject position. The examples found in the quotation from the Scriptures are excluded here since they are not written by the authors themselves. For the sake of comparison, the examples of the commonest construction *those* + rel. will also be examined. Table 4.3 shows the distribution of *those/them/they* + rel. according to the modifying restrictive relative clauses.

Table 4.3: *Those/them/they* modified by restrictive relative clauses in the subject position

Modifying relatives	Standard *those* + rel.	Nonstandard *them* + rel.	*they* + rel.
who	80		6
that	11	5	
which	8		
whom	2		
prep. + *whom*	4		
whose			1
prep. + *whose*	2		
zero	4		
as		7	
Total	111 (85.4%)	12 (9.2%)	7 (5.4%)

The commonest construction of the three is *those* + rel., which has seven different patterns with six modifying relative pronouns (*who, that, which, whom, whose* and zero). The relative pronoun *as* is not used in this construction. The following are examples of the seven types of *those* + rel.

Those + rel.
(20) *Those who* are faithful know only the trivial side of love: (*Dorian*, p. 10)
(21) *Those that* wish to be clean, clean they will be; and *those that* wish to be foul, foul they will be.   (*Water*, p. 13)
(22) Small rooms are *those which* require costly fittings and rich furniture.
   (*Barchester*, I, p. 88)
(23) *Those whom* she sentenced were taken into custody by the soldiers, ...
   (*Alice*, p. 82)
(24) *Those to whom* no such happiness has ever been granted at least avoid the bitterest of disillusions.   (*Ryecroft*, p. 44)
(25) It was not to be supposed that any other people could be meant than *those with whom* she was connected.   (*Pride*, p. 143)
(26) Our weakest motives were *those of whose* nature we were conscious.
   (*Dorian*, p. 48)
(27) "... and then *those* you term weak are very capable of being as obstinate as you!"   (*Wuthering*, p. 87)

The constructions *them* + rel. and *they* + rel. show only limited variations. As for *them* + rel., only two relatives, *that* and *as*, are used, the latter appearing only after *them*. According to the *OED*, the relative pronoun *as* is occasionally used instead of *who* or *that* in dialectal speech. The earliest example of the form *those as* is attested in 1603.[4]

The antecedent *such* is also replaced by *that, those*, or entirely omitted, leaving *as* an ordinary *rel. pron.* = That, who, which. Cf. Norse use of *som*. *Obs.* in standard English, but common *dial.* in England and the United States. (s.v. *as, adv. [conj.*, and *rel. pron.*], B.24.*a*.)

Hosoe (1935: 217) states that since the relative pronoun *as* is occasionally used instead of *who* in dialectal speech, the standard *those who* generally becomes *them as* in dialects. This is the case with our 19th-century texts. The twelve examples of the form *them as/that* are used in dialectal speech by five lower-class characters. The users of *them as* are: Dolly (5 exx.), a wheelwright's wife in *Silas Marner*; Mrs. Hall (1 ex.), an innkeeper in *The Invisible Man*; and Nicholas Higgins (1 ex.), a millworker in *North and South*. Those using *them that* are Nicholas Higgins (2 exx.) again, Orlick (2 exx.), a Journeyman in *Great Expectations*, and Silver (1 exx.), a buccaneer in *Treasure Island*. It seems that the forms *them as/that* in the subject position belong to dialectical speech, whether regional or social.

Them + rel.
(28)   *Them as* stops in this house comes in by the doors, — that's the rule of the house, ... <Mrs. Hall: Innkeeper>   (*Invisible*, p. 35)
(29)   '... *Them that* die'll be the lucky ones.' <Silver: Buccaneer>
                                                            (*Treasure*, p. 108)

The pronoun *they* tends to be followed by *who* in the relevant construction just as the standard *those* does. All of the seven examples are used by the narrators of *Barchester Towers* (6 exx.) and *Wildfell Hall* (1 ex). This indicates that the usage was accepted as standard even in written language at that time, which conforms to what Murray mentions at the beginning of this section.

They + rel.
(30)   Work is now required from every man who receives wages; and *they who* have to superintend the doing of work, and the paying of wages, are bound to see that this rule is carried out. <Narrative>
                                                            (*Barchester*, I, p. 112)
(31)   *they whose* suspicions had been such gall and wormwood to my soul. <Narrative by Gilbert>   (*Wildfell*, p. 419)

I will next examine the use of *those/them* modified by a restrictive relative clause in the object position. There is no example of *they* + rel., probably due to case discrepancy between the nominative form and the object position. The combinations of *those/them* + rel. are shown in Table 4.4. The construction *them* + rel., when in the object position, represents 8.7 percent of the total examples, just below its rate of appearance in the subject position (9.2%), which suggests that *them* + rel. is almost equally used in both subject and object positions in our texts. From either a historical or dialectal perspective, it is not unusual for the nominative case to be replaced by the objective case, but the opposite transition is rare.[5]

Table 4.4: *Those/them* modified by restrictive relative clauses in the object position

Modifying relatives	Standard *those* + rel.	Nonstandard *them* + rel.
who	210	2
that	10	7
which	22	7
prep. + *which*	4	
whom	24	
prep. + *whom*	14	
whose	9	1
zero	43	
as		15
Total	336 (91.3%)	32 (8.7%)

The variation of relative pronouns after the objective *those* is quite similar to that of the nominative *those*; it is modified by six kinds of relatives (*who, what, which, whom, whose,* and zero) in eight different patterns, with the relative pronoun *who* enjoying the highest proportion. Prepositions are sometimes placed before such relatives as *which* and *whom*. The following are examples of the eight different types of *those* + rel.

Those + rel.
(32) You'd like to see her taken care of by *those who* can leave her well off, and make a lady of her; (*Silas*, p. 162)
(33) I was unwilling to quit the sight of *those that* remained to me; and, above all, I desired to see my sweet Elizabeth in some degree consoled.
(*Frankenstein*, p. 44)
(34) He was void of any of those feelings which actuate men to do good. But he was perhaps equally void of *those which* actuate men to do evil.
(*Barchester*, II, pp. 162–163)
(35) But I was guilty at times of mere self-indulgence; a book tempted me, a book which was not one of *those for which* I really craved, a luxury which prudence might bid me forego. (*Ryecroft*, p. 30)
(36) He believed *those whom* he wished to get under his hoof, the Grantlys and Gwynnes of the church, to be the enemies of that religion.
(*Barchester*, I, p. 136)
(37) And I do not think it of light importance that he should have attentive and conciliatory manners towards every body, especially towards *those*

CHAPTER 4 THE NONSTANDARD USAGE OF DEMONSTRATIVE PRONOUNS 153

to whom he owes his preferment. (*Pride*, p. 77)
(38) He loved to stroll through the gaunt cold picture-gallery of his country house and look at the various portraits of *those whose* blood flowed in his veins. (*Dorian*, p. 117)
(39) A small kindness from *those* she loved made that timid heart grateful.
(*Vanity*, p. 710)

The variant *them* is most frequently modified by *as* (15 exx.) followed by *that* (7 exx.) and *which* (7 exx.). The relative *as* is used only with the pronoun *them*. Unlike *them* + rel. in the subject position, which is considered nonstandard usage, the use of *them* + rel. in the object position is difficult to explain from a sociolinguistic standpoint. The 32 examples of the relevant construction are used by nineteen people: thirteen are of the lower class; the remaining six are well-educated, including two narrators. Concerning the relatives following *them*, fifteen examples of the form *them as* are used by nine people presumably as dialectal speech, as in example (40). The exceptional case comes from the narrator of *Barchester Towers*, in which the relative pronoun *as* is used in the collocation *such – as* (see example [41]). The variant *them* followed by a relative other than *as* is used by both the uneducated and the educated, as shown in examples (42) through (46).

Them + rel.
(40) '... and you could put your trust i' *Them as* knows better nor we do, seein' you'd ha' done what it lies on us all to do.'
<Dolly: Wheelwright's wife> (*Silas*, p. 81)
(41) And 'the fourteen' — or such of *them as* were old enough to hope and discuss their hopes, talked over their golden future. <Narrative>
(*Barchester*, II, p. 176)
(42) God forbid that I should say a sojer or sailor, or commercial gent from the towns, or any of *them that* be slippery with poor women!
<Sarah: Village girl> (*Jude*, p. 45)
(43) "I'll be preparing myself to go out as a missionary to preach liberty to *them that* are enslaved — your Harem inmates amongst the rest... ."
<Jane: Governess> (*Jane*, p. 269)
(44) Would not the first of *them who* saw me wring my neck like a snipe's?
<Narrative by Jim> (*Treasure*, p. 77)
(45) "Boy! Let your behaviour here be a credit unto *them which* brought you up by hand!"<Mr. Pumblechook: Corn-chandler> (*Great*, p. 54)
(46) '... Don't go taggin' araound efter *them whose* eyes bung out with fatness, accordin' to Scripcher.' <Salters: Fisherman> (*Captains*, p. 136)

We have above observed that the language of the Scriptures is closely involved in that of our 19th-century novels, but it is not always so. In example (46), Salters, an American fisherman, remarks on *"them whose* eyes bung out with fatness" in reference to Psalm 73:7 in the *KJV: "Their* eyes stand out with fatness." The disagreement between *them whose* and *their*, however, demonstrates that the form *them whose* here is not affected by the 17th-century Bible. The variant *them* in this case should therefore be considered as social dialect. As regards the use of the construction *them* + rel., it is not easy to see whether it is dialectal or archaic. In order to decide which usage is applied it would be necessary to examine what place the speakers are from, what social status they belong to, and how conservative they are.

4.3 Summary

The present section has discussed the usage of the demonstrative adjective *them* for *those* (e.g., *them books*) and the demonstrative pronouns *them/they* for *those*. As to the demonstrative adjective, the relevant examples are found only in dialogue. Since the speakers use *them books* for *those books* either as regional or social dialects, it is safe to say that the form was regarded as nonstandard at that time. Although the majority of users of this form belong to the lower class, upper-class people use it when inclined to dialectal usage in a given region. On the other hand, the usage of the demonstrative pronoun *those* is not so simple. The examples of the apparently nonstandard construction *them/they* + rel. are found both in dialogue and in narrative. The usage of *them* + rel. in the subject position is similar to that of *them books*; the construction is used either as regional or social dialect. When *they* + rel. and *them* + rel. are used in the subject position and in the object position, respectively, these constructions are either dialectal or archaic (or literary). It is to be noted, however, that the relative pronoun *as* following *them/they* is limited to dialectal speech. To sum up, the literary usage of *them/they* + rel. had been falling out of use in the 19th century, while the dialectal usage survived until it came to be labeled as nonstandard usage by later grammarians.

Notes
1 He notes that "[s]ince the craze for correctness was a predominantly middle-class feature, it could lead to the seeming paradox that 'non-standard' features were retained in the lower and upper classes."
2 The loss of *h* is seen in traditional dialects except for two geographically peripheral parts of

CHAPTER 4 THE NONSTANDARD USAGE OF DEMONSTRATIVE PRONOUNS   155

England, the northeast and East Anglia (Trudgill 1999: 28–30).
3 Russell Ash notes in the "Introduction" to *Alice's Adventures under Ground* (1985: 13) that in 1864, Carroll privately presented the manuscript as a Christmas gift to a girl named Alice Liddell, then aged ten, and published it in 1865 after many changes and much expansion.
4 "To those *as* have no children." – HOLLAND, *Plurarch's Morals*, 222.
5 The history of English shows that the second person pronoun nominative *ye* has been replaced by the objective *you* in Modern English, and today the objective case is used after a *be* verb instead of the nominative case as in "it is *me*." In dialectal usage it is common to use the objective case in the subject position as in "you and *me* are."

CHAPTER 5

The Rivalry between Relative Pronoun Variants

In Present-day English, the relative pronouns are *who, whom, whose, which, what, that* and the zero relative. Historically speaking, *that* is the oldest among them, tracing back to the demonstrative pronoun *þæt* in Old English. As a rule, the relative sentence was introduced by a demonstrative pronoun or a particle of probably demonstrative character. In Old English, the definite articles (*sē, sēo, þæt*) were first used as relatives, either by themselves or along with the indeclinable particle *þe*. At the end of the Old English period, the particle *þe* had become the most usual relative pronoun but early in Middle English its place was taken by *þæt* (*that*). This was a common relative all through the Middle English period. As for *wh*-relatives, the simple interrogative pronouns *who* and *which* occurred as generalizing relatives in late Old English and early Middle English. In the 15th century, *which* began to be alternately used with *that*. *Who* appeared frequently in the 16th century and eventually replaced *that* (partly) and *which* in reference to persons in the 18th century. (cf. Kellner 1892: 204–205, 208; Mustanoja 1960: 192; Hansen and Nielsen 2007: 157; Baugh and Cable 2002: 245).

The systematized guidelines for the use of relative pronouns were established by prescriptive grammarians in the 18th century and have been largely preserved ever since; it is required, for instance, that the *wh*-relative pronouns *who* and *whom* be used for persons and *which* for nonpersons, and except for certain cases *that* is alternately used in place of *which* but not of *who* or *whom*. However, there are some grammatical variations in the use of the relatives, as seen in the choice of *who* or *whom* in the objective function and that of *whose* or *of which* for non-personal antecedents, both of which I will investigate in this chapter.

5.1 *Whom* vs. *who*[1]

5.1.1 Overview

The originally nominative form *who*, which started to replace *whom* at the beginning of early Middle English, has become more common in the object function today than *whom*. Edward Sapir (1921: 156) indicates that this transition is part of the development of English from a synthetic to an analytic language, predicting the demise of *whom* within a couple of hundred years of his time.[2] The choice between *whom* and *who* now seems to be a matter more related to formal/informal contexts than to grammatical usage. Quirk et al. (1985: §6.35) state:

> In many ways the opposition between *who* and *whom* does not parallel the subjective/objective distinction in the personal pronouns. *Whom* is largely restricted to formal style, and can be avoided altogether in informal style, through the use of *who*, *that*, or zero.

However, *who* has only recently established its present common use. Criticism against this recent practice seems to have existed even in the 20th century.

> The form *whom* is chiefly written English, although <u>schoolmasters are persistently labouring to revive the form in the spoken language</u>; it is supposed to be required when the pronoun is a direct object or when it is used in a prepositional adjunct (Kruisinga 1932: §1045). (Underline mine)

This kind of voice was much louder in the previous century. Of the use of *whom/who*, the majority of grammarians in both the 18th and 19th centuries proposed a traditional prescription. As Lowth (1769: 105) says:

> The Relative is the Nominative Case to the Verb, when no other Nominative comes between it and the verb: but when another nominative comes between it and the Verb, the Relative is governed by some word in its own member of the Sentence: as, "The God, *who* preserveth me; *whose* I am, and *whom* I serve [8]."

Grammarians' influence on the use of *whom/who* seems to have been considerable. David Denison (1998: 277) describes the trajectory of its grammatical use as follows:

The *OED* is able to trace the use of *who* in object functions back to ME, though the editors of the first edition were reassured that relative *who* used 'ungrammatically' for *whom* was 'now' (i.e. 1924) rare or obsolete as a relative except in the indefinite sense of 'whomever'! (s.v. *who* pron. 13). If true, it suggests that prescriptivism had temporarily reversed a long-term trend; the second edition more realistically states that it is 'still common colloquially.'

On the other hand, it is also reported that the "errors" in the use of *whom/who* were most frequently seen at that time (Priestley 1769: 107; Cobbett 1819: 105). It would therefore be interesting to find out how the grammarians' rule worked to avoid the objective form *who* in the 19th century before it came to be commonly used.

5.1.2 Interrogative and relative pronouns

Since the case problem of *whom/who* is seen in the interrogative pronoun as well as the relative pronoun, both usages will be examined. In our 19th-century texts, there are 1,101 examples of the objective *whom/who* as a relative pronoun and 76 as an interrogative pronoun. As shown in Table 5.1, the objective *whom* is dominantly employed both in the relative (99.8%) and in the

Table 5.1: Distribution of the objective *whom/who* in the relative/interrogative pronoun

	Relative pronouns		Interrogative pronouns	
	whom	who	whom	who
Pride (f)	83		1	2
Frankenstein (f)	78	1	2	
N and S (f)	64		5	4
Vanity	308		11	
Great	80		7	
Barchester	123		9	1
Jane (f)	50		8	
Wuthering (f)	16		2	
Silas (f)	24			1
Water	13		1	
Wildfell (f)	41		7	1
Alice	3			
Jude	55		2	1
Treasure	14			
Dorian	26		2	
Satan (f)	77	1	7	
Ryecroft	21			
Scarlet	17			
Captains	5			2
Invisible	1			
Total	1,099 (99.8%)	2 (0.2%)	64 (84.2%)	12 (15.8%)

interrogative (84.2%), which represents a complete reversal of the situation today. The instructions by contemporary normative grammarians in the choice of *who* or *whom* is strictly observed. Our statistical data on the whole agree with Dekeyser (1975: 195), who concludes that no shift in favor of *who* in the objective case took place during the 19th century. He presents 1,179 occurrences (99.6%) for the relative *whom* as compared with five (0.4%) for *who* and 25 occurrences (69.4%) for *whom* in interrogative clauses compared with 11 (30.5%) for *who*.

The objective *who* is thus sparsely used throughout our texts and no signs are seen that report its increased use. Limited as its occurrence is, there is one noteworthy point concerning its usage in terms of authors' sex. Out of the nine texts where the objective *who* is found, six are written by female authors while out of the eleven texts where the form is not found, nine are written by male authors. This means that the women are less hesitant to use the deviant variant than are the men. Kruisinga (1932: §1055) insightfully writes that the objective *who* is sometimes used "either by writers who refuse to modify genuine English in obedience to traditional rules founded on ignorance, or by those who are willing to conform to them but in whom nature is occasionally stronger than the memory of school teaching." If our data correctly reflect the difference between men and women in the use of *whom/who* in this period, the female authors apparently fit those who preferred "ungrammatical" but less artificial forms and thus refused to be bound to the rule.

The above table also demonstrates that the objective *who* had started to be used in interrogative clauses. It is reported that the interrogative *who* in the object function gained ground faster than its relative counterpart (Schneider 1992a: 443). Our data support this observation. Jespersen (1933: 137) claims that the form *whom* tends to be displaced by *who* in the interrogative pronoun more than in the relative pronoun "evidently because the relative as object is not followed immediately by the verb." Apart from this syntactic factor, written/spoken contexts might be involved in the higher occurrence of *who* in the interrogative pronoun. That is, as seen in Table 5.2, the interrogative pronoun is more often employed in speech than in written language. In general, nonstandard forms are more casually used in speech. This might have something to do with the higher occurrence of the interrogative *who* in the object function as a whole.

Table 5.2: Distribution of the relative and interrogative pronouns *whom/who* in written/spoken language

	Written		Spoken	
	whom	*who*	*whom*	*who*
Relative	923	2	176	
Interrogative	25	1	39	11

The above table shows that both in the relative and the interrogative *whom* is preferred to *who* but the latter is chosen mostly in speech. Indeed, as to the interrogative pronoun, when *who* is used it appears in speech in all examples except for one. Whether for syntactic or contextual reasons, or both, it is assumed that the use of *who* began in spoken language. I will consider later two exceptional instances of the relative pronoun *who* in writing.

5.1.2.1 Interrogative *whom/who*

In reference to the historical transition from *whom* to *who* over the larger span, the proportion of the objective *who* in our texts is inexplicably low. According to Toshio Saito (1980), the proportion of the interrogative objective form *who* in prose dramatically increased in the latter half of the 16th century and outnumbered *whom* in the middle of the 17th century. The preference for *who* increased until the end of the 18th century, marking the establishment of the use of *who* in colloquial English. He separately surveyed the proportion of *whom* and *who* in plays in the latter half of the 20th century, presenting the overwhelming dominance of *who* (*whom* : *who* = 11: 95). In his diachronic study of the interrogative *whom/who*, the 19th century was somehow overlooked. He assumes the continual increase during the century, though indicating the possible influence of prescriptive grammars which made people "grammar-conscious." The overwhelming predominance of *whom* (*whom* : *who* = 64 : 12) in the middle of a transition from *whom* to *who* would have to be attributed to the influence of the grammarians in this period.

As is seen, the users of *who* are a minority in the grammar-oriented society. I would now like to investigate from a sociolinguistic standpoint who used the interrogative *who* in the object function and who avoided it. Table 5.3 shows the numbers of characters who use the variants *whom/who* according to their social class:

Table 5.3: Number of characters who use the interrogatives *whom/who* in the objective function classified according to social class

	whom	who
U	16	2
M	15	3
L		3
American		2

The table presents that *whom* is used only by the upper and middle classes while the objective *who* is used by characters with various social backgrounds. More specifically, the speakers of *whom* are limited to well-bred and/or educated people such as landowners, clergymen, high-ranking officers, schoolteachers (including a schoolmaster and a schoolmistress) and governesses, as if its grammatical usage were secured by learning. The users of *who*, on the other hand, vary in social class, consisting of two characters from the upper class, three from the middle, three from the lower and two Americans (a railway tycoon's son and a fisherman). Since the use of *who* in object functions was considered ungrammatical at that time, it is no surprise that those in the lower class use it, as in examples (1) to (3).

(1) 'Miss Marget — Miss Hale — th' oud parson's daughter — yo' known *who* I mean well enough, if yo'll only think a bit — '
<Nicholas: Millworker> (*N and S*, p. 421)

(2) 'Then you needn't tell *me who* you bought it of,' said the farrier, looking round with some triumph; (Italicized "me" in the original)
(*Silas*, p. 44)

(3) '... You know, I suppose, *who* I married?' <Arabella: Innkeeper's wife>
(*Jude*, p. 305)

Along with these lower-class characters, ladylike women also use the "ungrammatical" variant. Examples (4) and (5) are both from *Pride and Prejudice*, with the speakers being Mrs. Bennet and her youngest daughter Lydia respectively. Jane Austen sometimes illustrates vulgar speakers in her works and these two characters are described as such (Phillipps 1970; Suematsu 2004). In this text, their lack of propriety has almost ruined the marriage between Mr. Darcy and Elizabeth, the heroine and second eldest daughter of the Bennets. In contrast, educated Elizabeth properly uses the objective *whom* in a similar context as in example (6). These examples also suggest that although the gentry are not supposed to use *who* instead of *whom* even in speech, the objective *who* is used by people of the upper class in certain contexts.

(4) '*Who* do you mean, my dear? ...' <Mrs. Bennet: Gentleman's wife>
(*Pride*, p. 45)

(5) I am going to Gretna Green, and if you cannot guess with *who*, I shall think you a simpleton, for there is but one man in the world I love, and he is an angel. <Lydia: Gentleman's daughter> (*Pride*, p. 221)

(6) 'Of *whom* does Jane ever think ill? ...' <Elizabeth: Gentleman's daughter> (*Pride*, p. 215)

The use of *who* in the object function by the "ladies" may be thus explained by the authors' intentional choice of the form to show the speakers' vulgarity. However, vulgar speech, or lack of education, is not the only reason for the use of the objective *who*. Jespersen's remark mentioned above may be helpful here. He indicates that the objective form *whom* is more likely to be displaced in the interrogative because the interrogative as object is followed immediately by the (auxiliary) verb, as in example (7):

(7) 'What's your name? and what trade are you, and *who* do you work for?' <Mr. Plomacy: Steward> (*Barchester*, II, p. 136)

This leads us to reexamine our examples by separating them into the direct/ indirect questions or the main/subordinate clauses. Let us take the case of Mr. Thornton, a young educated mill owner in *North and South*, who uses both *whom* and *who* in his speech. In example (8), he utters three objective *who*'s, out of which two appear in main clauses while in (9) he employs *whom* in a subordinate clause.³ These examples by the same person indicate that the objective *who* tends to be used in main clauses. According to Schneider (1992a: 443), the sign that the use of *who* extends from main to subordinate interrogative clauses is already found in Early Modern English. If so, *who*, which was more commonly used in the direct question, was possibly considered more acceptable than in the indirect question in the 19th century.⁴

(8) '*Who* have you heard running the masters down? I don't ask *who* you have heard abusing the men; for I see you persist in misunderstanding what I said the other day. But *who* have you heard abusing the masters?' <Mr. Thornton: Mill owner> (*N and S*, p. 118)
(9) 'Once for all, they shall know *whom* they have got to deal with... .' <Mr. Thornton: Mill owner> (*N and S*, p. 146)

Two characters in *Captains Courageous* use the objective *who* in the interrogative but no one uses *whom* in a similar context, which is a peculiar feature not seen in the rest of our texts. Two examples by American characters are as follows:

(10) 'That is because we make you feesherman, these days. If I was you, when I come to Gloucester, I would give two, three big candles for my good luck.'
'Give *who*?' <Harvey: American railway magnate's son> (*Captains*, p. 52)
(11) Did ye see his face when Penn asked *who* he'd been charged on all these years? <Long Jack: Fisherman> (*Captains*, p. 94)

In his research on the use of *whom/who* in written British English and American English, Schneider (1992b: 237) indicates that the occurrence of *whom* in interrogative clauses is greater in American English. By contrast, our examples, though limited, hint that the usage of *who* in object functions had already been accepted in American English at that time.

5.1.2.2 Relative *whom/who*

This section will consider the use of *whom/who* as relative pronouns. The grammatical rule is more strictly observed in this function, with the objective *who* being used in only 0.2 percent of the total of the instances. This figure is amazingly low in view of the relatively frequent use of the objective *who* in the preceding periods. As to the use of *whom/who* in the Early Modern English period, Schneider (1992a) reports that Shakespeare replaces *whom* by *who* 7 percent of the time, though he says that the playwright is quite ahead of his time on that point. About the transition from *whom* to *who* in general, Schneider also states that "since then it has been a matter of usage in which the assessment of 'correctness' in language and prescriptive attitudes have played a role." He is right and the low percentage for the objective use of *who* in our 19th-century texts demonstrates that prescriptivism was successfully checking the usage during the century.

Before discussing the problematic examples of *who*, it may perhaps be helpful to shed light on the behavior of the normative form *whom*. Let us have a look at the distribution of *whom* from a chronological perspective. Figure 5.1 displays the frequency of *whom* per 10,000 words in each text; it shows not only that the form *whom* has become sparse in the later texts in spoken language but also that the frequency of *whom* as a whole has gradually declined over the course of the century. From our data it is obvious that the decline of *whom*, however, is not being compensated for by the rise of *who* in the objective function.

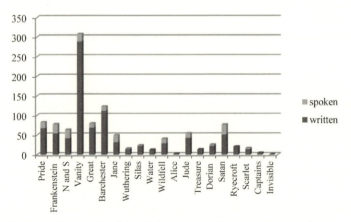

Figure 5.1: Frequencies of the relative pronoun *whom* per 10,000 words

According to Visser (1963–1973: §§ 627–33), the zero relative is rare in Old English and Middle English but rapidly increases from the 16th and 17th centuries through the present day, with a slight decrease during the 18th and 19th centuries. Saito (1961), who surveys the development of relative pronouns in modern colloquial English, also claims that during the 19th century the relative *whom* lost ground while the zero-form and *that* gained ground.[5] If this is the case, the decrease of *whom* in our 19th- century corpus is associated with the increase of its omission or the avoidance of the relative clause itself. As the competition between *whom* and *who* is yet to be started, it will be far into the following century before *who* begins to directly replace *whom*.

I will next investigate what kinds of characters use *whom* and in which way. As shown in Table 5.4, most users of *whom* belong to either the upper or middle classes, i.e., the form is generally restricted to educated society. This is especially true of written language, naturally so because at that time writing letters or diaries was a general engagement for those in the upper and middle classes, who were blessed with education.

Table 5.4: Number of users of the relative *whom* classified according to social class and register

	Dialogue	Letter/Diary	Narrative
U	38	5	
M	26	5	4
L	6		2

Note: Three people whose social status cannot be identified are omitted from this table.

Ten characters who use *whom* in their writing utter it in dialogue as well. The narrators using *whom* include two members of the lower class: Jim, an innkeeper's son and the protagonist of *Treasure Island*, and Nelly, a servant in *Wuthering Heights*. They use *whom* fifteen and eleven times respectively. Since Jim and Nelly use standard English throughout their narration, it would not be unexpected that they employ *whom*. Unlike upper- and middle-class people, however, they seldom use *whom* in dialogue. Jim never uses the relative *whom* in dialogue and Nelly, only once. These two narrators aside, the remaining characters in the lower rank number six: Jude the mason (6 exx.) in *Jude the Obscure*, Nicholas the millworker (3 exx.) in *North and South*, Justine the servant (2 exx.) in *Frankenstein*, Hope the cabman (2 exx.) in *A Study in Scarlet*, Nelly the housekeeper (1ex.) in *Wuthering Heights* and Silas the weaver (1 ex.) in *Silas Marner*. Again, not all of them are uneducated; Jude is a self-taught mason and Justine is originally from a higher-rank family in Geneva, where the manners of servants are more refined and moral.[6] Hope is not English either; he had been a pioneer in California before coming to London to work as a cabman. Two nameless characters who do not belong to any class are the monster

(17 exx.) in *Frankenstein* and a phantom (1 ex.) in *Jude the Obscure*. The monster, who has attained a sophisticated style of English, uses *whom* ten times in dialogue and seven in narrative. On the whole, the relative *whom* is used by those with education. See examples (12) and (13), which are uttered by the bishop and the monster.

(12) 'Of course,' continued the bishop; 'there can be only one man *whom* I could wish to see in that situation... .' <Bishop>   (*Barchester*, I, p. 103)

(13) "Now is the time! — save and protect me! You and your family are the friends *whom* I seek. Do not you desert me in the hour of trial!" <Monster>   (*Frankenstein*, p. 135)

The exceptional use of *whom* by the lower class can be explained in view of its syntactic constructions. When a relative clause is connected with its main clause, there are some cases in which the relative pronoun cannot be omitted: when the relative pronoun appears in non-restrictive clauses and when a preposition is placed before the relative pronoun. These conditions apply to examples (14) and (15) by lower-class characters.

(14) '... Yo' try that, miss; try living a year or two among them as looks away if yo' look at 'em; try working within two yards o' crowds o' men, who, yo' know, have a grinding grudge at yo' in their hearts — to *whom* if yo' say yo'r glad, not an eye brightens, nor a lip moves, — to *whom* if your heart's heavy, yo' can never say nought, because they'll ne'er take notice on your sighs or sad looks (and a man's no man who'll groan out loud 'bout folk asking him what's the matter?) — just yo' try that, miss — ten hours for three hundred days, and yo'll know a bit what th' Union is.' <Nicholas: Millworker>   (*N and S*, p. 232)

(15) '... And him as I'd gone out and in wi' for ten year and more, since when we was lads and went halves — mine own famil'ar friend, in *whom* I trusted, had lifted up his heel again' me, and worked to ruin me.' <Silas: Weaver>   (*Silas*, p. 139)

Concerning the omission of the relative pronoun, Charles T. Onions (1932: 74) states that in the spoken language the tendency is to omit the relative as much as possible while in the written language its omission is often felt to be undignified. In dialogue the relative *whom* is omissible in 60 (34.1%) out of the total instances of 176, and in writing it is omissible in 265 (28.7%) out of the 923. These figures may indicate that the relative *whom* is comparatively preserved in speech in our 19th-century texts even when omissible, but at the same time it should be mentioned that there are some cases in which the speaker dares to use a *whom* that could be omitted. This usage can be explained in terms of "dignity." See the following examples.

(16)   and thirdly — which perhaps I ought to have mentioned earlier, that it is the particular advice and recommendation of the very noble lady *whom* I have the honour of calling patroness.
       <Mr. Collins: Clergyman>   (*Pride*, p. 81)
(17)   'Do you know Me now, man *whom* my millions of dross have made wretched? — or do you need me to tell you WHO I am?'
       <Lucio: Noble and Satan>   (*Satan*, p. 368)
(18)   "… Look here; to gain some real affection from you, or Miss Temple, or any other *whom* I truly love, I would willingly submit to have the bone of my arm broken, or to let a bull toss me, or to stand behind a kicking horse, and let it dash its hoof at my chest, — " <Jane: Schoolgirl>
                                                                    (*Jane*, p. 69)
(19)   'I've been thinking, ever sin' I saw you, what a marcy it were yo' did na take me on, for that I ne'er saw a man *whom* I could less abide. But that's maybe been a hasty judgment; and work's work to such as me. So, measter, I'll come; and what's more, I thank yo'; and that's a deal fro' me,' <Nicholas: Millworker>   (*N and S.* p. 326)

In example (16) Mr. Collins, a clergyman, uses *whom* in referring to his noble acquaintance with "the very noble lady" in a dignified (or rather an affected) manner. Example (17) is found in one of the most thrilling scenes, where Lucio is finally revealing his identity to Geoffrey in an imposing manner. In (18), Jane, a schoolgirl, claims that she will do anything for her beloved one by using the relative *whom* emphatically. And in example (19), Nicholas, a millworker, also uses *whom* to illustrate his previous view of his master, Mr. Thornton, in a very cynical way. The talk between the worker and master in this scene is conducted in a grave mood. All these instances similarly illustrate that the grammatically omissible relative *whom* is retained for the sake of dignity in dialogue.

Lastly, I would like to discuss the examples of *who* in the objective function found in *Frankenstein* and in *The Sorrows of Satan*.

(20)   yet I have found a man *who*, before his spirit had been broken by misery, I should have been happy to have possessed as the brother of my heart. <Robert Walton: Poet>   (*Frankenstein*, p. 27)
(21)   You, as a student and lover of ancient history, will be interested to know that his ancestors were originally princes of Chaldea, who afterwards settled in Tyre — from thence they went to Etruria and there continued

through many centuries, the last scion of the house being the very gifted and genial personage *who*, as my good friend, I have the pleasure of commending to your kindest regard.
<John Garrington: Oxford-graduate businessman>   (*Satan*, p. 19)

Given the extremely low frequency of the relative *who* in the object function, the above examples can be regarded as the most exceptional. Interestingly, these examples have a couple of elements in common. Firstly, in both examples, the objective *who* is not used in dialogue by uneducated persons but in letters by educated men. This eliminates the possibility that the authors used the form to demonstrate substandard speech of the lower class or ungrammatical use in an agitated mood, which occasionally causes people to speak ungrammatically. Secondly, neither of the authors uses the interrogative *who* in object functions, which is more likely to be used than its relative counterpart. And thirdly, both *who*'s are used in rather complex structures, which could make the correct choice difficult. Taking these elements together, we cannot reject the possibility that those writers unintentionally use *who* instead of *whom* in these two cases. In regard to the use of the relatives *who* and *whom*, therefore, apart from the two female authors, it is concluded that the grammatical use of *whom* in the object function was common at that time.

5.1.3 Summary

I have discussed the rivalry between *who* and *whom* in the object function in the 19th-century novel from several perspectives. The tendency to stick to the traditionally grammatical variant is far stronger in the 19th century than today and even than in earlier centuries, which demonstrates significant influence of prescriptivism on the use of the relative pronoun at that time. Moreover, in the transition from *whom* to *who* in the relative, *whom* was not directly replaced by *who*: while *whom* is on the decline during this century, the usage of the objective *who* is not proportionally on the increase. The change is not, however, completely halted. Although the objective *who* is not used very often, it is beginning to appear as a spoken interrogative pronoun. While the users of this *who* in our novels are generally less educated, there are signs that the form is being accepted when used in the direct question. The female authors seem to show comparatively less hesitance in employing the objective *who* in their works.

CHAPTER 5 THE RIVALRY BETWEEN RELATIVE PRONOUN VARIANTS

5.2 *Of which* vs. *whose*

5.2.1 Overview

The relative pronouns *who* and *whom* today are used in exclusive reference to persons while the genitive *whose* is used for both persons and non-persons. According to Biber et al. (1999: 618), generally, *of which* is considerably less common than *whose* though their frequencies are equal in academic prose. The popular use of *whose* for non-persons is only a recent phenomenon. It had been strenuously criticized by the normative grammarians until the early 20th century. However, it is also true that, despite the criticism, many eminent writers have continuously employed the variant to avoid the clumsy and inconvenient prepositional phrase *of which* (Fernald 1904: 292). In the short term, this usage can be seen as part of the recent grammatical development from *of which* to *whose*. From a longer historical perspective, however, it is observed that there was a completely opposite transition at an earlier time. Hansen and Nielsen (2007: 157) note:

> [*Whose*] in OE (*hwæs*) was gender-neutral, but in ME it was not normally used for non-persons until the fourteenth century; *of which* reflects the development from synthesis to analysis and the two variants have been differentiated functionally so that *of which*, supported by the restricted use of non-personal *which*, was used in connection with non-persons, and the main function of *whose* is still to refer to persons.

Going with this synthesis-to-analysis development, *of which* on the whole had gained ground to a certain extent during the 17th century but after that "it has not been as successful as one might have expected" (Schneider 1993: 238).[7] As for the genitive *whose*, it seems to have been continuously used to refer to persons. Rydén (1966: 47) notes that *whose* mainly occurs with personal antecedents but more rarely after a non-personal antecedent. On the other hand, Masakatsu Mizuno (1993) argues that in the later 16th century the genitive *whose* was used with non-persons quite commonly, though he does not present statistical data.[8] This suggests that the use of *whose* varies among writers.

Regarding a setback in the synthesis-to-analysis development after the 17th century, prescriptive grammarians in the 18th century are said to have been partly responsible. They attempted to limit *whose* to personal reference just like *who* and *whom*. Murray (1806: 151) writes:

> The word *whose* begins likewise to be restricted to persons; yet it is not done so generally, but that good writers, even in prose, use it when

speaking of things. The construction is not, however, generally pleasing, as we may see in the following instances: "Pleasure, *whose* nature, &c." "Call every production, *whose* parts and *whose* nature," &c.

In view of the present-day usage, the use of *whose* for non-persons has eventually survived despite these grammarians' efforts. Burchfield (1996: 849) describes how the rule was unrealistic.

> The twists and turns of grammatical teaching from the 18c. onward produced the folk-belief that while *whose* was the natural relative pronoun when the antecedent was human, or at a pinch was an animal, it should not be used with an inanimate antecedent. The OED (1923), by contrast, demonstrated that in all kinds of circumstances from medieval times onwards *whose* had been used as a simple relative pronoun with an inanimate antecedent.

In the following sections, I will examine how successfully, or unsuccessfully, the grammatical instructions were observed to confine *whose* to personal reference in the grammar-conscious 19th-century English society.

5.2.2 Genitive *whose* and its alternative variants

Although our main interest lies in the usage of the genitive relative for non-personal reference, it would be necessary to see how the genitive relatives are used in the 19th century as a whole.[9] Firstly, let us have a look at the distribution of *whose* and its alternative genitive relatives according to personal and non-personal antecedents. Nouns, pronouns and proper names which denote people, the deity and other spiritual beings are regarded as personal antecedents[10] while all the rest are treated as non-personal antecedents. In order to investigate the rivalry between genitive *whose* and its equivalent forms, partitive constructions and other accidental combinations of *of which* are excluded.[11] Similarly excluded are the construction "the like(s) + *of which*," the instances of *of which* in which the relative *which* refers to its previous sentence or clause, and those of "*of which* + noun"[12] since in such constructions *of which* is not replaced with *whose*.

Genitive *whose* is alternately used in place of either *of whom*, *of which* or limitedly the archaic form *whereof* in 19th-century English. There are 956 instances of these four variants together, out of which 619 are used for persons and 337 for non-persons. The distribution of these genitive relatives is presented per text in Table 5.5.

Table 5.5: Distribution of genitive relatives *whose* and its variant forms for persons/non-persons

	Persons		Non-persons		
	of whom	whose	whereof	of which	whose
Pride (f)		56		9	3
Frankenstein (f)		39		16	10
N and S (f)		36		24	8
Vanity	1	152	13	57	5
Great		28		10	7
Barchester		59		14	3
Jane (f)		27		11	30
Wuthering (f)		5			8
Silas (f)	1	33			2
Water		3		1	
Wildfell (f)	1	24		10	8
Alice		4		2	
Jude	1	38		5	20
Treasure				1	2
Dorian		27		4	17
Satan (f)		51		5	8
Ryecroft		21		5	4
Scarlet		6		5	3
Captains		4			5
Invisible		2		1	1
Total	4 (0.6%)	615 (99.4%)	13 (3.9%)	180 (53.4%)	144 (42.7%)

The table shows that *whose* is used for both persons and non-persons while *of whom* is restricted to persons and *of which* (as well as *whereof*) to non-persons. In reference to persons, *whose* is almost exclusively used with 99.4 percent of the cases while there are as few as four instances (0.6%) of *of whom*, which are given below.

Of whom
(22) then official characters — such men as Governor-generals and Lord-lieutenants, in whom he took little interest; Chief-justices and Lord chancellors, silent, thin-lipped figures *of whom* he knew barely the names.   (*Jude*, p. 74)
(23) He delivered this box into Eppie's charge when she had grown up, and she often opened it to look at the ring: but still she thought hardly at all about the father *of whom* it was the symbol.   (*Silas*, p. 142)
(24) The dreadful secret was told to him by Firkin with so frightened a look, that for the first moment Mr. Bowls and his young man thought that robbers were in the house; the legs *of whom* had probably been discovered by the woman under Miss Crawley's bed.   (*Vanity*, p. 431)
(25) I then wrote three letters of adieu: the first to Esther Hargrave, in which I told her that I found it impossible to stay any longer at Grassdale, or to

leave my son under his father's protection; and, as it was of the last importance that our future abode should be unknown to him and his acquaintance, I should disclose it to no one but my brother, through the medium *of whom* I hoped still to correspond with my friends.

(*Wildfell*, pp. 369-370)

The analytic form *of whom* might look pedantic but as far as these four examples are concerned, the form seems to have been chosen for other reasons. In example (22), for instance, *of whom* corresponds to *in whom* in the preceding clause to produce a syntactic parallelism. Concerning such cases as example (23) where an objective relation is to be denoted, Poutsma (1916: 960) states that the form *of whom* is common enough. In (24) and (25), *of whom* seems to be used for emphasis, perhaps seriously for the latter and comically for the former.

Concerning non-personal antecedents, the situation is completely different. It is not only that both *of which* and *whose* are equally used but that *of which* enjoys even the greater proportion. The grammatical restriction of the use of *whose* to persons is observed in more than half the cases. That is, the use of *whose* for non-persons was not as common as today.

As Table 5.5 shows, apart from *of which*, the variant *whereof* is also used for non-persons. Schneider (1993) states that *whereof* completely disappeared in Early Modern English. In effect, all thirteen examples of *whereof* are attested solely in *Vanity Fair*. This fact may signify the author's exceptional predilection for this archaic variant and *whereof* in the relevant function is virtually out of use in this period. Some examples are as follows:

Whereof
(26) Lights went about from window to window in the lonely desolate old Hall, *whereof* but two or three rooms were ordinarily occupied by its owner. (*Vanity*, p. 506)
(27) She grows daily more careworn and sad: fixing upon her child alarmed eyes, *whereof* the little boy cannot interpret the expression.
(*Vanity*, p. 623)

5.2.3 *Of which* vs. *whose* for non-personal antecedents

As for the constructions of genitive relatives for non-personal reference, four different types are attested in our 19th-century texts.[13] The number of instances of each type and their examples are shown below.

CHAPTER 5 THE RIVALRY BETWEEN RELATIVE PRONOUN VARIANTS   173

Whose: 144 instances
(28)   ... the terrible portrait *whose* changing features showed him the real degradation of his life,   (*Dorian*, p. 115)

Headword + *of which*: 125 instances
(29)   I was passing the back parlour, or teachers' sitting-room, the door *of which* was half open,   (*Jane*, p. 90)

Of which + headword: 19 instances
(30)   He spoke of it as a certain event, *of which* the time alone could be undecided.   (*Pride*, p. 151)

Of which ... headword: 36 instances
(31)   Passing on into the front court-yard, I hesitated whether to call the woman to let me out at the locked gate *of which* she had the key,
         (*Great*, p. 397)

There are 144 instances of *whose* and 180 instances of *of which*, which will be analyzed with reference to chronological and sociolinguistic factors, register, types of antecedents, and syntactic factors.

5.2.3.1 Chronological and sociolinguistic analyses

Figure 5.2 shows the proportions of *whose* and *of which* for non-personal antecedents per text. Although the ratio of these two forms varies from text to text, *of which* seems to be preferred in the earlier texts and *whose* in the later texts on the whole. In order to clarify the possible chronological change of

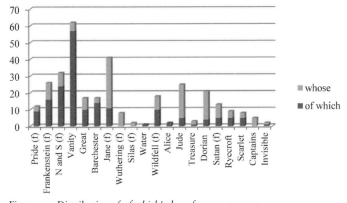

Figure 5.2: Distribution of *of which/whose* for non-persons

these two alternatives, let us compare the situation in the earlier texts and that in the later texts. Since the chronological boundary appears to lie somewhere between *Alice*, published in 1865 and 1872, which has no example of *whose*, and *Jude the Obscure*, published in 1895, in which *whose* is far better liked, the twenty texts will be grouped into the twelve earlier texts and the eight later texts. The results are shown in Table 5.6 below.

Table 5.6: Chronological difference in the use of *of which* and *whose* for non-persons

	of which	whose	Total
12 earlier texts	154 (64.7%)	84 (35.3%)	238
8 later texts	26 (30.2%)	60 (69.8%)	86

In the earlier texts *of which* claims around 65 percent of the total, while in the later texts the situation is reversed, with *whose* claiming about 70 percent. This indicates that *whose* came to be used with greater liberty over the course of the 19th century. However, the increased use of *whose* seems not to be related to the chronological factor alone.

Table 5.7: Distribution of *of which* and *whose* for non-persons according to sex

	of which	whose	Total
Female authors	75 (49.3%)	77 (50.7%)	152
Male authors	105 (61.0%)	67 (39.0%)	172

Table 5.7 presents which form is generally preferred by the male and female authors. The figures in the table clearly show that the female authors use *whose* more frequently than the males. Moreover, it is noted that out of the eight female authors as many as seven are associated with the earlier texts, which tend to prefer *of which*. Thus this supports the hypothesis that women used *whose* more freely in this period while men stuck to *of which*, and that men who refrained from using *whose* for non-persons at first gradually accepted it towards the end of century, as clearly shown in the below table.

Table 5.8: Distribution of *of which* and *whose* with male authors according to chronological difference

	of which	whose	Total
First 5 males	84 (84.8%)	15 (15.2%)	99
Last 7 males	21 (28.8%)	52 (71.2%)	73

Since both male and female characters use *of which* and *whose* in dialogue, let us next focus on how these characters use these forms in terms of gender and social background. There are twenty characters using *of which* and 23 characters using *whose*.

Table 5.9: Number of the characters who use *of which/whose* for non-persons classified according to social class and sex

	of which			*whose*		
	Male	Female	Child	Male	Female	Child
U	3	3		4	3	
M	10	2		8	3	
L			1	2	1	2
Monster	1					
Total	14	5	1	14	7	2

Table 5.9 shows that many of the characters using these relative variants belong to the higher social class. There is no indication that the higher class prefers the grammatical *of which* to *whose*. The frequent use of the relatives *of which* and *whose* by upper- and middle-class characters suggests that the use of the relative pronoun itself illustrates the attainment of education. As for *whose*, five lower-class characters are included in its users. However, except for Nicholas, a millworker in *North and South*, all the rest are educated enough to read and talk properly. (I will consider Nicholas's usage later in a different light.) All in all, the authors seem not to have regarded the use of *whose* for non-persons so poorly as the purists thought.

Another point to be noted here is that there is no salient disparity found between the male and female characters. As we have found above, however, our authors themselves differed in the choice of *whose* and *of which* according to sex (see Table 5.7). These facts reveal that the authors were unaware of there being such gender-related difference in the use of *whose* and *of which*.

5.2.3.2 Spoken and written

In Present-day English, *of which* and *whose* are used primarily in writing, especially in the case of the former. According to Biber et al. (1999: 618), regardless of head nouns, *whose* as well as *of which* is extremely rare in conversation and *whose* is moderately common in all written registers. I would like to examine in which register these variants are likely to appear.

Table 5.10: Distribution of non-personal relatives *of which/whose* according to register

	of which	*whose*	Ratio
Dialogue	6	13	1: 2.2
Written language	174	131	1: 0.8
• letter	3	5	1: 1.7
• diary	9	7	1: 0.8
• poetry		4	0.0: 1
• narrative (1st pers.)	51	56	1: 1.1
• narrative (3rd pers.)	111	59	1: 0.5

Ratio = *of which* : *whose*

Table 5.10 presents the distribution of *of which* and *whose* according to the spoken/written language with the written language further classified into five subcategories; letter, diary, poetry[14] and two types of narrative. The table clearly shows that both *of which* and *whose* are mostly attested in written language. It is also found that in writing *of which* is a little more frequently used than *whose*, but in dialogue *whose* is more often employed than *of which*. As to the written language, the ratio of *of which* to *whose* differs by subcategory. While the third-person narrative employs *of which* far more than *whose*, the first-person narrative slightly prefers *whose*. *Whose* is relatively more freely used than *of which* in letter and poetry. Though narrative is generally considered closer to written language than to speech, the first-person narrative tends to be conversational. In the first-person narrative, the way characters narrate varies. Some narrators tell the story to the readers as in *Great Expectations* and *Jane Eyre* while others talk to another character like housekeeper Nelly in *Wuthering Heights* and scientist Frankenstein in *Frankenstein*. In regard to letter, linguistic contexts tend to be more colloquial than writing in general. Taken all together, although both variants are likely to be used in writing, it is assumed that *whose* would seem more colloquial than *of which*.

5.2.3.3 **Types of antecedents**
With the increase of acceptance of *whose* for nonpersons, many more kinds of objects should have come to be employed as antecedents. Our next concern therefore is about the types of non-personal antecedents of these two genitive relatives. For this analysis, the antecedents are classified into four groups according to their characteristics: human-associated objects, existences in nature, artificial objects and abstract objects. These four are then further grouped into nine subcategories: (a) parts of a person, (b) groups,[15] (c) animals, (d) plants, (e) inanimate nature, (f) buildings/yards, (g) furniture/articles, (h) vehicles, (i) events/actions and (j) ideas/feelings. The results are summarized in Table 5.11 and Figure 5.3 below.

CHAPTER 5 THE RIVALRY BETWEEN RELATIVE PRONOUN VARIANTS 177

Table 5.11: Non-personal antecedents of *of which* and *whose*

	of which	*whose*
Of human	12 exx.	25 exx.
a. Parts of a person	*face, hair, hands, head* (2), *tears*	*eye(s)* (3), *face* (2), *heart, mind, body and mind, voice* (4), *smile*
b. Groups	*army, circle, crowd, hospital, the Union, regiment*	*cavalry, college, crowd, family* (2), *firm, march, army, organization, race, regiment, throng*
Of nature	10 exx.	39 exx.
c. Animals	*puppy*	*animal(s)* (2), *bees, birds, butterflies, dog* (2), *eagle, frogs, mare, nightingale, Skulker* [the dog], *spaniel, hawks and carrion crows, turtle doves, vultures, flies*
d. Plants	*tree* (2), *blossoms*	*beech, flowers, forest-tree, lime-tree, horse-chestnut, trees, laburnum, plant, weeds*
e. Inanimate	*bay, field, rainbow, river, horizon, hill*	*half-moon, Alps, dell, hill(s)* (2), *lake, mountains* (3), *rock, rookery, swamp, scenery,*
Artificial objects	63 exx.	40 exx.
f. Buildings/yards	*barouche, bedroom* (2), *door, drains, drawing-room* (2), *farm-house, garden* (2), *gutter, house* (3), *inclosure, gate, lodge-gate, lodge-house, Number 46* [the room], *parlour, passage, room(s)* (4), *sitting-room, tailors' shops, courtyard, grass-plot, walk, church, lodgings, stair passage, farm, grass-plot*	*alley, apartment, cottage, dining-room, hamlet, porch, arch, college, lane, room* (3), *saloon, sitting-room, window, temple* (2), *the Old Green Copper Rope-Walk*
g. Furniture/articles	*letter(s)* (4), *note, novel, map, port-wine, money, book* (2), *utensils, tools, cards, a band of velvet, newspaper, sofa, coat, articles, stove, chain, work* 'book,' *box, dress, grass-plot, furniture, mask, shawl and brooch*	*accordion, book, box, cabinet, candle, china plate, clock, drawer, drawings, lantern, machine, object, portrait, silver pint, spirit-lamp, stools*
h. Vehicles		*cab, fleets* (2), *steamer, the Hispaniola* [the ship], *vessel*

Abstract objects	95 exx.	39 exx.
i. Events/actions	*alteration, banquet, dinners, panegyric, discoveries* (2), *trial, pantomime, order, kiss, proposal, workings of the system, rejection, inquest, walk* (2), *recital, intercourse, interview, complaint, combat, tale 'talk,' mesmerism, meal, transactions, arrest, talk, undertaking, receipts, fall, event, task, voyage, dialogue, altercation, conversation*	*action, rejections* (2), *undertaking, whisper, the Great Wessex Agricultural Show, itinerant concerns, experience*
j. Ideas/feelings	*favour, trust, familiarity, spirituality, promise, crime, duty, idea* (3), *liberty and self sacrifice, disappointment, joy, language, feelings and passions, propensities and passions, mystery, song, passion, Eastern tongue, shock, apprenticeship, subject, opinion, noise, ignorance and stupidity, pleasure, feeling, hymn, facts, fortune, neatness and consistency, something* (2), *scheme, a new time, life, things, opinions, lifetime, remainder, partiality, calamity, message, narrative and calculations, sum, impulse, Christmas Day, charades, words, silence, indignation, belief, world* (2), *parish, town, village, district*	*death, desire, dreams, everything, existence, form, ideal, life, matter, motives, passion* (2), *sight, sins* (2), *spirit, sympathies, term, thing* [love], *thoughts, virtues, words, October morning, error, world, city* (2), *England, the New West, village, spirit-land*

Note: In this table, the number of examples of *whose* is 143 instead of 144 since one antecedent (*race*) is used for two instances of *whose*. The figures in brackets stand for frequencies for the antecedents appearing more than once. For the sake of conciseness, adjuncts of the antecedents are omitted.

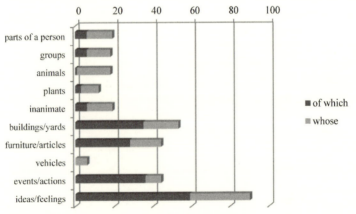

Figure 5.3: Non-personal antecedents of *of which* and *whose*

CHAPTER 5 THE RIVALRY BETWEEN RELATIVE PRONOUN VARIANTS 179

The figure (as well as the table above) illustrates that the types of the antecedents greatly affect the choice of the relatives. Roughly speaking, there is a tendency for *whose* to be preferred for antecedents in reference to something associated with people, animals and others in the natural world, and for *of which* to be preferred for inanimate objects, either artificial or intangible. Let us see how the types of the antecedents are related to the choice of the relatives from category to category.

Whether physical (e.g., *eyes, face*) or nonphysical (e.g., *heart, mind*), the parts belonging to a person could be metonymically categorized as person although *of which* and *whose* are both possible in all the cases.[16] *Voice, tears* and *smile*, which are not parts of a human body, are also considered part of the people who produce them. Groups and organizations consisting of people tend to be dealt with as people, which is quite the same usage as today. For all these categories, both *of which* and *whose* are applicable. See examples (32) to (36)

a. Parts of a person
(32) 'Certainly,' said she, smiling up in *his face*, the expression *of which* was somewhat anxious and oppressed, and hardly cleared away as he met her sweet sunny countenance, (*N and S*, p. 124)
(33) ... I found him to be a dry man, rather short in stature, with *a square wooden face, whose* expression seemed to have been imperfectly chipped out with a dull-edged chisel. (*Great*, p. 169)
(34) I did not raise my eyes, but I suppose mamma looked, for *a clear, melodious voice, whose* tones thrilled through my nerves, exclaimed —
(*Wildfell*, p. 459)

b. Groups
(35) Emmy found herself in the centre of *a very genteel circle* indeed; the members *of which* could not conceive that anybody belonging to it was not very lucky. (*Vanity*, p. 781)
(36) Jefferson Hope began to think that they were fairly out of the reach of *the terrible organization whose* enmity they had incurred. (*Scarlet*, p. 102)

Animals are the nearest to humans among all the non-personal objects, and perhaps plants are the next. In most cases *whose* is preferred, which is especially the case with animals. One exception in the category of animals is example (38). The choice of *of which* here has something to do with the syntactic construction of its relative clause, in which the relativizer is used to express how the headword (a little waddling puppy) is related to Sancho (a setter's name). In constructions of this type, *whose* is rarely used (Poutsma 1916: 960).[17]

c. Animals

(37) They were buzzards, *the vultures* of the west, *whose* coming is the forerunner of death. (*Scarlet*, p. 73)

(38) My first pretext for invading the sanctum, was to bring Arthur *a little waddling puppy of which* Sancho was the father, and which delighted the child beyond expression, and, consequently, could not fail to please his mammá. (*Wildfell*, p. 68)

For plants such as trees and flowers, *whose* is also used in preference to *of which*. It is noteworthy that while *whose* is always chosen for natural plants, *of which* is preferred for artificial and abstract ones; in example (39) from *Dorian Gray*, *whose* is used for a natural plant called "laburnum" while *of which* is chosen for embroidered "long-stemmed white blossoms" in (40). Similarly, in example (41) from *The Sorrows of Satan*, *whose* is used for natural flowers whereas in example (42) *of which* is chosen for a metaphorical tree of knowledge.

d. Plants

(39) Another cope was of green velvet, embroidered with heart-shaped groups of acanthus-leaves, from which spread *long-stemmed white blossoms*, the details *of which* were picked out with silver thread and coloured crystals. (*Dorian*, p. 114)

(40) Lord Henry Wotton could just catch the gleam of the honey-sweet and honey-coloured blossoms of *a laburnum, whose* tremulous branches seemed hardly able to bear the burden of a beauty so flame-like as theirs; (*Dorian*, p. 1)

(41) Our wisdom came from the devil in the first place, according to the legend of *the tree of knowledge* — the fruit *of which* taught both good and evil, but which still apparently persuades man to evil rather than good, and leads him on to a considerable amount of arrogance besides, (*Satan*, p. 177)

(42) — the little harmless souls of *flowers, whose* task in life, sweetly fulfilled, had been to create beauty and fragrance by their mere existence, expired to gratify the vanity of one woman to whom nothing was sacred. (*Satan*, p. 239)

For the landscape (e.g., *mountains, hills, fields, rivers, rocks*, etc.), *whose* is more likely to be used than *of which*, though the difference is not as distinct as in the case of animals and plants. Though they are inanimate, such objects might be felt as part of nature just as animals and plants.

e. Inanimate (nature)

(43)   I lighted the dry branch of a tree, and danced with fury around the devoted cottage, my eyes still fixed on *the western horizon*, the edge *of which* the moon nearly touched.   (*Frankenstein*, p. 138)

(44)   Away to the south-west of us we saw two low hills, about a couple of miles apart, and rising behind one of them *a third and higher hill, whose* peak was still buried in the fog.   (*Treasure*, p. 63)

As we can see, *whose* is employed more often for natural objects than for artificial objects; as for buildings, yards, furniture and physical articles, *of which* appears more frequently than *whose*

f. Buildings/yards

(45)   As she said this, she came upon *a neat little house*, on the door *of which* was a bright brass plate with the name 'W. RABBIT' engraved upon it.
(*Alice*, p. 31)
(46)   Mr. Collins invited them to take a stroll in *the garden*, which was large and well laid out, and to the cultivation *of which* he attended himself.
(*Pride*, p. 120)
(47)   *A little hamlet, whose* roofs were blent with trees, straggled up the side of one of these hills;   (*Jane*, p. 99)
(48)   and there was *the Old Green Copper Rope-Walk* — *whose* long and narrow vista I could trace in the moonlight,   (*Great*, p. 370)

g. Furniture/articles

(49)   He waited in the light of *the stove*, the door *of which* she flung open before going out,   (*Jude*, p. 194)
(50)   "... and an intricate lace veil; lying of course on *a marble sofa*, from among the legs *of which* Death will be creeping out and poking at his victim with a small toasting-fork."   (*Barchester*, II, p. 165)
(51)   and she had *a small drawer* in a cabinet in the library which she would trifle over for hours, and *whose* key she took special care to remove when she left it.   (*Wuthering*, p. 198)
(52)   Dan lay at length in his bunk, wrestling with *a gaudy, gilt-stopped accordion, whose* tunes went up and down with the pitching of the *We're Here*. (Italicized "We're Here" in the original)   (*Captains*, p. 51)

As far as vehicles are concerned, *whose* is used in all of the six cases, but it should be mentioned that out of the six vehicles, five are ships. It is common to refer to a ship by the feminine singular *she*. This could lead *whose* to be chosen for ships. The vehicle in the remaining example, example (54), is a *cab*, but the vehicle is described as if it were the owner of the horse.

h. Vehicles

(53) *The Hispaniola* herself, a few yards in *whose* wake I was still being whirled along, seemed to stagger in her course, and I saw her spars toss a little against the blackness of the night; (Italicized "Hispaniola" in the original) (*Treasure*, p. 124)

(54) As a sort of objective commentary on Jude's remarks there drove up at this moment with a belated Doctor, robed and panting, *a cab whose* horse failed to stop at the exact point required for setting down the hirer; who jumped out and entered the door. (*Jude*, p. 317)

With abstract objects, *of which* is more common than *whose*, especially in the case of events/actions, where *whose* appears least often. Interestingly enough, *whose* is used relatively more frequently for ideas/feelings than events/actions. This is probably because ideas/feelings are more likely to be associated with humans. James J. Paxson (1994: 40) states that "[t]he 'personified' can be found among a range of abstract essences, inanimate objects, animals, etc." According to Elizabeth Closs Traugott (1972: 155), the relative pronouns *whose* and *whom* were used with personified inanimate antecedents in the later 16th century.

i. Events/actions

(55) The second piece was *the last new grand comic Christmas pantomime*, in the first scene *of which*, it pained me to suspect that I detected Mr. Wopsle with red worsted legs under a highly magnified phosphoric countenance ... (*Great*, p. 379)

(56) Luckily, at this time he caught *a liver complaint*, for the cure *of which* he returned to Europe, and which was the source of great comfort and amusement to him in his native country. (*Vanity*, p. 27)

(57) By every law of nature and sex *a kiss* was the only rejoinder that fitted the mood and the moment, under the suasion *of which* Sue's undemonstrative regard of him might not inconceivably have changed its temperature. (*Jude*, p. 151)

(58) but I clung to every pretence of delay, and shrunk from taking the first step in *an undertaking whose* immediate necessity began to appear less absolute to me. (*Frankenstein*, p. 150)

(59) he repeated in *a whisper whose* despairing bitterness precluded all resentment. (*Wildfell*, p. 327)

j. Ideas/feelings
(60) it only gave my nerves *a shock*; *of which* I feel the reverberation to this day. (*Jane*, p. 20)
(61) And by *some impulse*, *of which* I cannot explain the meaning, she took George in her arms and kissed him with an extraordinary tenderness.
(*Vanity*, p. 498)
(62) she was a most active magistrate in *her own parish*, the minutest concerns *of which* were carried to her by Mr. Collins; (*Pride*, p. 130)
(63) There were *sins whose* fascination was more in the memory than in the doing of them, (*Dorian*, p. 133)
(64) Onward he still went, under the influence of a childlike yearning for the one being in the world to whom it seemed possible to fly — *an unreasoning desire*, *whose* ill judgment was not apparent to him now.
(*Jude*, p. 116)
(65) And now one can only watch the encroachment of his rule upon *that old, that true England whose* strength and virtue were so differently manifested. (*Ryecroft*, p. 157)

Personification occurs in more than one-third of the cases (or eleven instances) of ideas/feelings, where *whose* is always chosen. In examples (63), (64) and (65), *sins*, *desire* and *England* are personified respectively. As to the antecedents of events/actions, no instance of personification is found except for example (57), in which *kiss* is personified. There, the variant *of which* is used, possibly for some syntactic reason, which I will discuss in the next section.

5.2.3.4 Syntactic factors
As we have seen above, the relative *whose* is likely to be used in reference to natural objects, *of which* to artificial or abstract objects. However, it is not only the types of the antecedents that decide the choice between these two variants. Some of our examples have already suggested that the use of *whose* could be avoided for syntactic reasons. Let us now examine which syntactic factors could affect the choice of the relevant variants.

According to the syntactic functions in the relative clause, the headwords of the relative are classified into four different groups: (1) subject, (2) object, (3) prepositional object and (4) complement. Firstly, I would like to examine the rivalry between *of which* and *whose* in these four syntactic functions.

Table 5.12: Syntactic functions of the headword

	of which	whose	Ratio
Subject	72	103	1 : 1.4
Object	40	19	1 : 0.5
Prepositional object	53	21	1 : 0.4
Complement	15	1	1 : 0.1

Ratio = of which : whose

The table shows that the choice between *of which* and *whose* is considerably affected by syntactic factors. The variant *whose* outnumbers *of which* when its headword serves as the subject of a relative clause while *of which* is preferred otherwise. Judging from the fact that two-thirds of the total instances of *whose* appear with its headword being in the subject function, it is highly possible that the transition from *of which* to *whose* started in this function. As for the categories "object" and "prepositional object," *whose* counts for around 30 percent, with the former securing slightly more ground than the latter. When the headword appears as a complement of *be* verb, the variant *of which* is used in all the instances except for one. This indicates that this structure strongly requires the analytic form. The following are examples of *of which* and *whose* in each function.

Subject
(66) She was in a room the folding-doors *of which* stood open: (*Jane*, p. 104)
(67) he repeated in a whisper *whose* despairing bitterness precluded all resentment. (*Wildfell*, p. 327)

Object
(68) Fortunately the books were written in the language, the elements *of which* I had acquired at the cottage; (*Frankenstein*, p. 127)
(69) He seemed to hear voices, *whose* words he repeated as if to gather their meaning. (*Jude*, p. 381)

Prepositional object
(70) Presently we steamed into a great bay, in the narrow mouth *of which* lay an island. (*Ryecroft*, p. 101)
(71) Our punch was cooling in an ornamental lake, on *whose* margin the bower was raised. (*Great*, p. 205)

Complement
(72) — the Union, *of which* Higgins was the representative to the poor woman, (*N and S*, p. 301)

(73) — all made up one great army of personal enemies, *whose* fault it was that she was now a helpless widow.   (*N and S*, p. 301)

We have thus found that both the types of the antecedents and their syntactic functions play an important role in the choice between *of which* and *whose*. Let us next see the correlation between these two factors in the occurrence of the relatives. Table 5.13 presents the distribution of *of which* and *whose* according to the function of the headword and the type of the antecedents. When the headword serves as the subject, *whose* is mainly used for the human-related objects as well as natural objects while it is used slightly more often than *of which* for artificial objects. With abstract objects, the variant *of which* is more employed than *whose*. When the headword serves as an object, the situation is similar except that *of which* is more often employed than *whose* for the artificial or abstract objects. In the case of the headword as a prepositional object, *whose* is not necessarily preferred even for the human or nature-related antecedents while *of which* is predominantly chosen for artificial or abstract

Table 5.13: Distribution of *of which* and *whose* according to headword's function and antecedents' type

Of human (parts of a person, groups)

	of which	*whose*	Ratio
Subject	6	14	1 : 2.3
Verbal object		6	0.0 : 1
Prepositional object	3	5	1 : 1.7
Comp. of *be* verb	3	1	1 : 0.3

Of nature (animals, plants, inanimate nature)

	of which	*whose*	Ratio
Subject	3	32	1 : 10.7
Verbal object	1	4	1 : 4.0
Prepositional object	4	3	1 : 0.8
Comp. of *be* verb	2		1 : 0.0

Artificial objects (buildings/yards, furniture/articles, vehicles)

	of which	*whose*	Ratio
Subject	25	31	1 : 1.2
Verbal object	12	3	1 : 0.3
Prepositional object	25	6	1 : 0.2
Comp. of *be* verb	1		1 : 0.0

Abstract objects (events/actions, ideas/feelings)

	of which	*whose*	Ratio
Subject	38	26	1 : 0.7
Verbal object	27	6	1 : 0.2
Prepositional object	21	7	1 : 0.3
Comp. of *be* verb	9		1 : 0.0

Ratio = *of which* : *whose*

objects. When the headword functions as a complement of *be* verb, *of which* is the norm.

Our examination demonstrates that the types of the antecedent and the syntactic function of its headword are closely related with each other; *whose* is preferred for human-related antecedents in general while the variant tends to be avoided when the headword occurs as a prepositional object or a complement of *be* verb; *of which* appears to be preferred for abstract objects, although it is not necessarily the case when its headword functions as a subject. Let us take some examples to illustrate how the type of an antecedent and the syntactic function of its headword affect each other. Abstract nouns denoting positions or parts (e.g., *centre, middle, top, end*) usually require *of which* in adverbial phrases, as in example (74). However, even these positional terms can be employed with *whose* when they are given a concrete description, i.e., when they appear with an adjective, as in (75).

(74)   Miss Pinkerton did not understand French; she only directed those who did: but biting her lips and throwing up her venerable and Roman-nosed head (*on the top of which* figured a large and solemn turban),
   (*Vanity*, pp. 9–10)

(75)   stools still more antiquated, *on whose cushioned tops* were yet apparent traces of half-effaced embroideries, wrought by fingers that for two generations had been coffin-dust.   (*Jane*, p. 105)

5.2.4 Summary

The forms *of which* and *whose* for non-personal reference are far more competitive than is the case between *who* and *whom*, although the variant *whose* was not as freely used as today. The analytic form *of which* is slightly more frequent in use than *whose*; the transition from *of which* to *whose* is in progress in the 19th century, apparently led by females. Both *of which* and *whose* are equally used by the educated, which signifies that *whose* was not regarded as ungrammatical, contrary to what many grammarians of the day thought. The type of antecedent plays a significant role in the choice between *of which* and *whose*; *whose* is preferably used for human-related antecedents, animals and other natural objects, while *of which* is preferred for artificial and abstract objects. The syntactic function of the headword also influences the choice between the variants: *whose* is most frequently used when its headword is in the subject function; when the headword serves as a compliment of *be* verb, *of which* is the norm.

Notes
1 Whether to use *whom* or *who* in the object position can be treated as a subject of the case problem discussed in Chapter 3 but I will discuss it here as part of the grammatical change of the relative pronouns in the 19th century.
2 Sapir (1921: 156) states that "[n]o logical or historical argument will avail to save this hapless 'whom.' "
3 The second *who* in example (8), which is supposed to be *whom*, might have been caused by being placed between the other two *who*'s.
4 If the use of *who* in the main clause less offends educated English ears, Mrs. Bennet's speech in example (5) may not sound as vulgar as that of her youngest daughter.
5 His diagram shows that although *that* has been declining in its popularity on the whole, it slightly regained ground during the 19th century.
6 "The republican institutions of our country have produced simpler and happier manners than those which prevail in the great monarchies that surround it. Hence there is less distinction between the several classes of its inhabitants; and the lower orders, being neither so poor nor so despised, their manners are more refined and moral. A servant in Geneva does not mean the same thing as a servant in France and England." (*Frankenstein*, p. 65)
7 According to Schneider, who surveys the rivalry between *of which*, *whereof* and *whose* using Helsinki Corpus, *of which* increased up to 17 percent in the period 1640-1710 from 12 percent in the period 1500-1640.
8 Mizuno's study is mainly based on Shakespeare's histories.
9 As to the genitive interrogatives, there are no instances of *of which* or *of whom* though there are 39 instances of *whose*, which makes it needless to discuss the situation in this syntactic construction.
10 The deity and other spiritual beings are included in the group of personal antecedents since usually each is referred to by either *he* or *she*.
11 Partitive constructions are: (1) "infinite pronoun + *of which*" such as *one [some, most, all,* etc.] *of which*, (2) "the superlative + *of which*" such as *the youngest of which*, (3) *the former [latter, half, other* etc.] *of which*, and (4) "(ordinal) number + of which" such as *the third of which* and *forty of which*. Some examples of accidental combinations of *of which* are as follows: "the period of which I speak" (*Wuthering*, p. 289), "the sort of love of which I am capable" (*Jane*, p. 301), "books of which I had passionate need" (*Ryecroft*, p. 30) and "the door, out of which she went" (*Jude*, p. 63).
12 *Which* in this construction is called relative adjective as in "When Mr. Wemmick had put all the biscuit into the post, and had paid me my money from a cash-box in a safe, the key *of which safe* he kept somewhere down his back ..." (*Great*, p. 197).
13 As for *of which*, on top of the three mentioned above, another type, "*which* ... headword *of*," is also possible, but there is no example of this type found in our corpus.
14 Poems written by the authors of our texts are counted here; those quoted from other texts are excluded.
15 Although "groups" could occasionally stand for people, they are more often than not treated as an organization or a system working for people. In our texts, there are not a few instances of this type in which *of which* is chosen. I therefore deal with these antecedents as non-personal in order to find their preference in the use of *whose/of which*.
16 According to Wales (2001: 252), "metonymy" is an indexical sign in semiotic terms: there is a directly or logically contiguous relationship between the substituted word and its referent.
17 Poutsma (1916: 960) states that "the analytical construction may be common enough when the noun modified expresses how one person is related or disposed to another, or when an

objective relation is to be denoted."

CHAPTER 6
Concord with Indefinite Pronouns[1]

Biber et al. (1999: 351) define the indefinite pronouns as those "used to express entities which the speaker/writer cannot or does not want to specify more exactly," presenting four main groups: the *every* group (e.g., *everybody, everyone, everything*), the *some* group (e.g., *somebody, someone, something*), the *any* group (e.g., *anybody, anyone, anything*) and the *no* group (e.g., *nobody, no one, nothing, none*). In addition to these, *all, both, each, (n)either, one, (an) other* are generally listed as indefinite pronouns. In using indefinite pronouns, it is perhaps the concord pattern that is most problematic. Grammatically, most of the indefinite pronouns are singular. It is known that the singularity of the indefinite pronoun was first prescribed by grammarians in the 18th century. They insisted that the indefinites only agree with singular nouns, pronouns and verbs. However, in Present-day English it is not rare to treat them as plural even in formal usage because they usually indicate more than one person as seen in the examples below:

> *Everyone* thinks *they* have the answer.
> Has *anybody* brought *their* camera?
> *No one* could have blamed *themselves* for that. (Quirk et al. 1985: 770)

In using indefinite pronouns, fluctuations are found in pronoun-verb agreement and pronominal co-reference. Since concord is more controversial for some pronouns than others, I would like to deal with the following pronouns which have often been regarded as problematic by grammarians: *everybody, everyone, somebody, someone, anybody, anyone, nobody, each one, no one, none, either, neither, each* and *any*. Compound pronouns such as *anybody* and *anyone* are sometimes written in two words (e.g., *any body, any one*) in our 19th-century texts. Jespersen (1909-49: II, §17.21) states that in the 17th and 18th centuries both spellings are common. Our study deals with both types of compound pronouns without discriminating between them. The pronouns *every, some, any, no, each,* and *(n)either* used as adjectives or indefinite modifiers (e.g., *every man, any person, no human,* etc.) will be examined in comparison with their pronoun usage. For the sake of convenience, I will hereafter call indefinite pronouns in pronominal usage 'the *everybody* type' (e.g., *everybody, anyone*) and those in adjectival usage "the *every man* type" (e.g., *every man, any person*).

Dekeyser (1975) conducted research on concord with the indefinite on the basis of works by fifty-eight British authors published or made public between 1800 and 1899. The size of his corpus is estimated at 3,000,000 words. After surveying how contemporary grammarians viewed some particular usages of the indefinite pronoun in terms of number agreement, he observes the transition from singular to plural patterns in terms of verb agreement and pronominal agreement. For verb agreement, he examines *each* (*of*), *everybody, everyone, every/each* + head, *any* (*of*), *anybody, anyone, nobody, no*(*t*) *one,* (*n*) *either* and (*n*)*either* + head in terms of chronological and stylistic (spoken/written) difference. As for pronominal agreement, he investigates the indefinite pronouns mentioned above and a few nouns which express humans[2] in chronological, stylistic and sociolinguistic (male/female) standpoints. He treats *none* separately because its behavior is apparently different from the others. He also gives a special reference to indefinites modified by plural *of*-adjuncts. In his study on the indefinite pronoun, Dekeyser concludes that as for pronoun-verb concord, there is virtually no discrepancy between prescription and description, while as to co-referential pronouns prescriptivism had no impact on the actual usage in the 19th century. He also notes that, on the whole, plural concord is more common in speech than in written language. On the basis of his sociolinguistic analysis, Dekeyser argues that women are more inclined to use the plural co-referential pronouns than men. According to him, the usage of *none* enjoys plural concord more frequently than singular concord; this is especially so when the pronoun is followed by a plural modifier *of*-phrase.

Although the findings obtained from Dekeyser's research are supported by statistical data, there is still room for further investigation. I will therefore re-examine his results on the basis of a corpus and method different from his. I would also like to compare our data with those of Suematsu (2008), who conducted similar research on her 18th-century corpus,[3] whenever necessary.

6.1 Pronoun-verb concord

6.1.1 Overview

In English today, indefinite pronouns usually govern a singular verb, but

CHAPTER 6 CONCORD WITH INDEFINITE PRONOUNS   191

sometimes contextual meaning can lead to the use of a plural verb (Burchfield 1996: 35). According to Biber et al. (1999: 184), the pronouns *anybody/anyone, everybody/everyone, nobody/no one, somebody/someone* and *each* co-occur with singular verbs even though they may be co-referred to by plural pronouns. On the other hand, *either, neither, any* and *none* combine with both singular and plural verbs. Vacillation in number with *any* and *none* is similarly described early in the 20th century. Kruisinga states that *any* is plural and seldom singular in meaning and that *none* is oftener taken in a plural sense (1932: §§1220, 1347). In grammars of the 18th and 19th centuries, the singularity of indefinite pronouns is applied more broadly; starting with Lowth, it was advocated by Murray and Hazlitt. All three grammarians prescribe the following rule: "the distributive pronominal adjectives *each, every, either*, agree with the nouns, pronouns, and verbs, of the singular number only ..." (Lowth 1769: 92; Murray 1806: 151; Hazlitt 1810: 120). In regard to *none* and *any*, though little attention is paid to their usage at that time, Murray (1806: 159) considers the plural usage of *none* standard, noting that its usage became acceptable through continuous practice.[4]

6.1.2 The *everybody* type

Let us first have a look at the pronoun usage of the *everybody* type. There are a total of 618 instances, in which 13 different indefinite pronouns are employed.[5] Singular verbs are used in 553 instances (89.5%) and plural verbs in 65 instances (10.5%).[6] These figures indicate that singular concord is clearly the norm for indefinite pronoun-verb agreement in our 19th-century texts. Suematsu (2008: 24), who conducted a similar investigation on the basis of her 18th-century corpus, also found the dominant proportion of about 80 percent

Table 6.1: Number concord between indefinite pronouns and verbs

	Sing. verb	Plu. verb	Ratio
everybody/every body	94		1: 0.00
everyone/every one	35		1: 0.00
anybody/any body	32		1: 0.00
anyone/any one	46	1	1: 0.02
somebody/some body	29		1: 0.00
someone/some one	32		1: 0.00
nobody	120	3	1: 0.03
no one	112	2	1: 0.02
each	27		1: 0.00
either	6	2	1: 0.33
neither	2	5	1: 2.50
none	18	37	1: 2.06
any		15	0.00: 1

Ratio = Sing. verb : Plu. verb

for the singular verb form, but in comparison with our data the singular pattern seems less predominant.[7] The increased and monopolized use of the singular concord in our 19th-century texts may suggest that the newly installed grammar had a growing influence on the usage of the indefinite pronouns.

As seen in Table 6.1, the distribution of the concord patterns differs among individual indefinite pronouns. Some indefinite pronouns are more likely to be used with a singular verb, others less. Let us next look into the behavior of each pronoun in more detail.

The indefinite pronouns *everybody/every body*, *everyone/every one*, *anybody/any body* and *each* co-occur with the singular verb only. The following are some examples.

Everybody/every body: sing. 94 instances; plu. o instances
(1)   *Everybody was* in ecstasy; and Becky too, you may be sure.
                                                                                         (*Vanity*, p. 653)
(2)   It is what *every body says*.   (*Pride*, p. 33)

Everyone/every one: sing. 35 instances; plu. o instances
(3)   *Every one*, I suppose, *is* subject to a trick of mind which often puzzles me.   (*Ryecroft*, p. 100)
(4)   '*Does not everyone* approve and admire you?'   (*Satan*, p. 191)

Anybody/any body: sing. 32 instances; plu. o instances
(5)   but the argumentative Mr Macey, clerk of the parish, shook his head, and asked if *anybody was* ever known to go off in a fit and not fall down.   (*Silas*, p. 6)
(6)   "... *Has any body* hurt *you*?" (Italicized "you" in the original)
                                                                                    (*Wuthering*, p. 52)

Somebody/some body: sing. 29 instances; plu. o instances
(7)   How do you know that *somebody has* not?   (*Water*, p. 45)
(8)   You know it was reported a month ago, that *some body was* going to take Wildfell Hall — and — what do you think?   (*Wildfell*, p. 11)

Someone/some one: sing. 32 instances; plu. o instances
(9)   *Someone was* close behind, I knew not whom.   (*Treasure*, p. 112)
(10) Just as if *some one was* kissing the window all over outside. (*Alice*, p. 126)

Each: sing. 27 instances; plu. o instances
(11) *Each was* protesting against the rapacity of the other; (*Vanity*, p. 340)

As for *anyone/any one*, *nobody* and *no one*, the singular verb is predominantly employed although they have a few exceptions. Two instances of the typical singular usage and all the examples of the plural one are given below.

Nobody: sing. 120 instances; plu. 3 instances
(12) Nobody heeded me, *nobody was* aware of me. (*Invisible*, p. 113)
(13) *Nobody* ever *commits* a crime without doing something stupid.
(*Dorian*, p. 139)
(14) 'And before I take any bills or get any breakfasts, or do any such things whatsoever, you got to tell me one or two things I don't understand, and what *nobody don't* understand, and what everybody is very anxious to understand... .' <Mrs. Hall: Innkeeper> (*Invisible*, p. 35)
(15) And where he came from, *nobody don't* seem to know. <a mariner>
(*Invisible*, p. 66)
(16) *Nobody*, neither Hareton, nor Zillah *are* to know. <Linton Jr.: landowner's son> (*Wuthering*, p. 249)

Anyone/any one: sing. 46 instances; plu. 1 instance
(17) The stranger has gradually improved in health, but is very silent, and appears uneasy when *any one* except myself *enters* his cabin.
(*Frankenstein*, p. 27)
(18) 'But supposing *anyone applies*, I have no ring.' (*Scarlet*, p. 43)
(19) 'Look at my brother Pitt; look at the Huddlestons, who have been here since Henry II; look at poor Bute at the parsonage; — *are any one* of them equal to you in intelligence or breeding? ...' <Lady Crawley>
(*Vanity*, p. 127)

No one: sing. 112 instances, plu. 2 instances
(20) He was her dear Wickham on every occasion; *no one was* to be put in competition with him. (*Pride*, p. 242)
(21) '... *no one believes* it, surely, Ernest?' (*Frankenstein*, p. 79)
(22) Then it blow some more fresh, and we go down below and drive very fast — *no one know* where. <Manuel: Seaman> (*Captains*, p. 85)
(23) and *no one don't* seem to have been aware of his misfortune, it says, aware of his misfortune, until in an Alteration in the inn, it says, his bandages on his head was torn off. <a mariner> (*Invisible*, p. 67)

The use of the plural verbs in the examples (14), (15), (16), (19), (22) and (23) is "incorrect" in light of the grammar of the 19th century as well as of today. These examples can be put into the category which Biber et al. (1999: §3.9.4) call "non-standard concord in conversation" since this usage not infrequently occurs in spoken language.[8] In our texts, the plural concord of this kind is practiced by lower-class people such as an innkeeper, a mariner and a seaman as seen in (14), (15), (22) and (23) while it is sometimes used by upper-class people as in (16) and (19). Example (19) is uttered by Lady Crawley, whose usual language is hardly ever regarded as nonstandard. In this example, however, a list of names would impress her that she is talking about more than one person, which can cause her to employ the plural verb for *each*. Example (16) is another instance of plural concord by a person of the upper class. In this instance, there is a possibility that the phrase "neither ... nor ..." placed after *nobody* contributes to the production of the plural verb form since the phrase is often treated as plural. These instances indicate that other interposed elements can lead to plural concord.

In regard to *either* and *neither*,[9] both singular and plural verbs are used while it is not certain which form is preferred. In Present-day English, these pronouns generally govern a singular verb, but sometimes the number of the verb varies "because of the fundamental plurality of the conception" (Jespersen 1909–49: II, §6.44.). The situation of the usage in the 19th century may be the same. Burchfield (1996, s.v. *either* 4) states that plural concord tends to occur in the type "(*n*)*either* + *of*-phrase." Let us find out whether this tendency is true of *either* and *neither* in our 19th-century texts though the number of instances is small.

Table 6.2: Pronoun-verb concord: *either/neither* with/without an *Of*-phrase

	With *of*-phrase		Without *of*-phrase	
	Sing. verb	Plu. verb	Sing. verb	Plu. verb
either	4	1	2	1
neither	2	5		1

As far as our data go, there is no significant imbalance between the constructions with *of*-phrase and those without. Dekeyser (1975: 74–75), on the other hand, claims that the rule may be true of his eighteen instances of (*n*)*either*;[10] his study shows that the singular-plural ratios are 4 : 8 for "with *of*-phrase" and 3 : 3 for "without *of*-phrase." Different ratios between his data and mine would probably be statistically insignificant due to the paucity of examples in both of our data. Poutsma (1916: XL, 43) presents a more general observation that *either* and *neither* are used in two shades of meaning: (A) one and the other, (B) one or (the) other, no matter which.[11] When our sample is sorted into these two types, out of eight instances of *either*, three instances (plural 2: singular 1) belong to Type A; five (all singular) to Type B. Among eight instances of *neither*, six instances (all plural) fall into Type A and two (both singular) into Type B. See examples (24) to (31) below.

Either: sing. 6 instances: plu. 2 instances
Type A
(24)   *Either* of these young ladies *is perfectly qualified* to instruct in Greek, Latin, and the rudiments of Hebrew; (Italicized "perfectly qualified" in the original)   (*Vanity*, p. 117)
(25)   I was not present to close her eyes; nor *were either* of her daughters.
                                                                                                     (*Jane*, p. 240)

Type B
(26)   'Yes, I suppose. If *either cares* for another person, for instance.'
                                                                                                     (*Jude*, p. 201)
(27)   I do not think *either* of these soi-disant friends *is* overflowing with love for the other;   (*Wildfell*, p. 310)

Neither: sing. 2 instances; plu. 5 instances
Type A
(28)   To do them justice, *neither* of the sisters *were* very much displeased.
                                                                                                     (*Vanity*, p. 275)
(29)   The heart was thrilled, the mind astonished, by the power of the preacher: *neither were* softened.   (*Jane*, p. 352)

Type B
(30)   "But he is accused of it. So might you or I be. Either of us might be accused of it, you know."
        "Only *neither* of us *is*," I remarked.   (*Great*, p. 256)
(31)   "It's disapinting to a man," he said, in a coarse broken voice, "arter having looked for'ard so distant, and come so fur; but you're not to blame for that — *neither on us is* to blame for that.   (*Great*, p. 311)

The examples above indicate that in the case of *either* and *neither* plural forms are restricted to Type A. The choice of plural verbs here is perhaps due to the contextual meaning ("both") that (*n*)*either* bears. Poutsma (XL, 44) states that *either* in the first meaning ("one and the other") is getting more and more unusual and that when the separative idea is not prominent, *both* is used instead of *either*.

The behaviors of *none* and *any* are obviously different. Both indefinite pronouns tend to occur with a plural verb. In regard to *none*, the ratio of the singular and plural is 18: 37, marking 67 percent in favor of the plural. Dekeyser's results similarly illustrate the dominant plural patterning in 19th-century English literature with 26 examples (38.8%) for singular and 41 (61.2%) for plural. In her 18th-century texts, Suematsu (2008: 24) finds that *none* is used with a singular verb in 19 instances (27.5%) and a plural verb in 50 (72.5%). Although in 19th-century English the proportion of the plural verb form with *none* is high in comparison with the other indefinites, it still seems slightly lower than that in the previous century. In the use of *none*, there might have been a dilemma between grammatical correctness and notional naturalness. The examples of *none* occurring with singular or plural verbs are as follows:

None: sing. 18 instances; plu. 37 instances
(32) he would fly up in a passion of anger at a question, or sometimes because *none was put*, and so he judged the company was not following his story. (*Treasure*, pp. 3–4)
(33) I was alone; *none were* near me to dissipate the gloom, and relieve me from the sickening oppression of the most terrible reveries.
(*Frankenstein*, p. 166)

Unstable as the use of *none* in concord is, there seem to be some particular constructions which encourage the writers to decide which number to choose. One such construction is that including the modifying plural *of*-adjunct. As indicated in Table 6.3, this is the case with the indefinite *none*; plural concord is more likely to occur with an *of*-phrase than otherwise. It is undoubtedly assumed that plural (pro)nouns in the *of*-phrase lead to the use of plural concord.

Table 6.3: Pronoun-verb concord: *none* in the construction with/without an *of*-phrase

	Sing. verb	Plu. verb
With *of*-phrase	1	14
Without *of*-phrase	17	23

Compare the two examples found in *Jane Eyre*; in (34) *none* with an *of*-phrase is associated with a plural verb while in (35) a singular verb is used without an *of*-phrase.

(34) Yet, I thought, I ought to have been happy, for *none of the Reeds were* there; they were all gone out in the carriage with their mama: (*Jane*, p. 20)
(35) "... I wished to see Jane Eyre, and I fancy a likeness where *none exists*: besides in eight years she must be so changed." (*Jane*, p. 238)

Another construction which can affect the choice of number is an existential sentence or the *there* + *be* construction. This construction appears in almost half of the 53 examples of *none* where the singular *be* form is more often used in existential sentences (see Table 6.4). Michiko Yaguchi (2010) suggests that *there*-constructions without concord, while often attested in Present-day

English, already existed in Early Modern English.¹² Indeed, the usage is found in our texts.¹³

Table 6.4: Pronoun-verb concord: *none* in the existential sentences

there + be + none		otherwise	
Sing. verb	Plu. verb	Sing. verb	Plu. verb
11	15	7	22

(36) "The path of my departure was free;" and *there was none* to lament my annihilation. (*Frankenstein*, p. 128)
(37) Some people think that there are no fairies. Cousin Cramchild tells little folks so in his *Conversations*. Well, perhaps *there are none* — in Boston, USA, where he was raised. (Italicized "Conversations" in the original) (*Water*, p. 39)

These findings indicate that while *of*-phrases encourage plural agreement, *there + be* constructions tend to be linked with a singular verb. It seems possible, however, that both factors are relevant. There are three instances of this sort, in each of which the choice is the plural verb form. This would suggest that *of*-phrases play a stronger role in deciding the number than the *there + be* construction does. Compare (38) with (39) and (40) with (41):

(38) *There was none* to be had: the only one in the town was under repair. (*Wildfell*, p. 446)
(39) Happily, *there were none of Arthur's 'friends'* invited to Grassdale last autumn: he took himself off to visit some of them instead. (*Wildfell*, p. 314)
(40) 'The other swam after, and then *there was none*, And so the poor stone was left all alone; With a fal-lal-la-lady.' (*Water*, p. 158)
(41) At last, there *were none of us* left, except on the old Gairfowlskerry, just off the Iceland coast, up which no man could climb. (*Water*, p. 159)¹⁴

With regard to *any*, it has fifteen relevant examples, in each of which plural concord is employed. This indefinite pronoun thus turns out to be least tainted with singularity among the indefinites under discussion. The modifying plural *of*-adjunct is used in half of the examples but plural patterning is always selected whether with the phrase or not. Plurality of *any* has hence not been affected by grammar.¹⁵ The following are two examples of *any*: one occurring with the form *of*-phrase and the other without it.

Any: sing. 0 instances; plu. 15 instances

(42) 'I wonder if *any of those authors* are present!' (*Satan*, p. 223)
(43) 'I don't know of *any* that *do*,' Alice said very politely, feeling quite pleased to have got into a conversation. (*Alice*, p. 53)

6.1.3 The *every man* type

In addition to *–body* or *–one*, the pronominal adjectives or the indefinite modifiers (*some, every, any, no, each*) can be used before singular human-denoting nouns to form combinational terms similar to the compound pronouns (e.g., *every man, any woman*). According to Curme (1931: 52), the singular agreement is the norm after such adjectives although they have collective meaning.[16] This conforms to the rule in 19th-century English. There are a total of 147 instances of the *every man* type with no single violation in number concord found. The breakdown of the examples is as follows: *no* + sing. noun (61 exx.), *every* + sing. noun (45 exx.), *some* + sing. noun (19 exx.), *any* + sing. noun (19 exx.) and *each* + sing. noun (3 exx.). In our texts, 52 nouns denoting persons (or sometimes spiritual beings and animals) are used along with the five pronominal adjectives. The noun most frequently used is *man* (51 exx.), followed by *woman* (11 exx.), *person* (7 exx.), *gentleman* (6 exx.), *girl* (5 exx.), *God* (5 exx.), *child* (4 exx.), *artist* (4 exx.), *reader* (3 exx.), *human being* (3 exx.), *lady* (3 exx.), *boy* (3 exx.), *servant* (2 exx.), *lounger* (2 exx.) and *individual* (2 exx.); the remaining 37 words are used once each.[17] Some examples are as follows:

(44) '*Every man has* some little power in some one direction,' he would say.
 (*Jude*, p. 387)
(45) There *is no woman* to shield me here. (*N and S*, p. 180)
(46) Any one you love must be marvellous, and *any girl* that *has* the effect you describe must be fine and noble. (*Dorian*, p. 66)
(47) "... Go, and say *some person* from Gimmerton *desires* to see her."
 (*Wuthering*, p. 82)
(48) It is really wise and clever of us — for hence *each individual is* so much flesh-wall through which neither friend nor enemy can spy.
 (*Satan*, pp. 28–29)

It is to be noted that in (46) *any* combined with *girl* shows singular agreement. This is in sharp contrast to the pronominal *any*, which always shows plural concord. Poutsma (1916: XL, 19) states that "in Late Modern English this *any* is mostly to be understood as a plural, there being now a distinct tendency to place a prop-word after *any* when a singular is meant."

6.1.4 Spoken and written

Let us now examine the frequencies of single/plural concord in two different registers, spoken and written languages. Since there is no plural concord for the *every man* type as seen above, I will focus on the *everybody* type here.

Table 6.5: Pronoun-verb concord in written/spoken language: the *everybody* type

	Written			Spoken		
	Sing. verb	Plu. verb	Ratio	Sing. verb	Plu. verb	Ratio
everybody/every body	42		1 : 0.00	52		1 : 0.00
everyone/every one	20		1 : 0.00	15		1 : 0.00
anybody/any body	7		1 : 0.00	25		1 : 0.00
anyone/any one	19		1 : 0.00	27	1	1 : 0.04
somebody/some body	8		1 : 0.00	21		1 : 0.00
someone/some one	12		1 : 0.00	20		1 : 0.00
nobody	41		1 : 0.00	79	3	1 : 0.04
no one	62		1 : 0.00	50	2	1 : 0.04
each	21		1 : 0.00	6		1 : 0.00
either	2	1	1 : 0.50	4	1	1 : 0.25
neither		5	0.00 : 1	2		1 : 0.00
none	12	26	1 : 2.17	6	11	1 : 1.83
any		12	0.00 : 1		3	0.00 : 1
Total	246	44	1 : 0.18	307	21	1 : 0.07

Ratio = Sing. verb : Plu.verb

Table 6.5 shows that in the cases of indefinites such as the *–body/one* type pronouns and *each*, singular concord is the norm while the plural verb form occurs only in spoken language. Otherwise (i.e., *either, neither, none, any*), the plural form is found in both registers. Plural concord occurs in written language as often as in spoken language. The usage, being permitted in written language, is apparently not regarded as nonstandard or ungrammatical. Given that in the cases of *none* and *any* plural patterning is far more frequently or even exclusively used even in writing, the plural usage would have been accepted among the educated at that time. As to *either* and *neither*, as far as our data are concerned, it is not quite certain which pattering is preferred by the authors. It would be safe to conclude, however, that plural patterning is not strictly avoided even in formal language.

6.2 Pronominal co-reference

6.2.1 Overview

In pronominal reference, especially when indefinite pronouns like *everybody/ everyone* are referred to by a personal pronoun, concord becomes a problem not merely with number but also with gender. In Present-day English, there are choices of personal pronouns with reference to indefinite pronouns like *everybody/everyone*: *he or she*, *they*, and *he*. Among these three, *they* is commonly used while *he* is recommended; the disjunctive combination *he or she* is considered "clumsy" and sounds like "pedantic humour" and is thus to be avoided if possible (Fowler 1965, s.v. *number* 11). Rodney Huddleston and Geoffrey K. Pullum (2002: 492) state of the dilemma over whether to use *he* or *they* as follows:

> *He* has traditionally been regarded as the grammatically 'correct' choice in opposition to singular *they*; it is characteristic of relatively formal style. The issue of the choice between *he* and *they* has concerned writers on usage for some 200 years, but since this use of *he* represents one of the most obvious and central cases of sexism in language, the matter has received much more widespread attention since the early 1980s in the context of social changes in the status of women. (492)

The use of singular *they* is traced back to Middle English. Despite criticism from the prescriptive grammarians, singular *they* has continually been quite common in informal style (Huddleston and Pullum 2002: 493). The use of *he* in reference to *everybody/everyone* is supposed to be regarded as grammatical in the 18th and 19th centuries although there are few grammarians who gave explicit instructions on this issue. From the proper and improper examples presented by Lowth (1769: 83), Murray (1806: 160) and Hazlitt (1810: 120–121), it is presumed that the use of the third person singular masculine *he* for indefinite pronouns is recommended and that the plural form *they* is to be avoided.[18] The example presented as "proper" by the three grammarians is:

> "The king of Israel, and Jehosophat, the king of Judah, sat *each* on *his* throne:" (Italics in the original)

Some of those presented as "improper" by Murray and Hazlitt are:

> "Let *each* esteem others better than *themselves.*"
> "In proportion as *either* of these two qualities *are* wanting, the language

is imperfect."

"It is observable that *every* one of the letters *bear* date after his banishment." (Italics original)

Concerning the usage of the pronouns *each, one, either* and *neither,* Brown suggests that the singular was required; he (1851: 552) states that "the pronominal adjectives, *each, one, either,* and *neither,* are always in the third person singular; and, when they are the leading words in their clauses, they require verbs and pronouns to agree with them accordingly."

6.2.2 The *everybody* type

Let us first see how indefinite pronouns are co-referred to by other pronouns in terms of number. The total of our sample amounts to 253 instances, out of which 122 instances (48.2%) show singular agreement and 131 instances (51.8%) plural agreement. Unlike subject-verb agreement, on the whole, there is no striking preference for singular concord. The ratio of the singular and plural forms differs among the individual pronouns. *Any* and *(n)either* are (almost) always co-referred to by plural pronouns. The pronouns *–body/one* and *each* occur with singular and plural co-referential pronouns. The rule of singularity required by prescriptive grammarians seems not to be observed here. Comparison with the situation in the previous century, however, reveals a different story. According to Suematsu (2008: 17), plural pronouns are chosen in 61 percent of the relevant examples in her 18th-century corpus. Thus our figure of 51.8 percent may suggest that there was a move towards the singular in

Table 6.6: Number concord of pronominal co-reference: the *everybody* type

	Sing. pron.	Plu. pron.	Ratio
everybody/every body	5	27	1 : 5.4
everyone/every one	15	20	1 : 1.3
anybody/any body	6	6	1 : 1.0
anyone/any one	16	10	1 : 0.6
somebody/some body	5	2	1 : 0.4
someone/some one	12	1	1 : 0.1
nobody	4	5	1 : 1.3
no one	8	4	1 : 0.5
each one	1		1 : 0.0
each	44	28	1 : 0.6
either		11	0.0 : 1
neither	1	3	1 : 3.0
none	5	4	1 : 0.8
any		10	0.0 : 1
Total	122	131	1 : 1.1

Ratio = Sing. pron. : Plu. pron.

19th-century English because of grammatical regulation.

In our texts, where both singular and plural pronouns are "equally" used for the indefinite, let us now consider possible elements which affect the choice. *Merriam-Webster's Dictionary of English Usage* or *MWDEU* (1994: 416) points out that *everyone* is referred to by a singular pronoun twice as frequent as *everybody* in 20th century English probably due to "the underlying pressure toward singularity created by *–one*." This tendency conforms to the results based on our 19th-century texts. Table 6.6 above shows that in each pair the proportion of the singular is higher for the *–one* type than the *–body* type. A similar tendency is also found in the 18th-century English texts (Suematsu 2008: 22).[19]

Another noticeable point is that among the pronouns with *–body* or *–one*, the compounds *somebody* and *someone* appear with singular pronouns more often than the others, as seen in Table 6.7.

Table 6.7: Number concord of pronominal co-reference: compounds with *every/any/some/no*

	Sing. pron.	Plu. pron.	Ratio
everybody/everyone	20	47	1 : 2.4
anybody/anyone	22	16	1 : 0.7
somebody/someone	17	3	1 : 0.2
nobody/no one	12	9	1 : 0.8

Ratio = sing. pron. : plu. pron.

Indefinite pronouns are used to express entities "which the speaker or writer cannot or does not want to specify more exactly" (Biber et al. 1999: 351). *Somebody* and *someone*, for instance, are not infrequently used when the speaker does not want, or does not think it necessary, to specify the person. When a particular individual is meant by *someone* or *somebody*, singularity will be naturally chosen for a co-referential pronoun. Out of the seventeen instances of singular concord (*somebody*: 5 exx.; *someone*: 12 exx.) the speakers refer to a specific person in eleven cases (*somebody*: 4 exx.; *someone*: 7 exx.) but no such situation is found in the three instances of its plural counterparts. In example (49), the narrator does not know the name of *someone* and in (50) the speaker knows the name of *somebody* but does not mention it. In both examples, the speakers employ the singular masculine *he* for co-referential pronouns without hesitation because they *know* the referent is male. In example (51), in which *somebody* is not used to infer a specific person, plurality is chosen for it.

(49)   I was standing at the door for a moment full of sad thoughts about my father, when I saw *someone* drawing slowly near along the road. *He*

was plainly blind, for *he* tapped before *him* with a stick and wore a great green shade over *his* eyes and nose; *(Treasure,* p. 16)

(50) *Somebody* — I won't mention *his* name, but you know *him* — came to me last year to have *his* portrait done. *(Dorian,* p. 123)

(51) 'I guess *somebody* else made the country in these parts. It's not nearly so well done. *They* forgot the water and the trees.' *(Scarlet,* p. 73)

When the referent appears modified by *of us/you* (e.g., *each of us/you),* it occasionally happens that the first person plural *(we, our, us)* and the second person (plural) *you* are selected as co-referential pronouns. As shown in Table 6.8, there are only four examples in which the singular *he* is employed as co-referent: two examples each for the forms modified by *of us* and *of you.* That is, the plurality is more often used in reference to the indefinite of this type.

Table 6.8: Co-referential pronouns: indefinites + *of us/you*

	of + us		*of + you*	
	we	*he*	*you*	*he*
anyone		1		
each		1	1	2
either	2		1	
neither	2			
none	1			
any			1	
Total	5	2	3	2

Note: The co-referential pronoun *we* includes *us* and *our, you* includes *ye,* and *he* includes *his, him* and *himself.*

Singular concord

(52) I quite sympathize with the rage of the English democracy against what they call the vices of the upper orders. The masses feel that drunkenness, stupidity, and immorality should be their own special property, and that if *any one of us* makes an ass of *himself he* is poaching on their preserves. *(Dorian,* p. 7)

(53) The next moment *each of us* had taken to *his* heels in a different direction. *(Treasure,* p. 99)

(54) "... but you are not desolate: *each of you* has a comrade to sympathise with *him* in *his* decay." *(Jane,* p. 276)

(55) '*Each of us* has Heaven and Hell in *him,* Basil,' cried Dorian, with a wild gesture of despair. *(Dorian,* p. 128)

Plural concord

(56) Estella took no notice of *either of us,* but led *us* the way that I knew so

	well. *(Great*, p. 98)
(57)	'... and *neither of us* ride so light as *we* did when *we* first entered the corps.' *(Vanity*, p. 689)
(58)	They acted their part and I acted mine — *none of us* were ever *our* real selves for a moment. *(Satan*, p. 236)
(59)	"I meant to give *each of you* some of this to take with *you*," said she; *(Jane*, p. 72)
(60)	If *any of you* gentlemen have ever pined for a thing, and longed for it during twenty long years, and then suddenly found it within *your* reach *you* would understand my feelings. *(Scarlet*, p. 117)

Biber et al. (1999: 192) state that discord in number tends to occur where there is considerable distance. It is highly possible that distance is involved in the choice of the pronoun. When the speakers or writers use the singular *he* in co-reference to the antecedent, the referring pronoun occurs relatively close to the pronoun referred to; both pronouns often appear in the same coordinate clause. On the other hand, there is a certain distance between the indefinite pronoun and the plural co-referents such as *us* and *you*. It is also noteworthy that the co-referent *he* is likely to be chosen when the speakers refer to people in general by the antecedents *us* or *you* as in examples (52), (54) and (55), while the co-referents *we* or *you* are preferred when the speakers refer to more specific people who are there in the scene. Examples (54) and (59) are both found in *Jane Eyre*; in the former Jane chooses the co-referent *him* since *each of you* stands for people in general while in the latter Miss Temple employs *you* in addressing her two students before her eyes.

6.2.3 The *every man* type

There are 177 examples of the pronominal adjective in which pronominal co-reference is observed, with 166 examples of the singular and eleven of the plural. The proportion of the singular marks about 94 percent of the total, showing that there is little fluctuation in number concord with the adjective usage, as opposed to the pronominal usage. The common use of singular pronouns for pronominal adjectives is attributed to the specificity of nouns following the pronoun. There are 59 different nouns which denote humans in our sample; the most frequently-used noun is *man* with 83 examples followed by *woman* (9 exx.), *lady* (6 exx.), *clergyman* (4 exx.), *girl* (4 exx.), *person* (4 exx.), *gentleman* (4 exx.), *father* (3 exx.), *member* (3 exx.), *servant* (2 exx.), *boy* (2 exx.), *millionaire* (2 exx.), *pupil* (2 exx.), and *stranger* (2 exx.), with the other 45 different nouns appearing just once.[20] Some examples are shown according to singular/plural concord below the table.

Table 6.9: Number concord of pronominal co-reference: the *every man* type

	Sing. pron.	Plu. pron.	Ratio
some + sing. noun	20		1 : 0.0
every + sing. noun	38	7	1 : 0.2
any + sing. noun	51	3	1 : 0.1
no + sing. noun	40		1 : 0.0
each + sing. noun	17	1	1 : 0.1
Total	166	11	1 : 0.1

Ratio = Sing. pron. : Plu. pron.

Singular concord

(61) 'Why, I would apply to *some good house-mother* to recommend me one known to *herself* or *her* servants.' (*N and S*, p. 92)

(62) *Every gentleman* is interested in *his* good name. (*Dorian*, p. 122)

(63) I looked as grateful as *any boy* possibly could, who was wholly uninformed why *he* ought to assume that expression. (*Great*, p. 50)

(64) 'You don't mean to say that *no man* can love a woman unless *he* be a fool?' (*Barchester*, I, p. 142)

(65) *Each man* had anchored where it seemed good to *him*, drifting and rowing round *his* fixed point. (*Captains*, p. 99)

Plural concord

(66) *Every gambler* there was selfish to the core, and as I studied *their* hardened faces, a thrill of honest indignation moved me — indignation mingled with shame. (*Satan*, p. 90)

(67) 'But to expose the former faults of *any person*, without knowing what *their* present feelings were, seemed unjustifiable... .' (*Pride*, p. 220)

(68) and she is not, on any account, to give out more than one at a time to *each pupil*: if *they* have more, *they* are apt to be careless and lose them. (*Jane*, p. 62)

6.2.4 Spoken and written

On the use of pronominal concord, Quirk et al. (1985: 342–343) state that the "evasive tactic" of the plural pronouns is common but less acceptable. The description of this problem by Biber et al. (1999: 316) is different. They clearly note that plural forms are commonly used in both speech and writing. I would like to investigate the usage of pronominal concord according to written/spoken contexts in our 19th-century texts.

Table 6.10: Number concord of pronominal co-reference in written/spoken language

	Written		Spoken	
	Sing. pron.	Plu. pron.	Sing. pron.	Plu. pron.
The *everybody* type	80 (48.8%)	84 (51.2%)	41 (46.1%)	48 (53.9%)
The *every man* type	94 (91.3%)	9 (8.7%)	72 (97.3%)	2 (2.7%)

Table 6.10 shows how singular and plural pronouns appear in written and spoken languages for the *everybody* type and the *every man* type. In terms of written/spoken contexts, no significant difference in proportion is observed with either type; regardless of register, the proportion of the plural forms is slightly higher than that of the singular forms for the *everybody* type while the singular form is the norm for the *every man* type. In the 19th century, therefore, it cannot be said that plural forms were commonly used either in speech or in writing. However, it is expected that the usage of the plural forms in our texts will lead to what Quirk et al. call the commonly used "evasive tactic." Since the end of the 20th century, the surge of feminism has helped to establish singular *they* as standard usage. This is why the plural form has been accepted regardless of register. The difference in the description of acceptance of the plural forms between Quirk et al. (1985) and Biber et al. (1999) above may indicate that singular *they* has increasingly gained in grammatical correctness since the time of Quirk et al.

6.2.5 Sociolinguistic analysis

I will next look into difference in the use of pronominal concord among individual authors. Dekeyser (1975: 81) indicates that women are less "grammatical" than men in the use of co-referential pronouns. His results show that females chose plural pronouns more often (52.5 percent rate) than the males (30.3 percent rate).[21] Let us see whether this is the case with our corpus. Since the proportion of number concord differs between the *everybody* type and the *every man* type, observation of the two will be conducted separately.

6.2.5.1 The *everybody* type
Table 6.11 shows difference in the choice of pronoun concord between the male authors and the female authors. The females apparently use plural pronouns more often than singular ones while the males prefer singular pronouns. Concerning women's preference for plural pronouns, Dekeyser (1975: 81) states that "being women they must be averse to exclusively employing singular (masculine) pronouns." However, neither Dekeyser's findings nor the overall rates and percentages obtained here may be sufficient to prove his presumption. Further analysis on this subject is needed to explain the prefer-

ence of plural forms by female authors.

Table 6.11: Number concord of pronominal co-reference according to sex

	Sing. Pron.	Plu. Pron.	Total
Male authors	87 (59.6%)	59 (40.4%)	146
Female authors	35 (33.0%)	72 (67.0%)	107

The sex of the entity expressed by an indefinite pronoun is important for the choice of co-referential pronouns. The entities are meant to be of both sexes in some cases, as when the speaker is talking about people in general, as in the examples (69) to (71), or when specified men and women are simultaneously referred to, as in (72).

(69) I cannot understand how *any one* can wish to shame the thing *he* loves.
(*Dorian*, p. 63)
(70) *Nobody* could be nearer than a mile to them without their seeing *him*.
(*Jude*, p. 47)
(71) 'I always forgive *everyone* the moment *they* tell me the truth of *their* own accord.' (*Water*, p. 139)
(72) Then he watched the sailors upon deck, and the ladies, with their bonnets and parasols: but *none* of them could see him, because *their* eyes were not opened — as, indeed, most people's eyes are not. (*Water*, p. 155)

In contrast, there are cases in which the speaker refers to only one sex. In the following examples, the underlined part makes it possible to decide which sex the speakers bear in their mind; the referent is supposed to be male in examples (73) and (74) and female in (75) and (76).

(73) It is one of the great beauties of our system, that a working-man may raise himself into the power and position of a master by his own exertions and behaviour; that, in fact, *every one* who rules *himself* to decency and sobriety of conduct, and attention to *his* duties, comes over to our ranks; (*N and S*, p. 84)
(74) "But there are several other handsome, rich young men in the world: handsomer, possibly, and richer than he is — What should hinder you from loving them?"
"If there be *any, they* are out of my way — I've seen none like Edgar."
(*Wuthering*, pp. 69–70)
(75) A distant bell tinkled: immediately three ladies entered the room, *each* walked to a table and took *her* seat; (*Jane*, p. 45)
(76) ... bridesmaids in bright attire and picture-hats — young girls all eager

and excited-looking, *each* of them no doubt longing fervently for the day to come when *they* might severally manage to secure as rich a husband as myself ... (*Satan*, p. 240)

Since the singular pronoun *he* can be used both for males individually as well as for people in general, sometimes it is not clear which the speakers are talking about. Still there are hints to help us designate the sex referred to. It is easy when we know who the referents are as in (77) and if the speaker knows who they are, that is most helpful as in example (78).

(77) Stangerson has a son, and Drebber has a son, and *either* of them would gladly welcome your daughter to *their* house. (*Scarlet*, p. 89)

(78) 'Only *some one* come about the pictures,' said she, in apology for her abrupt departure: 'I told *him* to wait.' (*Wildfell*, p. 45)

In the following example, since all the crew members of the fishing vessel are male, those inferred from *everybody* are naturally male.

(79) Then *everybody* shouted and tried to haul up *his* anchor to get among the school, and fouled *his* neighbour's line and said what was in *his* heart, and dipped furiously with *his* dip-net, and shrieked cautions and advice to *his* companions, while the deep fizzed like freshly-opened soda-water, and cod, men, and whales together flung in upon the luckless bait. (*Captains*, p. 98)

Generally, one presumes the sex of people from their occupations (MacKay and Fulkerson 1979). This is especially the case with Victorian society. It would be only natural to assume people who have academic positions are male,[22] as in (80) and (81).

(80) 'It is not *every one* who can <u>sit comfortably in a set of college rooms</u>, and let *his* riches grow without any exertion of *his* own... .' (*N and S*, p. 330)

(81) And I, a shabby, poverty-struck, hemmed-in demonstrator, <u>teaching fools in a provincial college</u>, might suddenly become — this. I ask you, Kemp, if *you* — Anyone, I tell you, would have flung *himself* upon <u>that research</u>. (Italicized "you" in the original) (*Invisible*, pp. 93–94)

The contexts given by the neighboring words are also of help. In example (82), the terms "like a man" imply that the speaker imagines any "man" as a male. In (83), the underlined part indicates that the narrator expects "any one" who will accompany Mrs. Graham for her security to be male.

(82) '... It isn't much of a walk to Kench's; and then, if it's me as is deppity, I'll go back with you, Master Marner, and examine your premises; and if *anybody*'s got any fault to find with that, I'll thank *him* to stand up and say it out like a man.' (*Silas*, p. 56)
(83) In fact, she would not hear of *any one*'s putting *himself* out of the way to accompany her, though Fergus vouchsafed to offer his services, in case they should be more acceptable than mine, and my mother begged she might send one of the farming-men to escort her. (*Wildfell*, p. 81)

The sex of the referent thus can be specified to a considerable degree with reference to sex-suggesting clues. Table 6.12 shows how the referent's sex is related to its co-referential pronoun after sorting our sample with such hints. Examples in which only males are referred to are grouped as MALE, those in which only females are implied are called FEMALE, and when the pronoun can refer to both sexes or either, those examples are labeled as BOTH. Since it is gender that counts, eighteen examples of inanimate entities and animals whose sex is unknown are excluded here.

Table 6.12: Relationship between the referent's sex and the co-referential pronoun*

	MALE			FEMALE			BOTH			
	he	they	you/we	she	they	you/we	he	he or she	they	you/we
everybody/every body	1			1			2	1	27	
everyone/every one	4	1		1			10		19	
anybody/any body	5						1		6	
anyone/any one	4	1		3			9		9	
somebody/some body	5								2	
someone/some one	10			1			1		1	
nobody							4		5	
no one				2			5	1	4	
each one				1						
Subtotal	29	2		9			32	2	73	
each	13	5		4	5	1	9	8	14	
either		3	2		1	1			2	
neither	1		1			1			1	
none	1						3		3	1
any		1	1						6	
Subtotal	15	9	4	4	6	3	12	8	26	1
Total	44	11	4	13	6	3	44	10	99	1

*The pronouns stand for those in a variety of cases; for instance *he* stands for *he, his, him* and *himself*.

There are 59 instances of MALE, 22 of FEMALE and 154 of BOTH. No example is found in which the third person singular feminine *she* represents people in general. As a matter of course, only BOTH has examples of the disjunctive combination *he or she*. Some interesting differences are found in the choice of singular/plural forms among the three categories. Firstly, while singular pronouns are more likely to be used in both MALE and FEMALE, the plural pronoun *they* is the favorite in BOTH. Secondly, in the cases of MALE and FEMALE, the choice between singular and plural pronouns appears to be significantly controlled by the type of pronoun. While in the categories of MALE and FEMALE the *–body/one* types are rarely employed with a plural pronoun, in BOTH they are used with a plural pronoun more often (73 exx.) than a singular one (32 exx.). These findings evidently indicate that the writers spontaneously choose singular *they* to refer to both sexes.

Here, I would like to reanalyze the examples obtained above in terms of the authors' sex. The following tables present the distribution of concord in the cases where the sex of the subject is designated as either male or female (Table 6.13a) and that in the case where both sexes are referred to (Table 6.13b). There is no significant difference between the male and female authors in the choice of concord for MALE and FEMALE: singular forms are more likely to be chosen by the authors of both sexes. On the other hand, Table 6.13b shows a remarkable difference in their use of pronouns; in BOTH, the male authors use *he* and *they* almost equally while the female authors choose *he* and *they* in the ratio of 1 : 9.

Table 6.13a: Number concord of pronominal co-reference according to the authors' sex: MALE and FEMALE

	Sing. Pron.	Plu. Pron.	Total
Male authors	33 (71.7%)	13 (28.3%)	46
Female authors	24 (68.6%)	11 (31.4%)	35

sing. pronoun: *he, she* ; plu. pronoun: *they, we, you*

Table 6.13b: Number concord of pronominal co-reference according to the authors' sex: BOTH

	he	he or she	they/you/we	Total
Male authors	38 (41.3%)	8 (8.7%)	46 (50.0%)	92
Female authors	6 (9.7%)	2 (3.2%)	54 (87.1%)	62

All those observations could be further evidence for Dekeyser's speculation that women resort to plural pronouns more often than men because as women they do not like to lump their sex together with men under the pronoun *he*. Only three female authors use singular masculine *he* for both sexes[23] while the male authors are far less hesitant to make the pronoun *he* represent both sexes. However, it is also worth noting that the proportion of plural pronouns by the male authors increases in reference to both sexes as opposed to one sex, which suggests they also care to some degree. Singular *they* had been commonly used before the singular form was prescribed as grammatical. During the 19th century, the presence of singular *they* seemingly diminished but women preserved and handed down the usage to the following century, when the use of singular *they* would become popular again.

One alternative that resolves both gender and grammatical problems is to use the combinational form *he or she*, which is regarded as "clumsy" or "awkward" by many grammarians (cf. McKnight 1928: 528; Fowler 1965: 404). Since there are only ten examples in our 19th-century texts, this expression seems not to have been common at that time either. The compound *he or she* co-occurs with *each* eight times and with *everybody* and *no one* once each. In most cases the form is selected when the referents are specific persons whose identities are clarified, as seen in example (84), or at least whose sexes are known to the speaker/writer, as in (85) and (86). Eight out of the ten examples of *he or she* are of these types. It is psychologically understandable that in referring to particular men and women, the speakers are all the more hesitant to inclusively use generic *he* for them.

(84) So these two were each exemplifying the Vanity of this life, and *each* longing for what *he or she* could not get. (*Vanity*, p. 552)
(85) There were three ladies in the room and one gentleman. Before I had been standing at the window five minutes, they somehow conveyed to me that they were all toadies and humbugs, but that *each* of them pretended not to know that the others were toadies and humbugs: because the admission that *he or she* did know it, would have made *him or her* out to be a toady and humbug. (*Great*, p. 79)
(86) Directly *each* of these young people had done, *he or she* made promptly for the door with such an expression of animation as I have rarely observed in a shop assistant before. (*Invisible*, pp. 111–112)

No matter how clumsy, sometimes *he or she* or its variant forms are necessary as in (87) and (88). Both of the examples are attested in *Barchester Towers*.[24]

(87) *Everybody* calling *himself* a gentleman, *or herself* a lady, within the city of Barchester, and a circle of two miles round it, was included.
(*Barchester*, I, p. 85)
(88) How much each of them had to tell the other, and how certain *each* was that the story which *he or she* had to tell would astonish the other!

(*Barchester*, II, p. 241)

6.2.5.2 The *every man* type

Let us move on to the survey of the *every man* type. The relevant examples are similarly grouped in three categories: MALE, FEMALE and BOTH. Nouns combined with an adjective modifier are often helpful to determine which sex the subject belongs to (e.g., *every lady, any boy*). The term *man*, however, can be a little complex since it expresses either "male" or "human." The relevant examples are categorized as MALE or BOTH depending on the context in which the term is used. For instance, the "man" who is referred to as one who give a woman pain in (89) will be male, while it is more natural to assume that the term "man" in (90) stands for "people in general."

(89) 'And *no man* can pardon *himself* for giving a woman pain. What would you feel, if *a man* were faithless to you?' (*Vanity*. p. 273)

(90) The professor, indeed, went further, and held that *no man* was forced to believe anything to be true, but what *he* could see, hear, taste, or handle.
(*Water*, p. 96)

All the examples of the *every man* type were similarly classified into MALE, FEMALE and BOTH according to the sex of the referent suggested by the context in which they are used (see Table 6.14).

Table 6.14: Relationship between the referent's sex and the co-referential pronoun: the *every man* type

	MALE		FEMALE		BOTH	
	he	*they*	*she*	*they*	*he*	*they*
some + sing. noun	10		8		2	
every + sing. noun	18	5	5		15	2
any + sing. noun	17		8		26	3
no + sing. noun	15		7		18	
each + sing. noun	5		2	1	10	
Total	65 (92.9%)	5 (7.1%)	30 (96.8%)	1 (3.2%)	71 (93.4%)	5 (6.6%)

Unlike the case of the *everybody* type, the singular forms are predominantly used in all the categories. Gender seems to have little influence on the choice of concord with the phrase "pronominal adjective + singular noun." For further analysis, the data in the above table are examined in terms of the authors' sex as shown in Tables 6.15a and 6.15b.

Table 6.15a: Number concord of pronominal co-reference for MALE and FEMALE according to the authors' sex

	Sing. Pron.	Plu. Pron.	Total
Male authors	51 (91.1%)	5 (8.9%)	56
Female authors	43 (97.7%)	1 (2.3%)	44

Table 6.15b: Number concord of pronominal co-reference for BOTH according to the authors' sex

	Sing. Pron.	Plu. Pron.	Total
Male Authors	40 (97.6%)	1 (2.4%)	41
Female Authors	32 (88.9%)	4 (11.1%)	36

The singular forms are overwhelmingly used by both male and female authors for not only one sex but also for both sexes. Females do not tend to avoid the generic *he* even in the category of BOTH, although they choose this option less frequently than men do. Singularity embedded in a singular noun seems too great to reject even for the fairness of gender.

6.3 Discrepancy in number

It sometimes happens that number agreement is shifted from one to the other in the same utterance although prescriptive grammar prohibits this practice.[25] There are two different types of concord shift for the indefinite pronoun: [1] a shift from a singular verb to a plural pronoun; [2] a shift from a singular pronoun to a plural pronoun. The examples of the two types are displayed in Table 6.16 according to written/spoken language.

Twenty-nine instances are found with type [1] and five with type [2]. In our texts, there is no instance of the transition from plural to singular forms. Although it is said that discrepancy in number is commonly found in speech, no register-related difference is observed as far as our 19th-century texts are concerned; in fact our sample shows that concord transition occurs more often in written than in spoken language. The Table also demonstrates that concord shift occurs more frequently from verbs to pronouns than from pronouns to pronouns. This can be easily explained with reference to distance, which can act as one of the several factors for discrepancies; while verbs are placed close to the subject, co-referential pronouns may not be. Concord shift in pronoun-verb agreement seems to be restricted to indefinite pronouns which have strong connection with a singular verb, such as the *everybody* type, *each*, and the *every man* type. A transition of this sort can be caused by a gap between the verb of the referent and a co-referential pronoun that is placed far enough away to weaken the consciousness of the singularity of the indefinite pronoun. Some examples are presented in the table below.

Table 6.16: Shift from singular to plural forms in written/spoken language

	Sing. verbs to plu. pronouns		Sing. pronouns to plu. pronouns	
	Written	Spoken	Written	Spoken
everybody/every body	4	3		
everyone/every one	5	1		
anybody/any body	1	3		
anyone/any one	1	1		
somebody/some body				
someone/some one	1			
nobody	1	2		
no one	1			
each one				
each	2		2	
either				
neither				
none				
any				
some + sing. noun				
every + sing. noun	3		2	
any + sing. noun				
no + sing. noun				
each + sing. noun				
Total	19	10	4	0

(91) 'when *anybody* pretends this has been a severe winter, I shall tell *them* I saw the roses blooming on New Year's Eve — eh, Godfrey, what do *you* say?' (Italicized "you" in the original) (*Silas*, p. 94)

(92) But no — confound it — there was *some one* coming down the avenue! Why couldn't *they* enjoy the flowers and sunshine of the open garden, and leave that sunless nook to me, and the gnats and midges?
(*Wildfell*, p. 77)

(93) And *no one has* a right to say that no water babies exist, till *they* have seen no water babies existing; (*Water*, p. 45)

(94) "There's the coachman, and the two gardeners; you'll surely not wait to be thrust into the road by them! *Each has* a bludgeon, and master will, very likely, be watching from the parlour windows to see that *they* fulfil his orders." (*Wuthering*, p. 103)

(95) Silver was in the stern-sheets in command; and *every man* of them was now provided with a musket from some secret magazine of *their* own.
(*Treasure*, p. 96)

As for the shift from a singular pronoun to a plural one, there are only four examples in our texts: two with the pronoun *each* and two of the form "*every* + singular noun." Although the pronouns *each* and *every* favor the singular in each instance, they are co-referred to as plural the second time or later. The examples are as follows:

(96) And it stands to reason that *every great man* having experienced this feeling towards *his* father, must be aware that *his* son entertains it towards *himself*; and so *they* can't but be suspicious and hostile.
 (*Vanity*, p. 592)

(97) Yet, although that was the case, *every man* on board the boats had picked a favourite of *his* own ere we were half way over, Long John alone shrugging his shoulders and bidding *them* wait till *they* were there. (*Treasure*, p. 172)

(98) they were not seated at table, — the supper was arranged on the sideboard; *each* had taken what *he* chose, and *they* stood about here and there in groups, *their* plates and glasses in *their* hands. (*Jane*, p. 204)

(99) They say cowardice is infectious; but then argument is, on the other hand, a great emboldener; and so when *each* had said *his* say, my mother made *them* a speech. (*Treasure*, p. 20)

Even in the same sentence/paragraph, the more remote the distance between the referring pronoun and the pronoun referred to, the more weakened the consciousness of "grammatically correct" singularity is. One may remember that a singular pronoun is the norm when the sex of the referent is clearly designated. Even in such cases, a plural pronoun is chosen if distance blurs the identity of the sex. See examples (96) and (97), where despite the underscored words, which clearly express their sex, the plural pronoun is employed later in the speech. Here another factor, notional concord, which would be often more effective than grammatical correctness, seems to be significantly involved in the choice of the co-referent pronouns. In all these examples except for (96), the speakers are referring to a group of people in their sight. They choose the plural *they* instead of the singular *he* because it is simply more natural for them to do so.

6.4 Summary

All in all, the prescribed singular form is better administered in concord with indefinite pronouns in our 19th-century texts than either today or in the previous century. There are, however, some cases in which the rule tends to be violated.

I first observed the situation of pronoun-verb agreement. The singular verb form occurs in nearly 90 percent of the cases on average. As for individual pronouns, singularity is chosen for the *everybody* type and *each*; the plural usage with those pronouns, which is restricted to speech in our texts, is regarded as nonstandard. *Either* and *neither* are used with both singular and plural verbs. The writers tend to choose plural verbs when they use the pronoun to mean "both." As for *none* and *any*, plural use is the norm. In the phrase *of* + plural (pro)noun, *none* is more likely to occur with a plural verb while in the existential *there* construction the proportion of the singular is increased. When the indefinite pronoun is used as adjective (i.e., Type *every man*), no plural concord is attested.

In pronominal reference, the singular and plural forms are almost evenly used although the singular form is a sole option with the *every man* type. Except for *any* and *(n)either*, no distinct disparity in number is recognized. Morphologically, the form *–one* is more closely connected with a singular pronoun than the form *–body*. The pronouns *somebody* and *someone* also show a stronger tendency towards singular patterning, as they are often used to refer to a specific person. From a sociolinguistic standpoint, female authors are seen to employ singular *they* far more frequently than their male counterparts. When only one sex is meant by an indefinite pronoun, women use the singular form *he* or *she* in accordance with the referent's sex, while they overwhelmingly prefer the plural form *they* for both sexes.

Discrepancy in number is found both in pronoun-verb agreement and pronoun co-reference. Distance and notional concord are both implicated in this phenomenon. The more remotely the co-referring pronouns occur, the more likely the grammatically correct singular concord is overshadowed by notional concord.

Notes

1 The term *concord*, as well as *agreement*, signifies "formal agreement between words as parts of speech, expressing the relation of fact between things and their attributes or predicates" (*OED*) (Burchfield 1996: 34). In my paper these two words are synonymously used.
2 These nouns are: *every/each* + noun, *anybody/anyone, any (of), any* + noun, *somebody, someone, one, nobody, no(t) one, no* + noun, *(n)either, who(ever), a person, a man, a being, a slave* and *a soul*.
3 She used twenty works written in the 18th century, such as novels, plays and essays, for her research.
4 Citing the sentence "*None* of them *are* varied to express the gender" (italics original), Murray calls it "strictly proper and justifiable" (1806: 159).
5 Out of the relevant fourteen pronouns under survey, *each one* has no examples.

6 The examples in which the verb is possibly considered subjunctive, as in "just as if there *were* none other in the world" (*N and S*, p. 127), are excluded. In *North and South* and *Wildfell Hall*, in some cases the term *come* is used for *came* as in "'Only some one *come* about the pictures,' said she, in apology for her abrupt departure:" (*Wildfell*, p. 45). These examples are also excluded.
7 Suematsu (2008) investigated all the variants discussed in the present paper except for *any*. Without *any*, the occurrence of singular concord in our corpus further increases to 92 percent.
8 They write that "the complexity of concord patterns is increased by the variability of verb forms in speech. Conversation and, less frequently, dialogue in fiction produce many examples which do not follow the ordinary rules of grammatical concord." (1999: 3.9.4)
9 The word-group "*neither* of + plural pronoun" used as an apposition of a noun or pronoun is not included: "We *neither of us* perform to strangers." (*Pride*, p. 135)
10 As he does not distinguish between the examples of *either* and *neither*, how differently the two forms are distributed is not known.
11 Examples of types (a) and (b) for *neither* exemplified by Poutsma (1916: XL, 43) are as follows: (a) On either side of the road stood a row of stately mansions, but as the sun was right above it, there was shade on *neither*.; (b) Did you give the book to either of my brothers? I gave it to *neither* (Italics original).
12 Yaguchi (2010) argues that *there's* was already grammaticalized at the beginning of Modern English.
13 One of the examples of this kind in our texts is as follows: "But at least there was dogs ..." (*Great*, p. 69)
14 In *The Water Babies* plural verbs are also used in the *there*-construction, e.g. "there were none to be seen" (p. 87).
15 Dekeyser (1975: 76) found one instance of *any* (without *of*-adjunct) for the singular verb form and five for the plural verb form in his 19th-century corpus. Yet the data are not sufficient to suggest the possible influence of the modification.
16 Curme (1931: 52) states as follows: "[j]ust as the singular is usually found after the pronouns *each one, everyone, either, neither*, it is also usually employed after the adjective forms *each, every, either, neither*, although the reference is to more than one."
17 The words used once are: *youngster, tramp, trainman, swain, soul, simpleton, sailor, relative, protector, personage, officer, nobleman, missis, millionaire, member, mediator, master, living thing, gambler, Frenchman, subscriber, fellow, Englishman, editor, devil, Deity, consoler, colourist, clerk, clergyman, butcher, brother, Brinton, biped, angel* and *agent*.
18 Prior to Lowth, John Kirkby (1746:117) advocates generic *he* on the basis of the idea that the masculine person is "comprehensive."
19 She investigated the rivalry among three pairs: *anyone* vs. *anybody, someone* vs. *somebody* and *nobody* vs. *no one*.
20 The words used once are: *bachelor, beast, biped, brother, captain, creature, creditor, dancer, Daphne, doctor, Dr. Proudie, editor, Englishman, friend, gambler, grocer, house-mother, fellow, subscriber, human being, individual, listener, lounger, lover, maiden, master, moralist, mortal, mother, Mr. Bell, Mr. Slope, other, passer-by, prebendary, scholar, simpleton, slave, soul, student, tenant, victim, villain, whipper-snapper, widow* and *wretch*.
21 Dekeyser (1975) investigated the indefinite pronouns observed in our research and the following items altogether: *every/each* + noun, *any* (*of*), *any* + noun, *no* + noun, *who*(*ever*), *a person, a man, a being, a slave* and *a soul*.
22 Girls in middle- and upper-class families in the 19th century were educated either at home or school following a curriculum that emphasized female accomplishments like music and

drawing. It was not until the twentieth century that educational equality for women was achieved (Brown 1985: 56–57).
23 The six examples of *he* for both sexes are used by Charlotte Brontë (4 exx.), Mary Shelley (1ex.) and Marie Corelli (1ex.).
24 Given that this text provides half the examples of this type, the author, Trollope, might have used it simply because he liked it.
25 G. H. Vallins (1955: 17) calls the mixed use of number for pronominal reference "a careless illiteracy."

CHAPTER 7
Conclusion

The present study has attempted to clarify grammatical usage of the pronoun in 19th-century English novels from several standpoints: historical, syntactic, morphological, phonological and stylistic as well as sociolinguistic and pragmatic. I have discussed the usage of the grammatical variants with reference to: (1) personal pronouns, (2) case problems, (3) demonstrative pronouns, (4) relative pronouns and (5) concord with indefinite pronouns. Since the findings of each chapter are summarized at its end, I would like to conclude this study by sketching an overall picture of the grammatical variation of the pronoun in our 19th-century novels. First, I will see which kinds of linguistic factors are involved in pronoun variation in our texts as a whole. I will consider how prescriptive grammar affected the use of nonstandard pronoun variants and how the grammatical change in pronouns proceeded over the course of the century.

7.1 Linguistic factors involved in the choice of pronominal variants

The pronominal variants dealt with in this study and linguistic factors involved in their occurrence are listed in Table 7.1. The table shows that most target variants are influenced by more than one factor and that some factors are widely involved in the use of forms while others are involved only limitedly. It is interesting to note that in our 19th-century texts, while different kinds of factors simultaneously play roles in producing a given variation, the chronological factor is relevant almost only to the use of the relative pronoun *of which/whose* for non-personal antecedents. Apart from the chronological factor, let us see how the other linguistic factors are involved in the occurrence of the variants.

As for the external factors, social class and spoken/written style are most relevant to the variation of the pronouns. In other words, the character's social background and the spoken/written context are the major factors for the pronominal variation in our 19th-century novels. Regional factors are involved in the occurrence of almost all the variants of the personal pronoun as well as the reflexive pronoun and some variants of the demonstrative pronoun (e.g., *them books, them + as*). Since most regional variants are found in dialogue, they are usually associated with spoken language. The exceptions are the forms *'tis/'twas, on't/o't, them* + rel., and *they* + rel., which are sometimes found in literary writing. Literary, poetic or religious usages are also observed in the archaic second person singular *thou* and nominative plural *ye*. As another stylistic factor, the speaker-hearer relationship influences the use of personal pronouns, especially in the case of the second person. This seems to be natural given that the speakers employ such pronouns to address their hearers. Difference in sex, another social factor, is partly observed in the usages of the personal pronoun (e.g., *thou*), the case (e.g., *It is I/me, I!/Me!, than myself, between you and myself*), and the relative pronoun (e.g., *who/whom* in the objective function, *of which/whose* for non-persons) and in pronominal concord with the indefinite pronoun (e.g., Type *everybody*). The difference in use between men and women is reflected in the characters' usage of *thou, It is I/me, I!/Me!* and the relative pronouns *who/whom*, as well as in the authors' usage of the reflexive pronoun (e.g., *than myself, between you and myself*), *of which/whose*, pronominal concord with the indefinite pronoun, and again, *who/whom*. Furthermore, psychological factors have no small influence on the use of variants of the pronouns. Quite a few variants or forms of personal pronouns are uttered on occasions of high emotion. This suggests that grammatical variation cannot be considered separately from people's psychological conditions.

With regard to the internal factors, syntactic factors such as the grammatical functions of the variants and word order seem to play crucial roles for the grammatical change of the case choice, the relative pronoun and concord with the indefinite pronoun. The choices of the relative pronouns *of which/whose* and pronominal co-reference are often semantically decided, i.e., decided on the basis of the meaning of the antecedents. Semantic factors are also relevant to the use of the reflexive pronoun and the case problems (e.g., *than myself, as myself, between you and myself*) when these pronouns are used for clarity or emphasis. Phonological factors such as elision and assimilation are not widely observed but are closely associated with the occurrence of the shortened forms *on't/o't/to't* and *'em*. In both cases, syntactic and phonological factors work together.

CHAPTER 7 CONCLUSION   221

Table 7.1: Linguistic factors involved in the use of pronoun variants*

	Internal factors				External factors						
					sociolinguistic			stylistic			
	syntactic	phonological	semantic	regional	social class	sex	spoken/ written	speaker-hearer's relationship	literary, poetic, religious	psychological	chronological
Personal											
thou				(+)	(+)						
ye (nom. pl.)				+		+	+	+	+	+	
ye for *you*	+			+	+		+	(+)	+	+	
'e/a 'he'				+	(+)		+				
en/'n/'im/um 'him'				+	(+)		+				
'is/uz 'his'				+	(+)		+				
shoo 'she'				+	(+)					+	
hoo 'she'				+			+				
ut 'it'				+	(+)						
'tis/'twas				+	+		+		+	+	
'tis/'twas + n't	+	+		+			+			+	
on't/o't/o't, etc.	+	+		+	+		+	(+)	+	+	
'em											

*+: a positive factor, (+): a possible factor; the forms in square brackets have no variation.

| | Internal factors | | | External factors | | | | stylistic | | | |
	syntactic	phonological	semantic	regional	sociolinguistic social class	sex	spoken/ written	speaker-hearer's relationship	literary, poetic, religious	psychological	chronological
Reflexive											
-sel' (e.g. *himsel'*)				+			+				
-seln				+			+				
hissel'			(+)	+			+				
hisself				(+)	(+)		+				
'emselves, yerself			+	(+)	(+)		+				
Type *their/theyselves*		(+)		+			+			(+)	
Case problems											
It is *I/me*	+						+			+	
I!/Me!	+				+	+	+			+	
than *I (am)/me*	(+)		+	+	+		+			+	
than *myself*	+					+					
as–as I (am)/me	(+)			+	+		+				
such (–) as I/me	(+)										
as myself	+		+			+					
but, save *I/me*					(+)						
except *myself*			+								
except *I/me*	+						+				
you and I/me are			+			+					
between *you and me/myself*			+								

CHAPTER 7 CONCLUSION

	Internal factors			External factors							
	syntactic	phonological	semantic	regional	sociolinguistic		spoken/ written	stylistic		psychological	chronological
					social class	sex		speaker-hearer's relationship	literary, poetic, religious		
Demonstrative											
them books	+			+							(+)
them + rel.	+				+				+		
they + rel.					+				+		
them + *as*				+	+		+				
Relative											
inter. *who/whom*	+				+	+	+		+		
rel. *who/whom*	+		+		+	(+)				+	
of *which/whose*	+					+	+				+
Pronoun-verb concord											
Type *everybody*	+				+						
(n)*either*	+										
none	+										
[*any*]											
[Type *every man*]											
Pronominal co-reference											
Type *everybody*	+		+			+					
Type *every man*			+								
Number discrepancy	+										

7.2 Influence of prescriptive grammar

The findings of our research have shown that there are various aspects of "nonstandard" variants in our 19th-century texts; the term "nonstandard" sometimes indicates archaism and dialectal use while in other cases it refers to casual or informal use as well as solecism, depending on where in England a given variant is used or who uses it in what way. Not all nonstandard usage was equally criticized by the contemporary grammarians. In order to examine the influence of prescriptive grammar on our 19th-century nonstandard variants, it is necessary to take into consideration the degree to which the prescriptive grammarians paid attention to them.

7.2.1 Archaic/dialectal use

Archaic and dialectal elements cannot be separated from each other since the variants which have become obsolete and dropped out of standard language occasionally continue to be used in dialectal speech.

The archaic second person pronouns *thou* for singular and *ye* for plural are no longer considered standard in the 19th century as evidenced by their extremely low occurrence. *Thou* is more often attested in the northern part of England and more likely used as a pragmatic marker to convey the speaker's psychological or emotional mood just as seen in the usage of the upper class in Elizabethan society. The archaic nominative plural *ye*, on the other hand, is fossilized as shown in Joseph's speech in *Wuthering Heights* and in a few other characters' speech of Northern England and Ireland. This old variant is otherwise used in poetic or grave contexts.

Our 19th-century corpus yielded dialectal variants of personal pronouns belonging to Northern England, Southern England, Ireland or America. The Northern dialect has local forms of second person singular (*yo*, *yah*), archaic second person plural (*ye*) and third person singular feminine (*shoo*, *hoo*). The Southern has local variants of the third person singular masculine (*'e*, *a* for *he*; *en*, *'n*, *'im* for *him*; *'s*, *uz* for *his*). As for the third person neuter singular, the unstressed variant *ut* is found in the speech of an Irish American. The reflexive pronoun also has a variety of dialectal forms. Variants ending with *–sel'* or *–seln* are restricted to the northern part of England while variants with "wrong" cases of personal pronouns in the form *–self* or *–selves* are more broadly attested in England. Dialectal variants have not merely a sense of local color but convey profound nuance that the equivalent standard form cannot deliver. In Lancashire dialect, for instance, when seniors use *hoo* in reference to a female junior, they occasionally show affection or pity towards her.

Although regional variants were not considered standard at that time, they were not necessarily taken up as "incorrect" examples in prescriptive grammar. This is because, although these variants were employed by many local people in the particular regions, their occurrence was sparse in the nation as a whole. None of the dialectal variants attested in our texts register at higher than 1 percent of the total cases. The dialectal variants as well as archaic ones were destined to disappear or be irreversibly recessive, largely due to the spread of education and to modern means of intercommunication such as railways (cf. Wright 1905: vii; Görlach 1999: 31; Beal 2010:3).

7.2.2 Casual use

While full forms are required in writing, ellipsis and contraction occasionally occur in colloquial language to be regarded as casual use. The shortened unstressed variant *ye* for *you* and the weakened form *'em* for *them* might be typical examples. Both forms are widely attested in our texts and uttered by characters of all ranks in society. Those in lower ranks habitually employ them while educated people do so once in a while, especially in haste or in an agitated mood. Since shortened or weakened forms are part of regional dialect, both *ye* and *'em* are seen in various regions across England. For the local people who utter *ye* and *'em*, these forms are part of their regional dialects. In our corpus, the same forms are found to be used across the ocean by the American seamen in *Captains Courageous*. For them, these forms are their community language. Many of these shortened forms widely employed in casual speech at that time are still common in informal usage today. These types of nonstandard forms are least affected by grammar; they are limited to speech and people uttering such informal forms usually can use their standard full form whenever necessary.

7.2.3 Solecism criticized by grammarians

Solecism is often illustrated in "bad" examples along with the standard ones in grammar books. It is this kind of usage which often attracts grammarians' attention. Some variants regarded as solecism in the 19th century are no longer considered such today. In the present study, solecism in the use of pronouns has to do with case problems, the definite pronoun, the relative pronoun, and number concord. The results are summarized in Tables 7.2 to 7.6.

Our data demonstrate that the "grammatical" usage is predominantly observed for some forms but not necessarily for others. The "grammatical" forms employed with around 90 percent or higher of the total relevant instances are as follows: *younger than I*, etc.; *those books*; *those* + relative pronoun; relative *whom* in the object position; and singular concord between an indefinite subject and a verb. It is noteworthy that the forms which are grammatically accepted today (e.g., *younger than me*, etc, *who* in the objective position) were strictly avoided just as those still considered nonstandard in Present-day English (e.g., *you and me* in the nominative function; the demonstrative *them* for *those*). In contrast, the grammatical instructions are not faithfully observed in the choice between *of which* and *whose* for non-personal antecedents and number concord of pronominal co-reference.

Table 7.2: Distribution of nominative/objective forms in different types of case problems

	Nominative	Objective	Total
It is I/me	90 (67.7%)	43 (32.3%)	133
I!/Me!	96 (82.8%)	19 (17.2%)	116
younger than I/me	124 (93.2%)	9 (6.8%)	133
as tall as I/me	73 (88.0%)	10 (12.0%)	83
such as I/me	31 (77.5%)	9 (22.5%)	40
you and I/me are	543 (92.5%)	44 (7.5%)	587
Total	957 (87.6%)	135 (12.4%)	1092

Table 7.3: Distribution of *them/those* books and *them/they/those* + rel.

	those	them	Total
them/those books	1037 (92.0%)	90 (8.0%)	1127
	those	them/they	
them/they/those + rel.	447 (89.8%)	51 (10.2%)	498

Table 7.4: Distribution of *whom/who* in the objective position

	whom	who	Total
Relative	1099 (99.8%)	2 (0.2%)	1101
Interrogative	64 (84.2%)	12 (15.8%)	76
Total	1163 (98.8%)	14 (1.2%)	1177

Table 7.5: Distribution of *of which/whose* for (non-)personal antecedents

	of which	whose	Total
Personal	0 (0%)	615 (100%)	615
Non-personal	180 (55.6%)	144 (44.4%)	324

Table 7.6: Distribution of number concord with indefinite pronouns

	sing. verb	plu. verb	Total
Subject and verb	553 (89.5%)	65 (10.5%)	618
	sing. pronoun	plu. pronoun	
Pronominal co-reference	122 (48.2%)	131 (51.8%)	253

CHAPTER 7 CONCLUSION

In the group where the "grammatical" use is overwhelmingly predominant, the "error" is usually found in the speech of the characters. The speakers contributing to the proportion of the nonstandard use in Tables 7.2, 7.3, and 7.4 mostly consist of those who employ the relevant variants in their dialectal speech to reveal their regional or social background. As to the case problems, the degree of solecism differs among the six types in Table 7.2, varying from 6.8 percent at the lowest (*younger than me*) to 32.3 percent at the highest (*It is me*).

The "grammatical" use is best observed with the relative *whom* (99.8%). In our texts, the use of the relative pronoun *who* in objective use is limited to only two examples, which are likely to have been chosen accidentally by two female authors. In comparison with the use of the relative *who*, the interrogative pronoun *who* in objective use yields twelve examples, or 15.8 percent of the total cases. This would indicate that the objective use of *who* first started with the interrogative pronoun.

Though the use of *them books* for *those books* cannot be regarded as common, its frequency (8.0%) is not quite so low as to be treated as merely a function of local dialects. Not only Nicholas (a northern millworker) and Dixon (a southern servant) in *North and South* but also American fishermen in *Captains Courageous* and seamen, including buccaneers, in *Treasure Island* use *them books*. That is, this form is seen in social dialect as well. This is also the case of *them/they that* for *those that*, the frequency of which is 10.2 percent. As to the forms *them/they that*, there is more to be taken into account: some instances of these forms indicate their dialectal use, as in Joseph's speech in *Wuthering Heights*, while other instances demonstrate their use in literature as proper usage. This archaic literary element disappeared towards the end of the 19th-century, and in Present-day English the forms *them/they that* have survived in nonstandard speech.

Among usages that the grammarians had difficulty controlling in spite of their strenuous criticism are the rule of *of which* for non-personal antecedents and that of singularity for pronominal co-reference, as shown in tables 7.5 and 7.6. Although *whose* is always used for personal antecedents, it is also used for non-personal antecedents in 44.4 percent of instances. As for the number concord with indefinite pronouns, singular forms are usually chosen for subject-verb agreement, while plural forms are preferred for pronominal co-reference 51.8 percent of the time. From a historical standpoint, the controversial usage of *whose* for non-persons as well as plural concord for indefinite pronouns (e.g., singular *they*) slightly decreased during the 19th century and gradually increased afterward. If there was a setback even in the use of these resilient "ungrammatical" forms in the 19th century, it would be due to the grammarians' influence.

7.3 How the grammatical change in pronouns proceeded in the 19th century

From a historical point of view, it is safe to say that prescriptive grammar had greater influence on the usage of pronouns in 19th-century English than during any other period. In our 19th-century novels, ungrammatical pronominal variants are generally restricted to dialectal speech or to the language of lower class characters, while the imposed grammatical rules are faithfully respected by those in the middle and upper classes. However, our study also reveals that, in choosing a certain variant, people do not blindly depend on the grammar books. Sometimes, what pronominal variants actually mean comes before what the normative grammar requires. All in all, the male authors tend to follow the rules, while the female authors are less hesitant to use the "ungrammatical" variants. In the use of the relatives *of which/whose* for non-personal antecedents, for instance, women are more likely to use *whose*, probably because the form *of which* felt pedantic and clumsy to them. In the case of number agreement of pronominal co-reference, the women would have found it unnatural to use the pronoun *he* to indicate a person who could be of their sex. Moreover, the use of the non-reflexive *-self* forms (e.g., *younger than myself, between you and myself*), which may not be strictly grammatical, is more frequently employed by the female authors than by their male counterparts, presumably for emphatic purposes. It is assumed that while the men strictly adhered to the rules of grammar, the women, being less bound to grammar, preferred the usage which was easier to use and felt semantically natural so long as it was not a grave mistake. In 19th-century England, girls generally studied at home without receiving university education, while boys were able to pursue higher education at public school and then college. Our eight female authors were not exceptions (see Appendix 1). The general educational background may have produced more grammar-bound writers and speakers on the men's side than on the opposite in Victorian society.

To sum up, the formerly ungrammatical variants, which were avoided by the majority as in the choice of case (e.g., *It is me; Me!*), spread from the lower class to the middle and upper classes on one hand and possibly from male to female on the other hand so as to become part of standard Present-day English. As to the variants on which the prescriptive grammarians' control was not fully enforced in the first place, women played a significant role in keeping the relevant variants in use during the 19th century against the logical but semantically unnatural rules stipulated by the normative grammar. In terms of register, although many of the dialectal variants examined in this thesis are thoroughly restricted to speech, there are signs that some of the ungrammatical variants (e.g., the interrogative *who* in the objective function; the relative *whose* for non-personal antecedents) were spread from spoken to written language. Thus, it is concluded that the grammatical change in pronouns was steadily proceeding during the 19th century with various factors simultaneously involved. Lastly, concerning the fate of the variants which have been categorically regarded as ungrammatical but customarily used by a certain number of people throughout the century and continuing to today (e.g., *you and me* in the nominative function; the demonstrative *them* for *those*), it remains to be seen if such variants will attain a standard position sometime in future.

7.4 Further investigation

The present study has revealed that the usage of pronouns conformed to the traditional prescriptive grammar in 19th-century English far better than in Present-day English although the grammarians' instructions were not so successful with some variants. Indeed, in some cases the grammarians' efforts would prove to have been in vain, with the proscribed variants winning recognition as standard usage. No doubt, it took several more decades for many such nonstandard variants to come to be regarded as standard, as they are today. Hence, it is necessary to expand our investigation further into 20th-century English to discover the process of their gaining acceptance.

Some of our findings suggest that there is a difference between the two sides of the Atlantic with respect to some variants, such as the shortened form *'em* for *them* and the choice of *who/whom* in the objective function. However, a lack of data prevented that question from being decided conclusively. Similar research on the target variants in contemporary American literature will be useful to resolving these issues.

The novels used as our corpus supplied us with invaluable instances to learn about the pronominal usage in 19th-century England. Nevertheless, as is often pointed out, the dialogue of a novel is not real conversation. In order to confirm the findings of this study, further research should be conducted on the basis of different types of texts. Books of proceeding, records of trials, correspondence — either official or private — and diaries should be linguistically studied, though there is little variation of register if they are used alone.

Language change is a complex phenomenon. One grammatical variant may be likened to a polyhedron; if you shed light on it from one direction, it shows only one face, but if you shed light from multiple directions, its whole body will clearly emerge. It is absolutely certain that in the 19th-century grammatical change among pronouns was in progress, and many more grammatical variants await close investigation in this field.

Appendix

Appendix 1

Provided below is information about the authors (years of birth and death, birthplace or hometown, education)[1] and the works (publication year, main place of the story, narrator) for the texts used in this study, which are chronologically arranged according to the authors' birth year.

Jane Austen (1775–1817); *Pride and Prejudice* (1813)
    Author: Birthplace — Steventon, Hampshire
                Education — Tutored at home by her father
    Story: Main setting — Southeastern (SE) England
                Narrator — Omniscient narrator

Mary Shelly (1797–1851); *Frankenstein* (1818)
    Author: Birthplace — London
                Education — Tutored at home by her father
    Story: Main setting — England and other European countries
                Narrator — Walton (in letters to his sister); Frankenstein (in discourse with Walton); Monster (in discourse with Frankenstein)

Elizabeth Gaskell (1810–1865); *North and South* (1854–55)
    Author: Birthplace — Knutsford, Cheshire; moves to Manchester in 1832.
                Education — Boarding school
    Story: Main setting — Northern England; London (SE England)
                Narrator — Omniscient narrator

W. M. Thackeray (1811–1863); *Vanity Fair* (1847–48)
    Author: Birthplace — Calcutta, India; returns to England in 1817.
                Education — Torinity College, Cambridge; leaves without a degree; the Middle Temple
    Story: Main setting — London
                Narrator — Omniscient narrator

Charles Dickens (1812–1870); *Great Expectations* (1860–61)
    Author: Birthplace — Portsmouth, Hampshire; moves to London in 1823
                Education — Private schools; starts to work aged 15 as a clerk at an attorney's office, while studying shorthand
    Story: Main setting — Kent; London (both in SE England)

Narrator — Pip (monologue)

Anthony Trollope (1815–1882); *Barchester Towers* (1857)
    Author: Birthplace — London
               Education — Hallow; Winchester College
    Story: Main setting — An imaginary cathedral city of Barchester (Southern England)
               Narrator — Omniscient narrator

Charlotte Brontë (1816–1855); *Jane Eyre* (1847)
    Author: Birthplace — Haworth, West Yorkshire
               Education — Clergy Daughters' School at Cowan Bridge, Lancashire; Miss Wooler's School at Roe Head; Mme Heger's school, Brussels
    Story: Main setting — Northern England
               Narrator — Jane (monologue)

Emily Brontë (1818–1848); *Wuthering Heights* (1847)
    Author: Birthplace — Haworth, West Yorkshire
               Education — Clergy Daughters' School at Cowan Bridge, Lancashire; Miss Wooler's School at Roe Head; Mme Heger's school, Brussels
    Story: Main setting — Northern England
               Narrator — Rockwood (monologue); Nelly (in discourse with Rockwood)

George Eliot (1819–1880); *Silas Marner* (1861)
    Author: Birthplace — Arbury, Warwickshire
               Education — Educated at home and in boarding schools
    Story: Main setting — The Midlands
               Narrator — Omniscient narrator

Charles Kingsley (1819–1875); *The Water Babies* (1863)
    Author: Birthplace — Holne, Devonshire
               Education — King's College, London; Magdalene College, Cambridge
    Story: Main setting — North Country; Water land (imaginary world)
               Narrator — Omniscient narrator

Anne Brontë (1820–1849); *The Tenant of Wildfell Hall* (1848)
    Author: Birthplace — Haworth, West Yorkshire

           Education — Miss Wooler's School at Roe Head
    Story: Main setting — Northern England
    Narrator — Gilbert (in letters to his brother-in-law)

Lewis Carroll (1832–1898); *Alice's Adventures in Wonderland* and *Through the Looking-Glass* (1865 and 1872)
    Author: Birthplace — Daresbury, Cheshire
           Education — Christ Church, Oxford
    Story: Main setting — Wonderlands (imaginary worlds)
           Narrator — Omniscient narrator

Thomas Hardy (1840–1928); *Jude the Obscure* (1895)
    Author: Birthplace — Higher Bockhampton, Dorset
           Education — Schooling in Dorset; serves as apprentice to an architect aged 16
    Story: Main setting — Wessex (SE England)
           Narrator — Omniscient narrator

Robert Louis Stevenson (1850–1894); *Treasure Island* (1883)
    Author: Birthplace — Edinburgh
           Education — Edinburgh University
    Story: Main setting — Southwestern (SW) England
           Narrator — Mainly Jim; partially Dr. Livesey (both in journals)

Oscar Wilde (1854–1900); *The Picture of Dorian Gray* (1891)
    Author: Birthplace — Dublin
           Education — Trinity College, Dublin; Magdalen College, Oxford
    Story: Main setting — West Sussex (Southern England)
           Narrator — Omniscient narrator

Marie Corelli (1855–1924); *The Sorrows of Satan* (1895)
    Author: Birthplace — London
           Education — Educated at home and a convent school in France
    Story: Main setting — London (SE England)
           Narrator — Geoffrey Tempest (monologue)

George Gissing (1857–1903); *The Private Papers of Henry Ryecroft* (1903)
    Author: Birthplace — Wakefield, West Yorkshire
           Education — Owens College, Manchester; later dismissed
    Story: Main setting — Devonshire (SW England)
           Narrator — Henry Ryecroft (in a diary)

Arthur Conan Doyle (1859–1930); *A Study in Scarlet* (1887)
    Author: Birthplace — Edinburgh
               Education — Edinburgh University
    Story: Main setting — London (SE England); North America
               Narrator — Dr. Watson (in a journal); Omniscient narrator

Rudyard Kipling (1865–1936); *Captains Courageous* (1897)
    Author: Birthplace — Bombay, India; moves to Portsmouth in 1871.
               Education — The United Services College at Westward Ho!, Devon
    Story: Main setting — The Grand Banks of the North Atlantic; America
               Narrator — Omniscient narrator

H. G. Wells (1866–1946); *The Invisible Man* (1897)
    Author: Birthplace — Bromley, Kent
               Education — The Normal School of Science, Kensington; University of London
    Story: Main setting — West Sussex (Southern England)
               Narrator — Omniscient narrator; Invisible man (in discourse with Mr. Kemp)

Note

1 The information about the authors is based on Michael Stapleton (1983) and on biological details published with the texts examined in this study.

Appendix 2

Figure A2.1: Dialectal demarcation presented by Wright (1905) (adapted from Hirooka 1965: xlix)

Figure A2.2: Geographical demarcation of Great Britain (2014)

Bibliography

Primary Sources

[*Alice*] Carroll, Lewis. *Alice's Adventures in Wonderland* and *Through the Looking-Glass*. 1865 and 1872. Oxford World's Classics. Oxford: Oxford UP, 1998.

[*Barchester*] Trollope, Anthony. *Barchester Towers*. 1857. Oxford World's Classics. Oxford: Oxford UP, 1998.

[*Captains*] Kipling, Rudyard. *Captains Courageous*. 1897. Oxford World's Classics. Oxford: Oxford UP, 1999.

[*Dorian*] Wilde, Oscar. *The Picture of Dorian Gray*. 1891. Oxford World's Classics. Oxford: Oxford UP, 1998.

[*Frankenstein*] Shelly, Mary. *Frankenstein*. 1818. Oxford World's Classics. Oxford: Oxford UP, 1998.

[*Great*] Dickens, Charles. *Great Expectations*. 1860–61. Oxford World's Classics. Oxford: Oxford UP, 1998.

[*Invisible*] Wells, Herbert George. *The Invisible Man*. 1897. Oxford World's Classics. Oxford: Oxford UP, 1996.

[*Jane*] Brontë, Charlotte. *Jane Eyre*. 1847. Oxford World's Classics. Oxford: Oxford UP, 1998.

[*Jude*] Hardy, Thomas. *Jude the Obscure*. 1895. Oxford World's Classics. Oxford: Oxford UP, 1998. Rev. ed. 2002.

[*N and S*] Gaskell, Elizabeth. *North and South*. 1854–55. Oxford World's Classics. Oxford: Oxford UP, 1998.

[*Pride*] Austen, Jane. *Pride and Prejudice*. 1813. Oxford World's Classics. Oxford: Oxford UP, 1998.

[*Ryecroft*] Gissing, George. *The Private Papers of Henry Ryecroft*. 1903. Oxford World's Classics. Oxford: Oxford UP, 1987.

[*Satan*] Corelli, Marie. *The Sorrows of Satan*. 1895. Oxford Popular Fiction. Oxford: Oxford UP. 1996.

[*Scarlet*] Doyle, Arthur Conan. *A Study in Scarlet*. 1887. Oxford World's Classics. Oxford: Oxford UP, 1999.

[*Silas*] Eliot, George. *Silas Marner*. 1861. Oxford World's Classics. Oxford: Oxford UP, 1998.

[*Treasure*] Stevenson, Robert Louis. *Treasure Island*. 1883. Oxford World's Classics. Oxford: Oxford UP, 1998.

[*Vanity*] Thackeray, W. M. *Vanity Fair*. 1847–48. Oxford World's Classics. Oxford: Oxford UP, 1998.

[*Water*] Kingsley, Charles. *The Water Babies*. 1863. Wordsworth Classics. Ware, Hertfordshire: Wordsworth Editions, 1998.

[*Wildfell*] Brontë, Anne. *The Tenant of Wildfell Hall*. 1848. Oxford World's Clas-

sics. Oxford: Oxford UP, 1998.
[*Wuthering*] Brontë, Emily. *Wuthering Heights*. 1847. Oxford World's Classics. Oxford: Oxford UP, 1998.

Other texts
Austen, Jane. *Northanger Abbey*. 1818. Oxford World's Classics. Oxford: Oxford UP, 1998.
Carroll, Lewis. 1863. *Alice's Adventures under Ground*. London: Pavilion, 1985.
Fitzgerald, F. Scott. *The Great Gatsby*. 1925. Oxford World's Classics. Oxford: Oxford UP, 1998.
Gaskell, Elizabeth. *Ruth*. 1853. Oxford World's Classics. Oxford: Oxford UP, 1998.
The Holy Bible, Containing the Old and New Testaments: New Revised Standard Version. 1989. New York; Oxford: Oxford UP.
The Holy Bible: King James Version, Otherwise Known as the Authorized Version Published in the Year 1611, Quatercentenary Edition and Exact Reprint in Roman Type Page for Page, Line for Line, and Letter for Letter Format. Oxford: Oxford UP, 2010.
Shakespeare, William. *The Merchant of Venice*. c1596. Oxford World Classics. Oxford: Oxford UP, 2008.
Twain, Mark. *The Adventures of Huckleberry Finn*. 1884. Oxford World Classics. Oxford: Oxford UP, 1999.

References
Aitchison, Jean. 2001. *Language Change: Progress or Decay?* 3rd ed. Cambridge: Cambridge UP.
Andersson, Lars and Peter Trudgill. 1990. *Bad Language*. Oxford: Basil Blackwell.
Anderwald, Lieselotte. 2002. *Negation in Non-Standard British English: Gaps, Regularizations and Asymmetries*. London: Routledge.
ARCHER=*A Representative Corpus of Historical English Registers*. http://www.projects.alc.manchester.ac.uk/archer/archer-versions/ [accessed May 29, 2017].
Ash, Russell. 1985. "The Story of *Alice's Adventures under Ground*." Introduction. *Alice's Adventures under Ground*. By Lewis Carroll. London: Pavilion. 11–20.
Auer, Anita. 2009. *The Subjunctive in the Age of Prescriptivism: English and German Developments during the Eighteenth Century*. Basingstoke: Palgrave Macmillan.
Bailey, Richard W. 1996. *Nineteenth-Century English*. Ann Arbor: U of Michigan P.
Barber, Charles. 1976. *Early Modern English*. London: André Deutsch; new ed. Edinburgh: Edinburgh UP, 1997.
Barber, Charles. 1981. "'You' and 'Thou' in Shakespeare's *Richard III*." *Leeds Studies in English* 12: 273–289. Rpt. in *A Reader in the Language of Shakespearean Drama*. Ed. Vivian Salmon and Edwina Burness. Amsterdam: John Benjamins, 1987. 163–179.

Barber, Charles. 1993. *The English Language: A Historical Introduction*. Cambridge: Cambridge UP.
Baugh, Albert C. and Thomas Cable. 2002. *A History of the English Language*. 5th ed. London: Routledge.
Beal, Joan C. 2004. *English in Modern Times: 1700–1945*. London: Arnold.
Beal, Joan C. 2010. *An Introduction to Regional Englishes: Dialect Variation in England*. Edinburgh: Edinburgh UP.
Biber, Douglas, Stig Johansson, Geoffrey Leech, Susan Conrad and Edward Finegan. 1999. *Longman Grammar of Spoken and Written English*. New York: Longman.
Blake, N. F. 1981. *Non-standard Language in English Literature*. London: André Deutsch.
Brinton, Laurel J. 2008. *The Comment Clause in English: Syntactic Origins and Pragmatic Development*. Cambridge: Cambridge UP.
Brook, G. L. 1958. *A History of the English Language*. London: André Deutsch.
Brook, G. L. 1963. *English Dialects*. London: André Deutsch.
Brook, G. L. 1970. *The Language of Dickens*. London: André Deutsch.
Brook, G. L. 1973. *Varieties of English*. London: Macmillan.
Brown, Goold. 1851. *The Grammar of English Grammars*. New York: Samuel S. and William Wood.
Brown, Goold. 1884. *The Institutes of English Grammar, Methodically Arranged; with Copious Language Lessons; Also a Key to the Examples of False Syntax, Designed for the Use of Schools, Academies, and Private Students*. Rev. ed. New York: William Wood.
Brown, Julia Prewitt. 1985. *A Reader's Guide to the Nineteenth-Century English Novel*. New York: Macmillan.
Brown, R. and A. Gilman. 1960. "The Pronouns of Power and Solidarity." *Style in Language*. Ed. Thomas A. Sebeok. Cambridge, Mass.: MIT P. 253–276. *Language and Social Context: Selected Readings*. Ed. Pier Paolo Giglioli. Harmondsworth, Middlesex: Penguin, 1972. 252–282.
Bruti, Silvia. 2000. "Address Pronouns in Shakespeare's English: A Re-appraisal in Terms of Markedness." *The History of English in a Social Context: A Contribution to Historical Sociolinguistics*. Trends in Linguistics: Studies and Monographs 129. Ed. Dieter Kastovsky and Arthur Mettinger. Berlin: Mouton de Gruyter. 25–51.
Burchfield, R. W. (ed.). 1996. *The New Fowler's Modern English Usage*. 3rd. ed. Oxford: Clarendon.
Busse, Ulrich. 2002. *Linguistic Variation in the Shakespeare Corpus: Morpho-Syntactic Variability of Second Person Pronouns*. Amsterdam: John Benjamins.
Busse, Ulrich. 2003. "The Co-occurence of Nominal and Pronominal Address Forms in the Shakepeare Corpus: Who Says *Thou* or *You* to Whom?" In Taavitsainen and Jucker, 193–221.

Clark, John W. 1975. *The Language and Style of Anthony Trollope*: London: André Deutsch.

Cobbett, William. 1819. *A Grammar of the English Language, in a Series of Letters.* A Reprint Ser. of Books Relating to the English Language 20. Tokyo: Nan'un-do, 1970.

Crossick, Geoffrey. 1991. "From Gentleman to the Residuum: Language of Social Description in Victorian Britain." *Language, History and Class.* Ed. Penelope J. Corfield. Oxford: Basil Blackwell. 150–178.

Crystal, David and Derek Davy. 1969. *Investigating English Style.* London: Longman.

Curme, George O. 1931. *Syntax.* Boston: D. C. Heath.

Dekeyser, Xavier. 1975. *Number and Case Relations in 19th Century British English: A Comparative Study of Grammar and Usage.* Antwerpen: Uitgeverij De Nederlandsche Boekhandel.

Denison, David. 1998. "Syntax." *The Cambridge History of the English Language.* Vol.4. 1776–1997. Ed. Suzanne Romaine. Cambridge: Cambridge UP. 92–329.

Dossena, Marina and Charles Jones (eds.). 2003. *Insights into Late Modern English.* Bern: Peter Lang.

Doughty, Peter, John Pearce and Geoffrey Thornton. 1972. *Exploring Language.* London: Edward Arnold.

Fernald, James C. 1904. *Connectives of English Speech: The Correct Usage of Preposition, Conjunctions, Relative Pronouns and Adverbs Explained and Illustrated.* New York: Funk and Wagnalls.

Filppula, Markku. 1999. *The Grammar of Irish English: Language in Hibernian Style.* London: Routledge.

Fowler, H. W. 1965. *A Dictionary of Modern English Usage.* 2nd ed. Rev. Sir Ernest Gowers. Oxford: Oxford UP.

Freedman, Penelope. 2007. *Power and Passion in Shakespeare's Pronouns: Interrogating 'you' and 'thou.'* Hampshire: Ashgate.

Fujii, Kenzo. 2004. *America eigo to Irishism* [Irishism in American English]. Tokyo: Chuo UP.

Fujii, Kenzo. 2006. *America no eigo: Gohō to hatsuon* [English in America: Its Usage and Pronunciation]. Tokyo: Nan'undo.

Görlach, Manfred. 1999. *English in Nineteenth-Century England: An Introduction.* Cambridge: Cambridge UP.

Görlach, Manfred. 2001. *Eighteenth-Century English.* Heidelberg: Universitätsverlag C. Winter.

Greenbaum, Sidney. 1996. *English Grammar.* Oxford: Oxford UP.

Greenbaum, Sidney and Gerald Nelson. 2002. *An Introduction to English Grammar.* 2nd ed. London: Longman.

Golding, Robert. 1985. *Idiolects in Dickens.* London: Macmillan.

Gwynne, Parry. 1879. *A Word to the Wise; or Hints on Current Improprieties of Expression in Writing and Speaking.* London: Griffith.

Halliday, M. A. K. 1978. *Language as Social Semiotic: The Social Interpretation of Language and Meaning.* London: Edward Arnord.

Halliday, M. A. K., Angus McIntosh and Peter Strevens. 1964. *The Linguistic Sciences and Language Teaching.* London: Longman.

Hansen, Erik and Hans Frede Nielsen. 2007. *Irregularities in Modern English.* 2nd ed. Rev. Erik Hansen. Odense: UP of Southern Denmark.

Hatanaka, Takami, Hiroshi Fuji, Satoshi Takada and Heather Kotake. 1983. *Eigo no Variation* [*Variation in English*]. Tokyo: Nan'un-do.

Hazlitt, William. 1810. *A New and Improved Grammar of the English Tongue: For the Use of Schools.* A Reprint Ser. of Books Relating to the English Language 20. Tokyo: Nan'un-do, 1970.

Hickey, Raymond. 2004. *A Sound Atlas of Irish English.* Berlin: Mouton de Gruyter.

Hickey, Raymond. 2007. *Irish English: History and Present-Day Forms.* Cambridge: Cambridge UP.

Hickey, Raymond. (ed.) 2010. *Eighteenth-Century English: Ideology and Change.* Cambridge: Cambridge UP.

Hirooka, Hideo. 1965. *Eibungaku no hōgen* [Dialects in English Literature]. Tokyo: Shinozaki Shorin.

Hirooka, Hideo. 1983. *Thomas Hardy's Use of Dialect.* Tokyo: Shinozaki Shorin.

Holmes, Janet. 2008. *An Introduction to Sociolinguistics.* 3rd ed. Harlow, England: Pearson Longman.

Hope, Jonathan. 1994. "The Use of *Thou* and *You* in Early Modern Spoken English: Evidence from Depositions in the Durham Ecclesiastical Court Records." *Studies in Early Modern English.* Ed. Dieter Kastovsky. Berlin: Mouton de Gruyter. 141–151.

Hosoe, Itsuki. 1935. *George Eliot no sakuhin ni mochiiraretaru eikoku chūbu-chi hōgen no kenkyu.* [Studies in the Midland dialect used in the Works of George Eliot: With Special Reference to Silas Marner and Adam Bede]. Tokyo: Taibundo.

Hosoe, Itsuki. 1956. *Eikoku chihōgo no kenkyu* [Studies in British Dialects]. Tokyo: Shinozaki Shorin.

Huddleston, Rodney and Geoffrey K. Pullum. 2002. *The Cambridge Grammar of the English Language.* Cambridge: Cambridge UP.

Hughes, Kristine. 1998. *The Writer's Guide to Everyday Life in Regency and Victorian England: From 1811–1901.* Cincinnati, Ohio: Writer's Digest.

Imahayashi, Osamu. 2006. *Charles Dickens and Literary Dialect.* Hiroshima: Keisuisha.

Imahayashi, Osamu. 2007a. "A Corpus-based Sociolinguistic Study on the Use of *Look*-forms in the 19th Century." *PALA 2007 Proceedings Online.* 5 November 2013 <http://www.pala.ac.uk/resources/proceedings/2007/>

Imahayashi, Osamu. 2007b. "A Stylistic Approach to Pip's Class-Consciousness in *Great Expectations.*" *Studies in Modern English* (The Modern English Association) 23: 1-21.

Jespersen, Otto. 1909-49. *A Modern English Grammar: on Historical Principles.* 7 vols. Copenhagen: Munksgaard. Rpt. London: Allen and Unwin, 1954-61.

Jespersen, Otto. 1933. *Essentials of English Grammar.* Rpt. Tuscalloosa; London: U of Alabama P, 1964.

Johnson, Anne Carvey. 1966. "The Pronoun of Direct Address in Seventeenth-Century English." *American Speech* 41: 261-269.

Joos, Martin. 1961. *The Five Clocks.* New York: Harcourt, Brace and World.

Joyce, P. W. 1910. *English As We Speak It in Ireland.* London: Longman; Green.

Jucker, Andreas H. and Irma Taavitsainen. 2013. *English Historical Pragmatics.* Edinburgh: Edinburgh UP.

Kellner, Leon. 1892. *Historical Outlines of English Syntax.* London: Macmillan.

Kent, Susan Kingsley. 1999. *Gender and Power in Britain, 1640-1990.* London: Routledge.

Kirkby, John. 1746. *A New English Grammar.* Rpt. Menston: Scolar, 1971.

Kortmann, Bernd. 2008. "Synopsis: Morphological and Syntactic Variation in the British Isles." *Varieties of English 1: The British Isles.* Ed. Bernd Kortmann and Clive Upton. Berlin: Mouton de Gruyter. 478-495.

Kranich, Svenja. 2010. *The Progressive in Modern English: A Corpus-Based Study of Grammaticalization and Related Changes.* Amsterdam: Rodopi.

Kruisinga, Etsko. 1932. *A Handbook of Present-Day English.* Part II, Vol. 2. 5th ed. Groningen: P. Noordhoff.

Kytö, Merja. 1993. "Third-Person Present Singular Verb Inflection in Early British and American English." *Language Variation and Change* 5: 113-139.

Kytö, Merja, Mats Rydén and Erik Smitterberg (eds.). 2006. *Nineteenth-Century English: Stability and Change.* Cambridge: Cambridge UP.

Labov, William. 1966. *The Social Stratification of English in New York City.* Washington, D. C.: Center for Applied Linguistics.

Lass, Roger. 2006. "Phonology and Morphology." *A History of the English Language.* Ed. Richard Hogg and David Denison. Cambridge: Cambridge UP. 43-108.

Leech, Geoffrey and Jan Svartvik. 1994. *A Communicative Grammar of English.* 2nd ed. London: Longman.

Leonard, Sterling Andrus. 1929. *The Doctrine of Correctness in English Usage 1700-1800.* New York: Russell and Russell, 1962.

Lowth, Robert. 1769. *A Short Introduction to English Grammar: With Critical Notes.* A Reprint Ser. of Books Relating to the English Language 13. Tokyo: Nan'un-do. 1968.

MacKay, Donald G. and David C. Fulkerson. 1979. "On the Comprehension and Production of Pronouns." *Journal of Verbal Leaning and Verbal Behavior* 18:

661–673.

Mair, Christian. 2006. *Twentieth-Century English: History, Variation, and Standardization.* Cambridge: Cambridge UP.

Mazzon, Gabriella. 2003. "Pronouns and Nominal Address in Shakespearean English: A Socio-affective Marking System in Transition." In Taavitsainen and Jucker, 223–249.

McIntosh, Carey. 1986. *Common and Courtly Language: The Stylistics of Social Class in 18th-Century English Literature.* Philadelphia: U of Pennsylvania P.

McKnight, George H. 1928. *Modern English in the Making.* New York: Appleton. Rpt. under the title *The Evolution of the English Language: From Chaucer to the Twentieth Century.* New York: Dover, 1968.

Milroy, James. 2000. "Historical Description and the Ideology of the Standard Language." *The Development of Standard English 1300–1800: Theories, Descriptions, Conflicts.* Ed. Laura Wright. Cambridge: Cambridge UP. 11–28.

Mitchell, Sally. 1996. *Daily Life in Victorian England.* Westport, Connecticut: Greenwood.

Mizuno, Masakatsu. 1993. "Non-Personal *Whose* and the Genitive Equivalents with *Of* in Shakespeare's Histories." *Aspect of Modern English: The Tenth Anniversary Issue of The Modern English Association.* Ed. under the auspices of The Modern English Association. Tokyo: Eichosha. 276–293.

Mugglestone, Lynda (ed). 2006. *The Oxford History of English.* Oxford: Oxford UP.

Mugglestone, Lynda. 2006. "English in the Nineteenth Century." In Lynda Mugglestone, 274–304.

Mulholland, Joan. 1967. "'Thou' and 'You' in Shakespeare: A Study in the Second Person Pronoun." *English Studies* 48: 1–9.

Murray, Lindley. 1806[1795]. *English Grammar, Adapted to the Different Classes of Learners.* 15th ed. A Reprint Ser. of Books Relating to the English Language 19. Tokyo: Nan'un-do, 1971.

Mustanoja, Tauno F. 1960. *A Middle English Syntax: Parts of Speech.* Part I. Helsinki: Société Néophilologique.

MWDEU = *Merriam-Webster's Dictionary of English Usage.* 1994. Springfield, MA: Merriam-Webster.

Nakayama, Masami. 2009. "*AIN'T* and *DON'T*: A Sociolinguistic Study of Nonstandard Negation in Victorian Novels." *Studies in English Literature* (The English Literary Society of Japan) 50: 1–23.

Nakayama, Masami. 2011a. "Linguistic Rivalry between Three forms of Negation: A Sociohistorical Study of English in Nineteenth-Century Novels." *Studies in English Literature* (The English Literary Society of Japan) 52: 53–75.

Nakayama, Masami. 2011b. "What Children's Literature Tells Us about Non-standard Language: The Use of *Ain't* and *Don't* in *The Water Babies*." *Language and Information Sciences* (Association for Language and Information Sciences, U of Tokyo) 9:

19–30.

Nevalainen, Terttu and Helena Raumolin-Brunberg. 2003. *Historical Sociolinguistics: Language Change in Tudor and Stuart England*. London: Longman.

Onions, Charles T. 1932. *An Advanced English Syntax: Based on the Principles and Requirements of the Grammatical Society*. 6th ed. London: Routledge and Kegan Paul.

Ono, Hayashi and Hiroyuki Ito. 1993. *Kindai eigo no hattatsu* [A History of the Development of Modern English]. Tokyo: Eichosha Phoenix.

Ormond, Leonee. 1995. Explanatory Notes. *Captains Courageous*. By Rudyard Kipling. Oxford: Oxford UP, 1999. 157–182.

Otsuka, Takanobu (ed.). 1970. *Shin eibunpō jiten* [*Sanseido's Dictionary of English Grammar*]. 2nd ed. Tokyo: Sanseido.

Paxson, James J. 1994. *The Poetics of Personification*. Cambridge: Cambridge UP.

Pérez-Guerra, Javier, Dolores González-Álvarez, Jorge L. Beuno-Alonso and Esperanza Rama-Martínez (eds.). 2007. *'Of Varying Language and Opposing Creed': New Insights into Late Modern English*. Bern: Peter Lang.

Phillipps, Kenneth. C. 1970. *Jane Austen's English*. London: André Deutsch.

Phillipps, Kenneth. 1978. *The Language of Thackeray*. London: André Deutsch.

Phillipps, Kenneth. 1984. *Language and Class in Victorian England*. London: Basil Blackwell.

Poutsma, Hendrik. 1914–29. *A Grammar of Late Modern English*. 5 vols. 2nd ed. (Part I), 1st ed. (Part II). Groningen: P. Noordhoff.

Poutsma, Hendrik. 1916. *A Grammar of Late Modern English*. Part II: *The Parts of Speech*; Section I, B: *Pronouns and Numbers*. Groningen: P. Noordhoff.

Priestley, Joseph. 1769. *The Rudiments of English Grammar, Adapted to the Use of Schools; With Notes and Observations, for the Use of Those Who have made some Proficiency in the Language*, new ed. A Reprint Ser. of Books Relating to the English Language 14. Tokyo: Nan'un-do, 1971.

Quirk, Randolph, Sidney Greenbaum, Geoffrey Leech and Jan Svartvik. 1985. *A Comprehensive Grammar of the English Language*. London: Longman.

Rissanen, Matti. 1986. "Variation and the Study of English Historical Syntax." *Diversity and Diachrony*. Ed. David Sankoff. Amsterdam: John Benjamins. 97–109.

Romaine, Suzanne. 1982. *Socio-historical Linguistics: Its Status and Methodology*. Cambridge: Cambridge UP.

Roach, Peter. 1991. *English Phonetics and Phonology: A Practical Course*. 2nd ed. Cambridge: Cambridge UP.

Ross, Alan S. C. 1956. "U and Non-U." *Noblesse Oblige: An Enquiry into the Identifiable Characteristics of the English Aristocracy*. Ed. Nancy Mitford. London: Hamish Hamilton. 11–36.

Rydén, Mats. 1966. *Relative Constructions in Early Sixteenth Century English: With Special Reference to Sir Thomas Elyot*. Uppsala: Almqvist and Wiksells.

Rydén, Mats. 1979. *An Introduction to the Historical Study of English Syntax*. Uppsala: Almqvist and Wiksell International.

Rydén, Mats and Sverker Brorström. 1987. *The Be/Have Variation with Intransitives in English*: With Special Reference to the Late Modern Period. Stockholm: Almqvist and Wiksell International.

Saito, Toshio. 1961. "The Development of Relative Pronouns in Modern Colloquial English: A Statistical Survey of the Development of Their Usage Seen in British Prose Plays from the 16th Century to the Present Time." *The Scientific Reports of Mukogawa Women's University* 8: 67- 89.

Saito, Toshio. 1980. "Gimondaimeishi *who* no mokutekikaku yōhō no hattatsu [The Development of the Interrogative Pronoun *Who* in the Objective Case]." *In Honour of Yoshinobu Mōri: Studies Contributed on the Occasion of His Retirement from Osaka University*, 35–54. Professor Yoshinobu Mōri retirement commemorative organization stored in the Department of Literature, Osaka University.

Sapir, Edward. 1921. *Language: An Introduction to the Study of Speech*. New York: Harcourt Brace Jovanovich.

Schneider, Edgar W. 1992a. "*Who(m)?* Constraints on the Loss of Case Marking of *Wh*-pronouns in the English of Shakespeare and Other Poets of the Early Modern English Period." *History of English: New Methods and Interpretations in Historical Linguistics*. Ed. Matti Rissanen, Ossi Ihalainen, Terttu Nevalainen and Irma Taavitsainen. Berlin: Mouton de Gruyter. 437–452.

Schneider, Edgar W. 1992b. "*Who(m)?* Case Marking of *Wh*-pronouns in Written British and American English." *New Directions in English Language Corpora: Methodology, Results, Software Developments*. Ed. Gerhard Leitner. Berlin: Mouton de Gruyter. 231–245.

Schneider, Edgar W. 1993. "The Grammaticalization of Possessive *of Which* in Middle English and Early Modern English." *Folia Linguistica Historica* 14, 1–2: 239–257.

Scholes, Robert and Robert Kellogg. 1966. *The Nature of Narrative*. London; Oxford: Oxford UP.

Simpson, J. A. and E. S. C. Weiner (eds.). 2004. *The Oxford English Dictionary*. 2nd ed. CD-ROM Version 3.1. Oxford: Oxford UP.

Simpson, Ron. 2001. *English Grammar*. London: Hodder Headline.

Smitterberg, Erik. 2005. *The Progressive in 19th-Century English: A Process of Integration*. Amsterdam: Rodopi.

Sørensen, Knud. 1985. *Charles Dickens: Linguistic Innovator*. Acta Jutlandica LXI, Humanistisk serie 58. Arkona: Aarhus Universitet.

Stapleton, Michael. 1983. *The Cambridge Guide to English Literature*. Cambridge: Cambridge UP.

Strang, Barbara M. H. 1970. *A History of English*. London: Methuen.

Suematsu, Nobuko. 2004. *Jane Austen no eigo: Sono rekishi, shakaigengogakuteki kenkyu* [Jane Austen's English: Its Historical and Sociolinguistic Study]. Tokyo: Kaibunsha.

Suematsu, Nobuko. 2008. "18 seiki eigo ni okeru huteidaimeishi no kazu no icchi [Number Agreement with Indefinite Pronouns in 18th-Century English]." *The Kyushu Review* 12: 15–34.

Svartvik, Jan and Geoffrey Leech. 2006. *English: One Tongue, Many Voices.* New York: Palgrave Macmillan.

Taavitsainen, Irma, Gunnel Melchers and Päivi Pahta (eds.). 1999. *Writing in Nonstandard English.* Amsterdam: John Benjamins.

Taavitsainen, Irma and Andreas H. Jucker (eds.). 2003. *Diachronic Perspectives on Address Term Systems.* Pragmatics and Beyond New Ser. 107. Amsterdam: John Benjamins.

Tieken-Boon van Ostade, Ingrid. 1987. *The Auxiliary* Do *in Eighteenth-century English: A Sociohistorical-linguistic Approach.* Dordrecht: Foris.

Tieken-Boon van Ostade, Ingrid. 1994. "Standard and Non-standard Pronominal Usage in English, with Special Reference to the Eighteenth Century." *Towards a Standard English: 1600–1800.* Ed. Dieter Stein and Ingrid Tieken-Boon van Ostade. Berlin: Mouton de Gruyter. 217–242.

Tieken-Boon van Ostade, Ingrid. 2006. "English at the Onset of the Normative Tradition." In Linda Mugglestone, 240–273.

Tieken-Boon van Ostade, Ingrid. 2008. "Grammars, Grammarians and Grammar Writing: An Introduction." *Grammars, Grammarians and Grammar Writing in Eighteenth-Century England.* Ed. Ingrid Tieken-Boon van Ostade. Berlin: Mouton de Gruyter. 1–13.

Tieken-Boon van Ostade, Ingrid. 2009. *An Introduction to Late Modern English.* Edinburgh: Edinburgh UP.

Tieken-Boon van Ostade, Ingrid. 2014. *In Search of Jane Austen: The Language of the Letters.* Oxford: Oxford UP.

Tieken-Boon van Ostade, Ingred and Wim van der Wurff (eds.). 2009. *Current Issues in Late Modern English.* Bern: Peter Lang.

Traugott, Elizabeth Closs. 1972. *A History of English Syntax: A Transformational approach to the History of English Sentence Structure.* New York: Holt, Rinehart and Winston.

Trudgill, Peter. 1974. *The Social Differentiation of English in Norwich.* Cambridge: Cambridge UP.

Trudgill, Peter. 1975. *Accent, Dialect and the School.* London: Arnold.

Trudgill, Peter. 1999. *The Dialects of England.* 2nd ed. Oxford: Blackwell.

Trudgill, Peter. 2000. *Sociolinguistics: An Introduction to Language and Society.* 4th ed. London: Penguin.

Vallins, G. H. 1955. *Better English.* 3rd ed. London: Pan.

Visser, F. Th. 1963–1973. *An Historical Syntax of the English Language.* 4 vols.

Leiden: Brill.
Wales, Katie. 1996. *Personal Pronouns in Present-Day English*. Cambridge: Cambridge UP.
Wales, Katie. 2001. *A Dictionary of Stylistics*. 2nd ed. London: Longman.
Wales, Katie. 2006. *Northern English: A Social and Cultural History*. Cambridge: Cambridge UP.
Walker, Terry. 2007. Thou *and* You *in Early Modern English Dialogues: Trials, Depositions, and Drama Comedy*. Amsterdam: John Benjamins.
Weigle, Luther Allan. 1963. "English Version since 1611: Acceptance of the King James Version." *The Cambridge History of the Bible: The West from the Reformation to the Present Day*. Ed. S.L. Greenslade. Cambridge: Cambridge UP. 361–382.
Wright, Joseph. 1892. *A Grammar of the Dialect of Windhill, in the West Riding of Yorkshire*. London: Trübner.
Wright, Joseph (ed.). 1898–1905. *The English Dialect Dictionary*. 6 vols. New York: G.P. Putnam.
Wright, Joseph. 1905. *The English Dialect Grammar*. Oxford: Henry Frowde.
Wyld, Henry Cecil. 1920. *A History of Modern Colloquial English*. London: T. Fisher Unwin.
Yaguchi, Michiko. 2010. "The Historical Development of the Phrase *there's*: An Analysis of the Oxford English Dictionary Data." *English Studies*. 91, 2: 203–224.
Yoshida, Takao. 1980. *Dickens no kotoba* [The Language of Dickens]. Rev. ed. Kyoto: Apollon.
Yule, George. 1996. *Pragmatics*. Oxford: Oxford UP.
Zachrisson, R. E. 1920. "Grammatical Changes in Present-Day English". *Studier i Modern Språkvetenskap* (Stockholm Studies in Modern Philology) 7: 19–61.

Index

A
age 21
America/the United States 45, 51, 66, 224
American 45, 78, 79, 80, 95, 163, 225
Americans 62, 72, 162

C
child 10
Cockney 48, 67
colloquial 46, 48, 60, 72, 100, 176, 225

D
demonstrative adjective 141
dialect 3, 4, 7
dialectal marker 35, 42
dialectal speech 7, 71, 150, 151, 153, 154, 224, 228
distance 204, 213, 215, 216
d'ye 39, 47

E
Early Modern English 5, 27, 79, 163, 164, 172, 197
Elizabethan period 69
Elizabethan society 224
emotion 19
emotional attitude 19, 31, 32, 35
emotionally 64
emotional marker 33, 36
emphasis 115, 129, 137, 138, 220
emphatic 24, 68, 69, 83, 84, 86, 87, 99, 103, 105, 108, 111, 113, 116, 119, 123, 128, 228
emphatic adjunct 83, 86

emphatically 54, 135, 167

F
female 10, 21, 72, 95, 98, 105, 114, 116, 123, 124, 136, 138, 160, 168, 174, 186, 206, 210, 213, 216, 228
female junior 57, 224
formal 7, 106, 123, 133, 141, 158, 199
formality 30

G
grammar-conscious 161

H
headword 184, 185, 186
hypercorrect 106, 109, 129

I
indefinite modifier 198
Industrial Revolution 9, 12
informal 7, 46, 71, 92, 126, 158, 200, 224, 225
Ireland 42, 51, 144, 224
Irish 42, 43, 45, 59, 60, 87, 88, 99

J
junior 21, 23

K
KJV=The King James Version 29, 30, 148, 149, 154

L
language-external factors 10
language-internal factors 10

Late Modern English   1, 2, 3, 4, 17, 36,
    51, 198
linguistic instinct   7
literary   36, 52, 61, 67, 154, 220, 227
local dialect (*see also* regional
    dialect)   227
look form   48
lower class   11, 12, 48, 62, 64, 72, 80,
    95, 97, 98, 102, 105, 119, 121, 131,
    138, 151, 154, 162, 228
lower rank   19, 27, 225

M

male   10, 21, 25, 95, 98, 114, 123, 124,
    136, 138, 174, 206, 210, 211, 213,
    228
middle class   12, 63, 72, 80, 95, 97,
    102, 105, 119, 154, 130, 133, 162,
    165, 228
Middle English   27, 52, 69, 91, 142,
    157, 158, 165, 200
Midlands/Midland   4, 14, , 52, 55, 56,
    65, 82, 85, 87, 143, 144

N

narrative   13, 14
narrative, first-person   13, 176
narrative, third-person   13, 176
negative emotions   33
nonhuman entities   21, 28, 29
non-personal antecedent   169, 170,
    172
nonstandard   2, 4, 9, 95, 153, 216, 224
northern   35, 42, 51, 55, 84, 108
North/Northern   4, 14, 18, 20, 21, 24,
    28, 38, 41, 43, 44, 48, 52, 56, 65, 67,
    68, 82, 85, 86, 87, 103, 118, 143, 224
notional concord   215, 216
notional naturalness   196
NRSV=*The New Revised Standard
    Version*   148, 149

n't   60, 61, 62, 65, 66, 69

O

object territory   127
obsolete   38, 49, 52, 55, 69, 159, 224
Old English   18, 52, 56, 69, 91, 157,
    165
omission of the relative pronoun   166

P

pedantic   92, 120, 172, 200, 228
personal antecedent   169, 170
personification   183
plural *of*-adjunct   190, 197
poetic   18, 29, 43, 49, 51, 60, 61, 220
politeness   30
positive emotions   33
power and solidarity   19
pragmatic marker   35, 47, 224
pragmatics   1
prescriptivism   159, 164, 168, 190
Present-day English   17, 18, 80, 92, 99,
    108, 113, 116, 117, 129, 133, 141,
    147, 157, 175, 189, 194, 196, 200,
    226, 227
progressive assimilation   77
pronominal adjectives   201

R

regional dialect   4, 70, 73, 149, 154,
    225
regional marker   143
register   12, 13
religious   18, 29, 30, 35, 43, 49, 51,
    148, 149, 220

S

semi-emphatic   113, 124, 128
senior   21, 23
sex   10, 21

Shakespeare 18, 25, 33, 35, 47, 69, 164
singular *they* 200, 211, 216
social class 4, 10, 11, 12
social dialect 142, 144, 154, 227
social distance 19, 31
social marker 45, 143
sociohistorical-linguistic approach 4
socio-historical approach 1
solecism 104, 105, 108, 224
South/Southern 14, 45, 46, 47, 52, 53, 54, 55, 64, 65, 66, 68, 85, 86, 87, 143, 144, 224
speech 105, 160, 190
spoken context 61, 94
spoken language 7, 13, 96, 101, 109, 116, 119, 138, 161, 164, 166, 194, 199, 220, 229
standard 9, 54, 87, 151
subject territory 127
substandard 61, 65, 109, 116, 121, 131

T
there + *be* construction 196, 197

U
upper class 11, 12, 33, 36, 48, 62, 72, 80, 95, 97, 102, 105, 119, 130, 131, 133, 154, 162, 165, 194, 224, 228
upper middle class 11, 12, 20, 39

V
variationist approach 1
Victorian people 11
Victorian society 10, 26
vulgar 48, 67, 144, 162

W
working class 11
writing 175
written context 61, 94, 147
written language 13, 14, 109, 116, 119, 133, 151, 165, 166, 199, 213, 229

中山匡美（なかやま まさみ）

略歴
2006年九州大学大学院比較社会文化学府
修士課程修了。
2015年東京大学大学院総合文化研究科
博士課程修了。博士（学術）。
現在、東京大学・神奈川大学非常勤講師。

Masami Nakayama was born in Oita, Japan. She received a Ph.D. degree from the University of Tokyo. Masami is currently an adjunct lecturer in the University of Tokyo and Kanagawa University.

主な論文
- "Multiple Negation in Nineteenth-Century English; As Seen in Victorian Novels." *Studies in Modern English* 23.(2007)
- "Linguistic Rivalry between Three Forms of Negation: A Sociohistorical Study of English in Nineteenth-Century Novels." *Studies in English Literature: English Number* 52.(2011)
- "The Complex Behavior of the Second Person Pronoun *Ye* in 19th-Century English Novels." *Studies in English Literature: English Number* 55.(2014)

Hituzi Linguistics in English No. 26
Grammatical Variation of Pronouns in Nineteenth-Century English Novels

発行	2018年2月16日 初版1刷
定価	12000円＋税
著者	©中山匡美
発行者	松本功
ブックデザイン	白井敬尚形成事務所
印刷所	株式会社 ディグ
製本所	株式会社 星共社
発行所	株式会社 ひつじ書房

〒112-0011 東京都文京区
千石2-1-2 大和ビル2F
Tel: 03-5319-4916
Fax: 03-5319-4917
郵便振替 00120-8-142852
toiawase@hituzi.co.jp
http://www.hituzi.co.jp/
ISBN978-4-89476-901-4

造本には充分注意しておりますが、
落丁・乱丁などがございましたら、
小社かお買上げ書店にて
おとりかえいたします。
ご意見、ご感想など、小社まで
お寄せ下されば幸いです。

刊行のご案内

ファンダメンタル英語学　改訂版
中島平三 著　定価 1,400 円＋税

ファンダメンタル認知言語学
野村益寛 著　定価 1,600 円＋税

ファンダメンタル英語史　改訂版
児馬修 著　定価 1,600 円＋税

刊行のご案内

ひつじ研究叢書（言語編）

第143巻 相互行為における指示表現
須賀あゆみ 著　定価6,400円+税

第151巻 多人数会話におけるジェスチャーの同期
「同じ」を目指そうとするやりとりの会話分析
城綾実 著　定価5,800円+税

第152巻 日本語語彙的複合動詞の意味と体系
コンストラクション形態論とフレーム意味論
陳奕廷・松本曜 著　定価8,500円+税

刊行のご案内

英語コーパス研究シリーズ
堀正広・赤野一郎監修　定価 各3,200円+税

第1巻　コーパスと英語研究（近刊）
第2巻　コーパスと英語教育
第3巻　コーパスと辞書（近刊）
第4巻　コーパスと英文法・語法
第5巻　コーパスと英語文体
第6巻　コーパスと英語史（近刊）
第7巻　コーパスと多様な関連領域

刊行のご案内

Hituzi Language Studies

No. 1　Relational Practice in Meeting Discourse in
New Zealand and Japan
村田和代 著　定価 6,000 円 + 税

No. 2　Style and Creativity
Towards a Theory of Creative Stylistics
斎藤兆史 著　定価 7,500 円 + 税

No. 3　Rhetorical Questions
A Relevance-Theoretic Approach to Interrogative Utterances in English and Japanese
後藤リサ 著　定価 10,000 円 + 税

刊行のご案内

Hituzi Linguistics in English

No. 24 Metaphor of Emotions in English
With Special Reference to the Natural World and the Animal Kingdom as Their Source Domains
大森文子 著　定価 9,500 円＋税

No. 25 A Comparative Study of Compound Words
向井真樹子 著　定価 13,000 円＋税

No. 27 *I mean* as a Marker of Intersubjective Adjustment
A Cognitive Linguistic Approach
小林隆 著　定価 8,500 円＋税